J. EDGAR HOOVER
AND
HIS G-MEN

Crime is a dangerous, cancerous condition which, if not beaten down, will soon eat at the very vitals of our country.

J. Edgar Hoover

May 10, 1936

J. Edgar Hoover
and
His G-Men

William B. Breuer

PRAEGER

Westport, Connecticut
London

Library of Congress Cataloging-in-Publication Data

Breuer, William B.
    J. Edgar Hoover and his G-men / William B. Breuer.
      p. cm.
    Includes index.
    ISBN 0–275–94990–7 (alk. paper)
      1. Crime—United States—Case studies. 2. Criminal investigation—
United States—Case studies. 3. United States. Federal Bureau of
Investigation. I. Title.
HV7914.B696   1995
364.1'0973—dc20   94–25967

British Library Cataloguing in Publication Data is available.

Library of Congress Catalog Card Number: 94–25967
ISBN: 0–275–94990–7

First published in 1995

Praeger Publishers, 88 Post Road West, Westport, CT 06881
An imprint of Greenwood Publishing Group, Inc.

Printed in the United States of America

The paper used in this book complies with the
Permanent Paper Standard issued by the National
Information Standards Organization (Z39.48–1984).

10 9 8 7 6 5 4 3 2 1

Dedicated to
W. RAYMOND WANNALL
who served the nation with
great honor and distinction
for 33 years as a
G-Man and Assistant Director
of the
Federal Bureau of Investigation,
the world's greatest
law enforcement agency

Contents

Acknowledgments

Most of the research material used in creating this book came from the archives of the Federal Bureau of Investigation in the J. Edgar Hoover Building in Washington, D.C. These documents included summaries of major criminal cases, transcripts of interrogations, backgrounds of perpetrators of crimes, field-office reports, and biographies of the many G-Men killed in the line of duty. Photographs were also obtained from FBI files.

In addition, my wife Vivien, a diligent researcher, dug out relevant articles from scores of magazines and newspapers published at the time the dramatic events described in this book were unfolding. These media stories were invaluable for injecting color, sparkle, and immediacy into the narrative.

Also, I have referred to passages of significance that have been published by authors of integrity, ability, and objectivity.

In particular, appreciation for their research assistance is expressed to Thomas A. Jones, FBI Assistant Director for Public Affairs, and his staff, and to Dr. Susan R. Falb, official historian for the FBI.

William B. Breuer

J. EDGAR HOOVER
AND
HIS G-MEN

1

"Little George Won't Panic!"

George Weyerhaeuser, a precocious, cheerful lad, was walking through the grounds of the Tacoma Lawn Tennis Club in Tacoma, Washington, after leaving Lowell School at the noon hour on May 25, 1935. The nine-year-old boy was destined to follow in the footsteps of his forebears who had built a veritable empire of timber, sawmill, paper, and bank holdings in the Great Northwest. Weyerhaeuser Timber Company was the largest of its kind in the nation, if not in the world.

George was to meet his 13-year-old sister Anne in front of the nearby Annie Wright Seminary, an exclusive girls' school, and they would be picked up by the family chauffeur and driven to the Weyerhaeuser mansion for lunch, a daily routine.

When George reached the street, he saw a tan sedan parked at the curb. A man was seated behind the steering wheel and another was standing beside the vehicle.

"Son, where is Stadium Way?" the stranger asked. The boy replied that he didn't know. Then the man moved toward him and said, "You're a shy little fellow, aren't you?" and grabbed George. Putting a hand over the boy's mouth, the man hustled him into the automobile, shoved him flat on the back floorboard, and covered him with a dirty blanket. As the car drove away, one kidnapper told George: "If you keep your mouth shut and don't yell, we won't hurt you."

After leaving Tacoma and driving for about an hour, the kidnappers put the boy in a pit (one that they had dug earlier) and chained him. One man remained on guard while the other drove back to Tacoma to mail a ransom note to the Weyerhaeuser family. Little George was kept in the pit, chained most of the time, until the next night, when he was moved to another predug hole in the ground 20 miles away.

On the following day, the boy was driven for many hours. At one point, when George was on the back floorboard, the abductors became excited when they spotted a police car, and one of the men reached back and shoved the lad down.

"Hey, you're hurting my arm!" the spunky youngster exclaimed.

"Don't worry, son, we ain't goin' to hurt you," one man chuckled. "You're too valuable to hurt!"

Periodically, the car halted and the boy, with his head still covered by the dirty blanket, was stuffed into the trunk before the two men continued the ride. Eventually, the car stopped once more and George was led blindfolded into what seemed to him to be a house. He was put in a room, and furniture was pushed up against the outside of the door to prevent him from sneaking out.

Meanwhile, back in Tacoma, the Weyerhaeuser chauffeur had picked up George's sister Anne in front of her school, and when the boy failed to appear, the driver headed for the family mansion, one of Washington State's show places. There he told the boy's parents, Mr. and Mrs. John Phillip Weyerhaeuser, Jr., that George must have tarried along the way and would probably walk the short distance to his home. When their son had not returned by 2:00 P.M., the frantic parents telephoned the police.

At 6:25 P.M., a special delivery letter arrived at the Weyerhaeuser home. It read in part:

> We have your boy and will give you five days to communicate with us through the advertising columns of the Seattle P-I (*Post-Intelligencer*) newspaper. If you give this any publicity, we will harm your son.
>
> —The Egotist

Neatly typed on white paper, the letter told the Weyerhaeusers to gather $200,000 in various denominations of unmarked bills. It also instructed the parents that their reply in the newspaper should be signed "Percy Minnie."

As directed, the Weyerhaeusers placed a classified advertisement in the *Post-Intelligencer* in nearby Seattle:

> Due to publicity beyond our control please indicate another method of reaching you. Hurry relieve anguished mother.
>
> —Percy Minnie

In the meantime, Federal Bureau of Investigation agents from as far away as Washington, D.C. flew into Tacoma. As they landed, each man—15 in all— was armed with a concealed Tommy gun and other paraphernalia. In keeping with Bureau policy, the G-Men (as agents were popularly called) remained out of the ransom negotiations and kept low profiles pending the safe return of the victim.

The ransom note was rushed to FBI headquarters in Washington, D.C. for scientific evaluation. Back came an analysis: It had been typed by a "woman of sensibilities." For instance, the word "kill" did not appear. Instead, she used the word "harm." The evaluators concluded: "We believe most of the contents were dictated to her, but that she used her own phrasing."

After Tacoma newspapers had hit the streets telling of the boy's abduction, streams of bumper-to-bumper traffic inched in both directions past the Weyerhaeuser mansion. Vehicle occupants craned their necks to see whatever there may have been to see. Swarms of gapers milled about on the sidewalk and the spacious green lawn, some of them pilfering flowers, presumably as souvenirs.

The commotion outside became unbearable for George's distraught mother Helen, who had to take refuge in the home of her parents in Seattle, a short distance to the north.

Mrs. Clara Walker, the boy's aged and ailing grandmother, remained in the Weyerhaeuser home, unaware that little George was in the hands of kidnappers. The family feared that telling her could endanger her life. Crowds around the mansion were explained to Mrs. Walker as pickets in a lumber strike then in progress.

Outwardly, the Weyerhaeuser family was displaying high morale despite their anguish. Mrs. Lucille Berg, George's teacher, didn't think the boy would be panicky. "He's one of the most lovable little chaps I've had in my teaching experience," Mrs. Berg told reporters. "He has a wonderful sense of balance and high intelligence. I don't think being held a captive would excite him. He'll take care of himself. Little George won't panic!"

Not only Tacoma, but the entire West Coast was tense. The offspring of wealthy parents were being "chaperoned" (protected by armed guards). Lawmen from Los Angeles to Canada were running down clues and chasing fruitless leads. In Tacoma, police rushed to a beach after getting a tip that three men were acting in a highly suspicious manner. They turned out to be frolickers— all of them well lubricated.

John Weyerhaeuser, in the meantime, was desperately trying to raise the $200,000 ransom. Most of his wealth was in his vast holdings, and his family had suffered enormous financial losses in recent years, mainly because of the ravages of the Great Depression. Therefore, his friends chipped in with cash to help meet the ransom demand.

Under a thick veil of secrecy, F. Rodman Titcomb, uncle of the kidnapped boy and an executive in the Weyerhaeuser timber empire, drove in his Cadillac sedan to a specified locale and turned the $200,000 over to the kidnappers. At gunpoint, the abductors confiscated Titcomb's automobile and he had to walk several miles to reach a telephone.

A few hours later, dawn was approaching when two men halted their car along a deserted stretch of road near Issaquah, Washington, 25 miles from Tacoma, handed little George Weyerhaeuser a one-dollar bill, and let him out.

"Wait here," one kidnapper said. "Your pa will pick you up." Then the car drove away.

George waited. And waited some more. When his father didn't appear, the boy set out on foot and trudged six miles to the home of chicken farmer John Bonifas, who had ten children of his own.

"I'm the little boy who was kidnapped," George said.

Bonifas didn't have a telephone, so he put the disheveled and wet boy in his decrepit automobile and drove toward Tacoma. He was nearly out of gas, and George gave him the kidnapper's one-dollar bill to make a purchase.

Arriving at Benton, the farmer sought entrance to the telephone company building to call the Weyerhaeuser home or Tacoma police. However, the on-duty operator wouldn't admit him, saying that it was against company rules to open its doors for business until 8:00 A.M.

Bonifas stopped next at a roadside gasoline station and telephoned the Tacoma police department after learning that the Weyerhaeuser phone had been discon-nected. An hour later, little George leaped into the outstretched arms of his tearful and joyous mother and father at their big white residence.[1]

With George safely back, the FBI joined in what would be the largest man-hunt ever in the Northwest. From the boy, G-Men learned many details of his ordeal. After being chained in pits for two nights, he said he spent four days and three nights in a house. His captors blindfolded him when they took him outside, George said.

When he was inside and not blindfolded, the boy related, his captors wore masks. "They looked so funny, walking around like that. I laughed at them and it made them mad," the chipper lad said.

George told the FBI that he thought he had been held in a two-story house, because he heard furniture being shifted around above his first-floor room. Once, when his blindfold was off for a few moments, he saw that the house had two gables, and he recalled that in his room was a large cupboard, where the kid-nappers locked him on occasion.

A small army of searchers thrashing across the heavily timbered and hilly regions around Issaquah and others scanning the region from airplanes could not locate a house matching the boy's description of his prison.

Despite intensive endeavor, the FBI and other lawmen had hit a dead end. No trace of the kidnappers was found, and agents hoped for a break in the case. Perhaps the abductors would get careless and pass some of the $200,000 ransom.

Earlier, as the stacks of bills had been put together, their serial numbers were recorded by the FBI—a time-consuming and tedious task. The list had been forwarded to headquarters in Washington, D.C. by airplane. Under normal cir-cumstances, the printing of many thousands of serial numbers would require three weeks. However, FBI Director J. Edgar Hoover personally contacted the manager of the Bureau's printing plant with orders to go all out on the big job.

Thirty-six hours after the list had reached headquarters it had been printed and bound into thousands of copies. These were sent by air to each newspaper, bank, department store, post office, and law enforcement agency west of the Mississippi River.

On June 8, two weeks after George Weyerhaeuser had been abducted, a young blond woman, wearing a house dress, sauntered into a chain store in Salt Lake City and offered a five-dollar bill for the purchase of a small item. Routinely, the clerk sent the bill to the cashier's cage to make change. There an alert employee quickly identified the five-dollar bill as part of the Weyerhaeuser ransom.

After the woman was given her change, the store manager called the police, and Salt Lake City detective W. M. Rogers and Patrolman L. B. Gifford rushed to the store. From neighborhood investigation, the officers learned that the woman and her husband were living in an apartment as Mr. and Mrs. Metz.

Now the pieces in the puzzling investigation were starting to fall in place. Little George had said he had heard a woman's voice and laughter in the house where he was a captive, and FBI analysis had determined that the ransom note had probably been phrased and typed by a woman of "tender sensibilities" who shrank from making the threat of possible harm more severe.

A raid on the Metz home was planned. G-Men and policemen concealed themselves near the place, and when a man approached the front porch, they leaped out with drawn weapons and arrested him. They were sure of their man, for he had the name "Metz" tattooed across the back of one hand.

The suspect and his wife were taken to a Salt Lake City police station, where they identified themselves as Harmon Metz Waley, 24, and Margaret, 19, his wife. Currency found in Waley's pockets and a large amount of money stashed in the rented house matched the serial numbers on the Weyerhaeuser ransom list.

Waley, tall, broad-shouldered, and handsome, had been in trouble with the law since the age of 15. After having been arrested several times for robbery and theft (for which he had spent time in the reformatory), Waley joined the army and soon received a dishonorable discharge. Back in the crime business, he was sentenced to the Idaho state prison for a term of one to 15 years for a burglary in which a shot was fired at a policeman.

In less than one year the articulate Waley persuaded the parole board to pardon him, pleading that he wanted to go home to support his widowed mother. Three weeks after being released from prison Waley was arrested for armed robbery and later convicted. However, he coerced the judge into giving him a suspended sentence. A short time later he was caught in a stolen car and sent to the Washington State Penitentiary for two to five years. In spite of a record as an unruly prisoner, Waley got out from behind bars once more, in September 1933.

Margaret Waley, one of 14 children in a devout family, had married Harmon when she was 16 years old, and spent most of her marital union waiting for her husband to be sprung from jail or prison. Now, in the Salt Lake City police station and under persistent questioning by the FBI, she broke first, tearfully confessing to her role in the Weyerhaeuser abduction and implicating her husband.

Confronted with his wife's statement, Harmon Waley admitted being involved in the crime. The couple fingered a 32-year-old ex-convict, William Dainard, alias William Mahan, as the mastermind in the abduction. Mahan had his share of the ransom money, $100,000, when he left them a few days earlier, the Waleys declared.

Acting on information provided by the Waley couple, FBI agents located a cache of $90,700 of the ransom money that had been buried in historic Immigration Canyon, five miles from Salt Lake City.

Based on information from the Waleys, FBI agents and local police found the house where the Weyerhaeuser boy had been held. It was in the center of a quiet residential neighborhood in Spokane, clear across the state in eastern Washington. The house was dirty and ill-kept, and to passersby it appeared to have been long vacant. With its two gables and cupboard as outlined by little George, the house precisely matched his description.

Neighbors who had seen mysterious people in and around the house identified them to the FBI as the Waleys and William Mahan. G-Men discovered that Mahan had a long record as a hard-core criminal.

When he was 19 years of age, Mahan had been charged with breaking into a liquor warehouse in Saskatchewan, Canada, and fled to Montana to avoid prosecution. A year later he was convicted of car theft and confined to the Montana State Penitentiary to serve a two- to four-year term. In less than 12 months, he was considered to be "reformed" and was freed.[2]

Shortly afterward, on January 31, 1927, Mahan and a companion held up the Oakville Bank in Oakville, Washington, and made off with $5,000. After blowing his cut of the loot on a wild binge, Mahan knocked off the Rathdrum State Bank in Rathdrum, Idaho, and hit the jackpot—$100,000 in cash and negotiable securities.

While living it up in Butte, Montana, for a few months, Mahan was captured by local police and returned to Idaho, where he was given a 20-year sentence for the Rathdrum bank job. In the state prison Mahan was pegged as an agitator and a troublemaker, and served 18 months in solitary confinement as a ringleader in a plot for a mass escape.

Despite his long rap-sheet, his record as an incorrigible convict, and his reputation for violence, Mahan was granted a full pardon by the governor of Idaho and was released on June 21, 1933.[3]

It was in the Idaho prison that William Mahan and Harmon Waley had become close cronies. When each had been released, the pair teamed up and hatched the scheme to kidnap George Weyerhaeuser. For three weeks prior to grabbing the boy, Waley and Mahan had stealthily observed the daily habits and routines of the Weyerhaeuser family.

In the meantime, on the same day that Harmon and Margaret Waley had been collared in Salt Lake City, police officer James Mooney spied a familiar face as he strolled past the corner of Iron and South Dakota Streets in Butte, Montana, a few minutes past seven o'clock in the morning. He thought it was the man he knew as William Mahan, whom he had arrested for bank robbery six years earlier.

As Mooney approached the gray-green Ford V–8 sedan the man had entered, the figure leaped out and started to run. In a mad scramble across a nearby back fence and an adjacent rooftop, Mooney was outdistanced before he could fire his revolver.

Officer Mooney and another patrolman went to the Ford and pried open the locked glove compartment, and a small fortune spilled out. Rushing to Butte police headquarters, the two patrolmen got out the 55-page booklet of ransom bill serial numbers that the FBI had compiled and distributed. One by one, Mooney and his partner checked the $15,155 in bills. All of them matched the serial numbers on the ransom list.

Butte police contacted FBI Agent Howard Walker, who arrived with a few of his men and took charge of the Ford V–8. There was no doubt about it: the fleeing suspect was William Mahan.

In Washington, D.C., J. Edgar Hoover had been directing the search. As quickly as G-Men in the field picked up information in Salt Lake City, Spokane, Seattle, Tacoma, Butte, and elsewhere, they dictated details to Hoover by long-distance telephone. Then the Director (as Hoover liked to be called) moved his men around like knights on a gigantic chess board in an effort to close in on Mahan.

With the memory of three G-Men shot to death in recent weeks by a mad-dog killer named "Baby Face" Nelson seared into his being, Hoover sent word to his men chasing Mahan: "At the least sign of resistance from the subject, shoot to kill!"[4]

Hoover spoke sarcastically to reporters about William Mahan. Clearly angry and biting off his words, he declared: "The gentleman has a magnificent record—arrests for burglary, grand larceny, with some paroles thrown in, of course."[5]

Elsewhere in the nation's capital, President Franklin Roosevelt now threw the weight of his personal influence behind a drive generated by Hoover to prevent widespread abuses of the parole system. On June 10, 1935, the FBI chief's boss, Attorney General Homer Cummings, received a letter from FDR at the White House:

> Newspapers report long criminal record in case of two men definitely suspected of Weyerhaeuser kidnapping, including not only arrests and convictions, but also paroles. Every decent citizen is interested in humane parole systems which seek rehabilitation of offenders, but at the same time, we should seek to prevent abuses of parole, especially in the cases of habitual criminals.
>
> Therefore I am glad that you are having a special study made of these two cases (William Mahan and Harmon Waley), investigating all facts

relating to their previous records in every jurisdiction where they have been apprehended or paroled.

Observers in Washington believed that the president's views would be a boon to correct a parole system that had operated more for the benefit of criminals in a manner not intended by the sponsors of the parole system.

On June 23, 1935, Harmon and Margaret Waley stood solemnly before Federal Judge E. E. Cushman in Tacoma and pleaded guilty to kidnapping charges. Harmon begged the judge to be lenient with his wife, claiming that she had known nothing of the abduction until three days after it occurred.

Judge Cushman was not impressed. Margaret Waley was sentenced to 20 years in prison and her husband was given a 45-year term. Less than one month after spunky George Weyerhaeuser had been abducted off a Tacoma street, prison doors slammed shut behind two of the three culprits.

At his big white house overlooking Puget Sound, John Weyerhaeuser praised the FBI and other law enforcement officers. "Damned fine detective work," he told reporters.[6]

Meanwhile, after hearing of the Waleys being caught, Bill Mahan sneaked back into Tacoma under cover of night, got a large amount of the ransom money that was cached there, and grabbed a freight train for southern California. Surely, he was one of the nation's richest hobos.

Reaching Los Angeles, Mahan tried to peddle the hot money at discount prices to underworld "shovers." None wanted anything to do with currency whose serial numbers had been printed in newspapers all along the West Coast. After obtaining various colored inks, he sat in a shabby hotel room for many hours and, with a safety razor and a blunt-ended needle as his tools, attempted to change the telltale serial numbers.

All the while, FBI agents had been tracking the kidnapper. Time after time, his trail was picked up, only to be lost again. Mahan, who used at least a dozen aliases, went through a string of purchased and stolen cars in his meandering flight to escape capture. Throughout the West he ran the back roads and slept in his car in hobo jungles and sleazy tourist courts.

For months, G-Men, backed by Washington, D.C. headquarters and the 37 field offices, ran down every tip or clue in pursuit of Mahan, who drove to Reno, Nevada; Cheyenne, Wyoming; Omaha, Nebraska; Kansas City, Missouri; and back to Los Angeles. At all of these places, telephone callers reported that altered ransom bills had turned up in store cash registers.

In the spring of 1936, FBI agents learned that Mahan was driving a 1929 model Chevrolet. Scores of vehicle registration lists were painstakingly checked, and after thumbing through thousands of license plate numbers, the G-Men came upon the signature of a William Byers, whose writing style matched that of William Mahan. Now the FBI not only knew the specific kind of automobile the fugitive was driving but its license number as well.

On the same day the license number had been ferreted out, Mahan drove north from Los Angeles and arrived in San Francisco late in the night. Leaving $29,000 in an old bag, he locked the Chevrolet and checked into a nearby flea-bag hotel.

Meanwhile, along the West Coast, FBI men backed by policemen and sheriff's departments searched through the night for the telltale license number. Garages, private storage places, parking lots, curbsides—all were checked out. Vehicles traveling on major highways were carefully monitored.

Early the next morning, May 7, 1936, William Mahan checked out of the hotel, walked to his automobile, and sat on the running board, no doubt to contemplate where to run now. On the seat of his car was a fully loaded automatic Colt.

Suddenly, there was a scuffle of feet and several men appeared from behind parked vehicles.

"FBI!" the leader called out. "Don't try to resist, Mahan!"

Mahan thrust both hands into the air, and with a shrug said, "I've known for a long time that it couldn't last."[7]

Mahan's year-long chess game with the FBI was over.

That afternoon in Washington, D.C., Director Hoover was being interviewed by a group of reporters on the subject of crime in general. When the gathering was about to break up, a newsman asked casually, "When are you going to nab William Mahan?"

Hoover enjoyed being impish at times. This was one such occasion. "Mahan, Mahan?" he queried. "The name sounds familiar." Then, with a broad grin, the Director said, "Oh, yeah, now I remember. We grabbed Mahan in San Francisco this morning!"[8]

Chairs were shoved backward as reporters leaped to their feet and bolted out of the room to telephone the blockbuster story to their newspapers and radio stations.

Back on the West Coast, Mahan was flown to Tacoma, the scene of the Weyerhaeuser kidnapping. A hardened criminal, Mahan knew how to play the game: he denied any knowledge of the abduction except "for what I read in the newspapers."

On the East Coast, Director Hoover told newsmen: "We don't need his confession. We've got enough (evidence) to convict him."[9]

Most of the $29,000 found in Mahan's car was Weyerhaeuser ransom money, the Director added. Some $60,000 of Mahan's share of the ransom was not accounted for, however. Apparently he had blown that amount of money in wild spending sprees throughout the West during the past year.

When G-Men questioning Mahan in Tacoma confronted him with the mountain of evidence that had been collected, the often-paroled ex-convict broke down and confessed. Arraigned before Judge E. E. Cushman, the same jurist who had sentenced Harmon and Margaret Waley a year earlier, Mahan pleaded guilty to kidnapping.

Branding Mahan as the ''brains'' behind the Weyerhaeuser abduction, Cushman sentenced him to 60 years in the federal penitentiary on McNeil Island, which is in nearby Puget Sound.

While being driven to the prison, Mahan, manacled hand and foot, asked his guards, ''What's that big building over there?''

''That's the insane asylum,'' a guard replied.

''Well,'' the prisoner declared, ''that's where they should have sent me for 60 years. I must have been crazy to pull off that kidnapping!''[10]

In the wake of the cracking of the Weyerhaeuser case, an avalanche of praise from the media, government officials, and average citizens was showered on J. Edgar Hoover and his posse of eager, tenacious G-Men. Most observers of the FBI found it difficult to comprehend that it had been only 11 years since Hoover had taken control of and revitalized a federal law enforcement agency that had been totally inept, a refuge for political hacks, and a disgrace to the nation.

2

"No Catch-All for Political Hacks"

In March 1924, Harlan Fiske Stone, whom President Calvin Coolidge had nominated for U.S. attorney general to clean up the scandal-ridden Department of Justice, was put under a congressional microscope and dissected. Stone, a former dean of the Columbia University School of Law, and Coolidge had been classmates at Amherst College, and the president was convinced that his old friend could get the job done.

"Silent Cal," as Coolidge was known, had been Republican President Warren Harding's vice president, and when the silver-thatched Harding died while on a trip to Alaska on August 2, 1923, Coolidge took the reins of government.

Hardly had Coolidge warmed up his swivel chair in the Oval Office than the nation was rocked by the startling allegations that hit the Department of Justice he had inherited. So bizarre had been the antics of the branch under Attorney General Harry M. Daugherty, Harding's poker-playing crony back in his Ohio days, that it was called the "Department of Easy Virtue."

Senate hearings in recent months had disclosed that agents of the Bureau of Investigation[1] (a component of the Justice Department) had sneaked into senators' private offices in the capitol, opened their mail, and searched their files in an effort to obtain damaging information that could be used to blackmail the legislators into halting their probe of the beleaguered Attorney General Daugherty.

No one would ever know if the Bureau of Investigation operative who gave that shocking testimony, a shady figure named Gaston B. Means, was telling the truth or fabricating lies to achieve some unknown goal. Whatever may have been the case, Means's revelations dovetailed nicely with the general pattern of Harding administration corruption that was being splashed across front pages in America.[2]

In the wake of the blockbuster disclosures against the Department of Justice, Calvin Coolidge launched a massive house cleaning. One of the first to be bounced, on March 28, 1924, was Harry Daugherty.[3]

At his confirmation hearings, Harlan Stone, a New Hampshire-born Republican, was criticized by a few senators for raising his voice in an unpopular defense of conscientious objectors during World War I. However, the Senate overwhelmingly confirmed his appointment on April 6, 1924.[4]

There began for Attorney General Stone the most momentous challenge of his long career—weeding out the misfits and returning an aura of integrity to the Department of Justice, especially its critically tarnished Bureau of Investigation. Five weeks after taking office in the mausoleum-like Department of Justice Building at 14th and K Streets, Harlan Stone fired William J. Burns as director of the Bureau of Investigation.

On May 10, only 24 hours after accepting Burns's "resignation," Stone summoned J. Edgar Hoover to his office. Twenty-nine-year-old Hoover, who had begun his career in the Bureau of Investigation as a filing clerk in 1917, was a graduate of Georgetown University School of Law and had earned a reputation in the Bureau as a bright and energetic executive.

While strolling down the hall toward Stone's office, young Hoover reflected on the reason for this call from on high. William Burns had just been fired, and rumors held that other heads would be lopped off. Was Hoover to be the next one to get the axe?

When Hoover entered the attorney general's office, he stood in front of Stone, a large, imposing figure who was seated behind his desk, scowling. A bad sign, Hoover reflected. Only later would all members of the Bureau realize that scowling was a Harlan Stone trademark.

"Young man, I've been looking into your background," Stone said. "I want you to be Acting Director of the Bureau of Investigation."

Hoover, expecting to be fired, was stunned. He couldn't believe that the venerable Harlan Stone would appoint a man not yet 30 years of age and with limited investigative experience to head the Bureau.

Hoover replied: "Sir, I'll take the job—but only on certain conditions."

Stone lifted a quizzical eyebrow. Here was a young man who barely had his feet wet in investigative techniques, who had been offered one of the Department of Justice's plums and now was laying down conditions for acceptance.

Stone grunted: "Well, what are they?"

"The Bureau must be totally divorced from politics," Hoover replied. "Not a catch-all for political hacks. Appointments and promotions must be based on merit and proved ability."

"Is that all?"

"Just one more thing, Mr. Stone. The Bureau will be responsible only to the attorney general."

"I wouldn't give it to you under any other conditions. That's all, Hoover. Good day."

No one had ever accused John Edgar Hoover of being a shrinking violet. Within 24 hours, the new acting director began throwing his weight around in an all-out crusade to reconstruct the Bureau from the shambles he had inherited. Hoover knew things were bad, but they were even worse than he had suspected.

Carefully studying the personnel file of each agent, the acting director confirmed what he had long suspected: the Bureau was saturated with hacks who had been given jobs as agents because members of Congress and the executive branch had used the Bureau as a dumping ground to reward the political faithful. Numerous agents had close ties to the underworld, Hoover found, and some were ex-convicts. A few were alcoholics who seldom had bothered to show up for work.

Daugherty's Department of Justice, Hoover discovered to his dismay, had handed one man an agent's badge because of his expertise in furnishing friendly chorus girls to a top government official. Another agent had received his job because of his skill in singing risque ditties in front of the Department of Justice Building for the entertainment of federal employees during lunch hours.

Within the first few months as head of the Bureau, J. Edgar Hoover fired more than 100 agents, about two-thirds of the total force. Once he had swept out the flotsam, Hoover set about elevating the standards for the appointment of Bureau agents. "We need decent, honorable, respectable young men," he declared. Applicants had to be between the ages of 25 and 35, and be able to pass a stiff physical examination. All agents had to have a degree from a recognized law school or be an accountant, and each had to pass a competitive entrance examination.

A character check then scratched a large number of otherwise qualified applicants. "We can't afford to merely *be* right," the Director asserted many times. "We must give every *appearance* of doing right to avoid criticism."[5]

Political pull was of no help to an applicant—indeed, it might work against his chances. Every candidate was investigated carefully and coldly, sometimes going back to his grade-school days, before he got his insignia. These investigations established whether the applicant was the kind of man Hoover wanted as an agent.

Before a candidate became a full-fledged agent, he had to endure an exhaustive, three-month course in crime-busting techniques and demonstrate a proficiency with several weapons. Agents were on call 24 hours a day, and Hoover sent out inspectors who dropped in unannounced to check on his men in the field.

New agents were handed a code of conduct designed by Director Hoover. Along with other strict admonitions, the code prohibited them from taking a drink of booze (an illegal act in itself since Prohibition was enacted by Congress in 1920) while on duty. That code of conduct became a way of life for everyone in the Bureau. Even the clerks, stenographers, and other employees had to measure up to strict standards. Since agents were not under the Civil Service, Hoover could (and did, on occasion) jettison any Bureau man who flagrantly violated the code of conduct.

Young Hoover's stern discipline brought hoots of derision. Outside the Bureau, he was known to some in Washington as the "Boy Scout Master" and the "Boy Sherlock." His men were jeered at as "college-trained gumshoes" and "briefcase detectives." And the Director's firm resolve to divorce the Bureau from politics brought howls of indignation from a few influential members of Congress, who had been using the Bureau to reward hacks who had aided in their campaigns for office.

In 1925, one prominent senator made a call on Director Hoover and demanded to know why a certain agent (a political supporter) had been abruptly transferred from the legislator's home state. Patiently Hoover explained the reason for the transfer, but refused to return the agent to his previous post, as the senator demanded.

"I'll see the attorney general about this!" the irate senator huffed as he stalked out of the room.

An hour later, Harlan Stone sent for Hoover and asked for the facts in the transfer of the senator's crony. After hearing the Director's explanation, the attorney general scowled and said, "I don't think you're on solid ground—you should have fired the agent instead of transferring him!"[6]

Stone had been keeping a close eye on his young Bureau chief, and he liked what he saw. On December 10, 1924, seven months after Hoover's appointment to the post, Stone dropped the "Acting" from the Director's title.

Hoover's revitalized Federal Bureau of Investigation attracted exceptional agents of high caliber and fierce integrity. Each man knew that he had measured up for acceptance into a small, elite group of lawmen. It was certainly not the niggardly pay that an indifferent Congress had prescribed that brought these eager young men to the FBI. Rather, the agent's compensation was in seeing his plan grow into full bloom until his case was complete, knowing that he had matched wits with crafty criminals and emerged the victor.

In 1925, an FBI agent's starting salary was a modest $2,700 per year, with a $4 per diem for expenses when out in the field on assignment. A year later, Congress raised the per diem to $6, but then someone bent on saving the government money slashed that figure back to $5.

Hoover's men were expected to stay in reputable hotels when away from their home offices and to dress in a style that would reflect well on the Bureau. When on government business, an agent had to stretch his $5 per day subsistence to pay for his hotel room, meals, laundry, and other items. Then, when the U.S. comptroller general ruled that an FBI man on government business could not be reimbursed for tips demanded by American tradition, the agent had to dig down in his own pocket to pay Pullman porters, redcaps, hotel bellhops, and taxi drivers.

Edward P. Shanahan was typical of the "new" FBI agents. Resourceful, dedicated, and bright, his cheerful disposition made him popular with his colleagues. On October 11, 1925, Shanahan received a tip from underworld sources that 25-year-old Martin Durkin, an automobile thief who was also wanted for murder, was planning to hide a stolen vehicle in a Chicago garage. It was a federal crime to transport a stolen auto into another state.

Shanahan, assisted by Chicago police officers, staked out the garage and waited. An hour later, the G-Man was alone in the garage when Durkin drove in. When the agent approached to make an arrest, Durkin poked a pistol out of the car window and fired at point-blank range, the bullet striking Shanahan in the chest. The fugitive sped out of the garage in his automobile as the agent fired one shot before toppling over, dead.

Edward Shanahan was the first FBI agent to be killed in the line of duty, and his death cast a pall over the entire organization. In Washington, Director Hoover was both saddened and furious. Although it was not a federal crime to kill an FBI agent, Hoover called in an assistant and declared: "We've got to nab Durkin. If one of our fellows is killed and the killer gets away, our agents will never be safe!"

An all-out FBI hunt for Martin Durkin was launched. After the fugitive killed a policeman in Chicago and wounded another, he was traced to San Diego, where a Cadillac had been stolen from an automobile agency. A salesman identified a man who had been in the display room earlier in the day as Martin Durkin.

The trail led through southern California, Arizona, New Mexico, and into Texas. Coordination between local officers and the FBI at this stage left much to be desired, which served as an aid to Durkin in his flight. In one instance, the sheriff at Pecos, Texas, checked out a new Cadillac parked along a street. A young man was at the wheel with a woman companion beside him.

The sheriff grew suspicious when he spotted a pistol lying in the seat between the two occupants. However, the stranger said that he was a deputy sheriff from California on vacation, thereby explaining the necessity for carrying the gun. If the Texas lawman would permit him to go to his hotel room, he would get his identification papers to prove that he was indeed a deputy sheriff.

When the driver assured the sheriff that he would soon return with the proof, he was allowed to depart. Martin Durkin drove madly out of town and the Cadillac, which had been stolen from the San Diego dealer, was later found wrecked and abandoned not far from San Antonio.

The Pecos sheriff notified the FBI office in El Paso by letter. "I thought you might have something on this bird," he wrote. By that time, multiple murderer Durkin was long gone. However, through painstaking sleuthing, FBI agents learned from ticket agents at the San Antonio railroad station that Durkin and his girlfriend had boarded the *Texas Special,* a passenger train that was due to arrive in St. Louis at 11:09 that same morning, only two hours away.

Frantic telephone calls were made to the St. Louis office of the FBI, and agents there hurriedly got in touch with detectives on the St. Louis police department. Knowing that a shootout might erupt, and innocent bystanders killed or wounded, if an effort were to be made to nab Durkin in cavernous, crowded Union Station, the G-Men arranged with railroad officials to halt the *Texas Special* at a small town outside St. Louis. If Durkin tried to flee, he would have to cross open fields and would be a highly visible target.

When the speedy train came to a halt, FBI agents and detectives scrambled on board. Having been advised by the G-Men in San Antonio of the car and the compartment in which Durkin was riding, the FBI men and the detectives, with weapons drawn, barged in before the fugitive could reach for the loaded gun in his overcoat pocket. He was removed from the train in handcuffs.

Martin Durkin confessed that he had gunned down Agent Edward Shanahan in the Chicago garage. Three months after the killing, Durkin was sent to prison for 25 years.[7]

It took J. Edgar Hoover three years to shake down the Federal Bureau of Investigation and to install a system and a basic organization that was prepared to act swiftly and decisively. Yet the Bureau was operating under enormous handicaps. A majority in Congress, concerned about creating a home-grown version of a national police force like Soviet Dictator Joseph Stalin's dreaded OGPU, refused to expand FBI powers.

Agents were prohibited from carrying guns, except in special circumstances when permission was obtained from an immediate superior. They were not empowered to make arrests except in the sense that any citizen can make an arrest, and had to call in local police or sheriffs to make the pinch.

Although ready and able to become the nation's crime-busters, Hoover's tightly knit and highly mobile force of 461 agents spent much of its time in the late 1920s chasing violators of such arcane federal laws as the Migratory Birds Act.

While Congress was satisfied to have the FBI functioning as a largely unarmed force engaged in apprehending car thieves and the like, gangsters in America's big cities (and many smaller ones) had shot and bribed their way to positions of enormous power through unholy alliances with crooked politicians, crooked police, and shady judges.

The advent of the big-city gangs had come hard on the heels of the burial of John Barleycorn on January 16, 1920, when the United States officially went "dry." However, millions of Americans refused to accept Barleycorn's demise, so an entirely new profession—bootlegging—sprang up to supply the illegal booze that so many otherwise honest citizens were demanding.

In major cities, bootlegging profits were gargantuan, and rival gangs engaged in bloody wars over the sales rights to choice locales. In the Chicago area alone during 1925–1926, there were 92 murders of rival mob members—only two of them were solved.

Lack of intense effort by Chicago police reflected the mood of the people. If the gangsters wanted to bump off one another, so what? Thus, apathy toward even brutal crimes seeped into America's consciousness.

With treasuries swollen by bootlegging, prostitution, gambling, and "protection'' rackets, big-city underworld kingpins carved out invisible empires, aided by public officials on the take. Chicago vice overlord Alphonse "Scarface Al" Capone, for one, was hauling in an estimated $300 million per year in 1928 before he reached the age of 28.

Congress saddled the Treasury Department with responsibility for enforcing Prohibition laws, a task akin to preventing Americans from breathing by order of Capitol Hill in Washington, D.C. Almost overnight, a force of more than 4,000 Prohibition agents was scraped up and dispersed to 105 field offices.

While there were notable exceptions, such as famed Eliot Ness and his small band of "Untouchables," who were burrs under Al Capone's saddle blanket, the newly hatched Prohibition agents were largely untrained in law enforcement. Soon aware of the hopelessness of their task and cognizant of the fact that most of the public regarded them, not the bootleggers, as the enemy, many of these agents were corrupted. A Prohibition agent being paid $40 per week by Uncle Sam learned quickly that he could pocket perhaps ten times that figure each week by merely looking the other way at the right time.

In 1929, America was struck a staggering blow: A stock market crash mired the nation in the Great Depression, the worst economic catastrophe in the history of the Western world. Before the full impact of the debacle would be felt, most Americans knew poverty only by reputation. Then a large segment of the richest nation on earth learned what it meant to be poor.

Business firms and factories shut down by the thousands. Twenty-five percent of the nation's work force—13 to 15 million people—were unemployed. White- and blue-collar workers had life savings wiped out in the failure of local banks. Once prosperous stock brokers, professional engineers, and storekeepers sold apples (at three cents each) on street corners or became panhandlers. Appropriately, the hit tune of early Depression years was *Brother, Can You Spare a Dime?*

Thousands of struggling farmers, earning 50 cents per bushel for wheat and a few pennies for a dozen eggs, lost their properties when banks foreclosed. "If they come to take my farm, I'm goin' to fight," a debt-ridden Texas farmer exclaimed. "I'd rather be killed outright than die by starvation." Bankers, in the eyes of many, emerged as villains.

Foreclosed farmers became migratory field hands in the West. An Arkansas family walked 900 miles from Arkansas to the Rio Grande cotton fields in southern Texas, only to be told that hiring had ceased.

Perhaps a million nomads—no one was counting them—roamed around the United States in desperate searches for work. Many had their belongings strapped to dilapidated old cars that almost invariably broke down along the road at some remote locale. These luckless legions had an expression for their plight: "Stalled, stranded, and starving!"

President Herbert C. Hoover was scorned and derided by large numbers of bitter Americans, and his administration was blamed for the nation's plight. In large cities there were Hoovervilles, squalid villages that sprang up in parks and on vacant lots where the homeless sheltered themselves in flimsy shacks made of packing boxes and scrap metal while they foraged for food in back-alley garbage cans. Long lines of dispirited, ragged men and women shivered in winter's biting cold and broiled in the hot summer sun as they waited for meager meals of stale bread and soup dished out by local charities.

While one-third of the nation was ill-housed, ill-clad, and ill-nourished, America's lucky two-thirds had also been hit hard by the Great Depression. Few people bought houses (a new six-room home in a large city sold for $2,800). Clothes were patched and shoes half-soled. Cars were driven longer and farther, simple meals were served, plans for sending offspring to college were cancelled.

For Americans fortunate enough to hold onto or find jobs, wages plummeted 60 percent in the three years after the stock market crash. In 1932, the average annual earnings of physicians was $3,382, lawyers $4,218, professors $3,111, bus drivers $1,373, registered nurses $936, and hired farm hands $216.

In early Depression years, a man's haircut cost 20 cents and a lady's bob was 30 cents. A sirloin steak meal in a restaurant sold for 32 cents, with a vegetable dinner going for a dime. A raincoat cost $2.59 and a wool dress was tagged at $1.95. A man's suit was priced at $9.95 and a pack of cigarettes went for ten cents. For the few able to afford one, a new Pontiac could be bought for $565.

Millions of Americans sought brief respite from harsh reality through the fantasy world of Hollywood movies. At theaters they plunked down a dime to watch such popular film stars as Jean Harlow (''The Platinum Bombshell''), handsome newcomer Clark Gable, cowboy hero Tom Mix, sultry Mae West, comedians W. C. Fields and Eddie Cantor, child star Shirley Temple, and the canine hero Rin Tin Tin.

Families gathered in their parlors around big Philco and Dumont radios heard plump Kate Smith (''The Songbird of the South'') belt out *When the Moon Comes Over the Mountain* and other ballads of the day, and they laughed over the antics of Edgar Bergen and his sassy puppet Charlie McCarthy. Each week-night at seven o'clock, telephone calls dropped 50 percent as 30 million people chuckled or guffawed over the *Amos 'n' Andy* black comedy broadcast.

While Americans (except for the extremely rich) were trying to cope with the ravages of the Great Depression, a ''reign of terror'' (as the *New York Times* described it) reached epidemic proportions. Gangs of ruthless marauders, riding in swift, high-powered automobiles and toting Tommy guns, rifles, and sawed-off shotguns, were crisscrossing America, perpetrating bank robberies, kidnappings, murders, and other acts of violence on a massive scale.

State and local law enforcement officers—undermanned, underpaid, undertrained, underequipped, and out-gunned—were almost powerless to deal with the crime onslaught. They were further handicapped by laws that prohibited them from pursuing fleeing criminals across state lines.

Against this national backdrop of moral chaos, economic disaster, and law enforcement breakdown, the FBI was called on to go to war against gangland forces, even though its role at first was limited to violations of federal laws.

Director J. Edgar Hoover held no illusions that the battle would be short-lived, easy, or bloodless. He estimated that crooks outnumbered carpenters by four to one, grocers by six to one, and doctors by twenty to one.

3

Bank Robbery:
A Growth Industry

Lincoln, Nebraska, was basking in the warm rays of early autumn sunshine on the morning of September 17, 1930. Shortly after the Lincoln National Bank opened its doors at 10:00 A.M., five unmasked men, armed with Tommy guns, charged inside and shouted, "This is a stick-up! Get your hands up!"

While one of the robbers went through the teller cages scooping up money, two companions went to the basement and forced Florence Zelser, the assistant trust officer, to open the vault.

Upstairs, the three robbers had their weapons trained on bank employees and a few customers who had been ordered to lie face-down on the floor. Philip L. Hall, vice president of the bank, and a teller, W. E. Barkley, were struck on the head with a Tommy gun butt when they got up to argue with the holdup men. Both were dazed and bleeding, and their cuts would require numerous stitches.

Outside, another bandit waited in a getaway car. At one point, a Lincoln policeman and a detective approached in a squad car, and when the gang's lookout waved and smiled, the two officers waved back and drove on.

The bold robbery was carried out with military precision by professionals who had thoroughly reconnoitered the bank and its routines. From a window across the street, a merchant watched idly as the bandits carried out boxes and bags of currency and loaded them into the getaway automobile. They got into the car with such little haste that the merchant and pedestrians didn't realize that the bank was being robbed.

As the six gunmen pulled away in their car, they turned on a siren. Vehicles on the crowded streets quickly moved to the side to permit the "police car" to race unimpeded out of Lincoln.

In the hours ahead, Lincoln National Bank officials conducted an inventory to tote up their losses. It had been an astonishing haul—$3 million in currency and negotiable securities—the largest bank robbery in U.S. history up to that time.[1]

Because the Lincoln National Bank had only $60,000 in insurance to meet the staggering loss, the institution was forced into liquidation. A scapegoat was required for the debacle, so the Lincoln chief of police "resigned."

Only much later would it be learned that the mastermind behind the Lincoln bank job was one of the slickest—and most unlikely—characters roaming the murky shadows of the underworld. His name was Edward Wilhelm Bentz, who was 35 years of age at the time the Nebraska bank was cleaned out.

Eddie Bentz had gained a special niche in gangdom because he had invented the technique of "casing" a bank before knocking it off. On entering a city, he would go to the public library and turn to the files of the local newspapers. There he would look up the advertisement of a particular bank in which he was professionally interested, and closely study its assets and liabilities.

Much as would a scholar researching for his Ph.D. thesis, Bentz would write down on a pad the cash on hand and the amount owed by other banks, the amount due from the Federal Reserve, and the bond inventory. From his years of study of banking practices, Eddie could read a statement as expertly as any skilled financier. With this knowledge, he created a system of deductions that allowed him to determine, often within $1,000, exactly how much loot would await him at the targeted bank.

Once his plan had been created, Bentz began assembling a team of specialists for the job. He knew of at least ten underworld hangouts throughout the nation to which he could telephone and recruit the men with the required skills.

Before hitting the bank, Eddie Bentz, like a master architect, painstakingly drew up a getaway chart in order to avoid narrow bridges, traffic bottlenecks, dead-end streets, and police stations. Then Bentz and his team of specialists "ran the road," practicing their getaway with the same dedication that a football coach would run his team through drills in search of precision.

In these practice runs, the odometer of the gang's car would be set at zero in front of the targeted bank, and the robbers would drive over a prescribed route, sometimes for 100 miles or more, with Eddie jotting on a note pad. He would precisely mark the distance between turns (2.3 miles, rt. turn) and the fastest rate of speed at which they might take the corners.

Bentz, a heavyset man with crinkly, light-red hair, wore overalls and a wide-brimmed straw hat when he bolted into a bank while brandishing a Tommy gun to terrorize employees and customers into meek submission to his orders. Then his keenly rehearsed gang swept through the cages and into the vaults, gathering thousands of dollars in a lightning-swift foray.

When the robbers scrambled into the getaway car, Bentz would sit next to the driver and, like a coxswain in a rowing regatta, call out the instructions as the vehicle traveled over its predesignated route.

Every big gang wanted Bentz for its personal caser, as most criminals didn't know a bank statement from a horse racing form. Then Eddie took another step in the free enterprise system that endeared him to fellow crooks. Bank robbers who worked with him would get a major part of the cash, if they would give him the bonds and other securities.[2]

Unlike his cohorts in a bank job, Bentz was in no hurry to cash in. During the course of his extensive career he cached hundreds of thousands of dollars worth of bonds and securities across the nation, then waited for them to "cool off" before cashing them. His nimble accountant's brain permitted him to keep track of his "stock portfolio" and where he had hidden it.

Psychiatrists could have had a field day analyzing Eddie Bentz. Bank robberies (he would later admit to "50 or 100") seemed in part to be an avocation, even a hobby. His associates felt that one of Bentz's motivations was the thrill of the hunt, the opportunity to outwit the law, a sort of "me against them" attitude.

Eddie, an easygoing type who liked to talk with cultivated people, owned a few hundred volumes of rare books, including old editions of *Pilgrim's Progress* and the works of Shakespeare. His collection of old coins brought him into correspondence (under assorted assumed names) with some of the nation's reputable collectors. Photography fascinated him, and on his travels he roamed public parks, art museums, and places of historical interest, snapping away with his expensive Kodak. (He was far too cagey to risk photographing a targeted bank.) Golf was a passion, and Eddie's goal was to play every major course in the nation.

When between bank jobs, especially in winter, Bentz was a guest in Miami luxury hotels as a gentleman sportsman or took the baths at Hot Springs or played golf at exclusive southern California resorts. At those fashionable locales, Eddie chatted amiably with wealthy Wall Street brokers, chairmen of oil giants, and Detroit automobile tycoons.

Gracious in manner and impeccably garbed, his years of boning up on high finance permitted Bentz to be accepted as the financier he portrayed himself to be. None of those he rubbed elbows with in the playgrounds of the rich and influential suspected that this pleasant young man had begun his crime career at age 13 and had been involved in countless burglaries, bank robberies, impersonations, and thefts.

While Eddie Bentz reverted to his aura of respectability, the Secret Six, a Chicago-based organization devoted to suppressing crime, had developed information that tied a lieutenant in the Al Capone empire, August "Big Mike" Winkler, with the landmark Lincoln National Bank heist. Three others identified were Thomas O'Connor, Howard Lee, and Jack Britt.

A few days later, law enforcement officers raided a hangout in East St. Louis, in southern Illinois, and collared the three suspects. Put on trial in Lincoln, Nebraska, O'Connor and Lee were sentenced to 25 years in the Nebraska State Penitentiary, but a jury could not agree in the case of Jack Britt.

Now the search widened for Gus Winkler, who apparently had been laying low. In addition to the Lincoln bank job, the Capone chieftain was also wanted for murder in Piqua, Ohio, and for bank robberies in Michigan, Wisconsin, and Illinois.

On August 6, 1931, two Michigan state troopers lurched their car from its place of concealment onto a main road and gave chase to a speeding automobile carrying two men. The troopers had no way of knowing that they had triggered one of the most bizarre scenarios in American crime history.

The pursuing officers turned on their siren and flashed their red light, but the other car drove even faster. Rounding a curve, the driver of the fleeing vehicle lost control and the car plunged off the road, smashing into a tree. Dazed and bleeding, the two men were lifted from the wreckage.

Rushed to a hospital at Benton Harbor on the eastern banks of Lake Michigan, the accident victims were placed side by side on cots. One man had a skull fracture. Believing he was going to die, he told police his real name: August Winkler. His companion, suffering from internal injuries and not expected to live, was John E. Moran, a St. Louis gangster, Winkler said.

Governments of two states put in a claim for Winkler. Illinois wanted him as a suspect in a bank robbery at Plano, and Nebraska wanted to put him on trial for the $3 million robbery that wiped out the Lincoln National Bank a year earlier.

Winkler stoutly protested his innocence in the Nebraska job, and offered an alibi. On the evening of September 17, 1930, the day the Lincoln bank was hit, he said he had registered under an assumed name at the fashionable Statler Hotel in Buffalo, New York.

Winkler's alibi was investigated, and he had indeed been in Buffalo as claimed. However, residents on the outskirts of Lincoln had told investigators about an airplane that landed in a nearby vacant field about two hours before the bank robbery. At about 11:00 A.M., an hour after the holdup, the airplane had vanished, although no one had seen it take off.[3] Winkler could have flown to Buffalo in time to register at the Statler.

When Gus Winkler was sufficiently recovered from the skull fracture to travel, he was taken to Chicago. There he agreed to submit to a test by a new-fangled lie detecting machine, which was operated by Professor Leonard Keeler at Northwestern University. Winkler, the tests indicated, had not been involved in the Lincoln bank robbery.[4]

Despite the lie-detector findings, Winkler was extradited to Nebraska to stand trial. In Lincoln, he made an astonishing proposal. In return for immunity from prosecution, he would use his connections with the Al Capone mob to return $600,000 of the bonds taken from the Lincoln bank. Furthermore, he promised to prove that most of the stolen nonnegotiable bonds had been destroyed.

Winkler said that it would cost him $75,000 to locate the missing securities and negotiate their return, but that he was willing to spend the money rather than take a chance with an angry Nebraska jury that "would be out to nail me."

Max Towle, the Nebraska prosecutor, was skewered on the horns of a dilemma. If he failed to prosecute Winkler, public damnation would be heaped on him. On the other hand, large numbers of Nebraskans felt that the important thing was to recover the bank loot, even if it meant cutting a deal with an alleged participant.

Gus Winkler was released on bail of $100,000.

Five weeks later, on January 4, 1932, the Chicago police department received a call from a man who refused to identify himself. After hurriedly giving instructions, the caller slammed down the telephone.

As directed by the mystery caller, Chicago Police Sergeants Roy Steffens and Charles Touzinski drove to a desolate street corner that night and, under the dim rays of an overhead light, opened a large suitcase packed with $583,000 worth of negotiable and nonregistered securities from the Lincoln bank job.

The next day, the bonds were turned over to officials of the Lincoln National Bank in the offices of the Chicago Secret Six and the destruction of $2,217,000 of registered securities by the robbers was established. This unique development wiped out the loss to the bank except for $15,000, which was covered by insurance.

Investigators were convinced that only one man could have engineered this bizarre deal in which nearly $3 million in securities had been stashed somewhere in the underworld shadows for 16 months, and had the clout to order the small fortune to be returned. That powerful figure was 29-year-old "Scarface Al" Capone, who had often boasted: "I own Chicago!"

For whatever his reasons, the heavy-jowled overlord of crime apparently had wanted to clear up the Lincoln bank robbery, perhaps to get the public spotlight off the underworld.

The theory that Al Capone had pulled the strings behind the scenes gained credence a short time later when lawmen intercepted (and then allowed to continue to its intended recipient) a letter from a Lincoln lawyer to Philip D'Andres, Capone's bodyguard. The attorney asked for additional funds to defray expenses of the "bond development" and for his fee. Telegraphic records showed that Capone sent the requested funds to the Nebraska lawyer.[5]

A few days after the meeting in the offices of Chicago's Secret Six, Nebraska prosecutor Max Towle dropped all charges against Gus Winkler, and he was released.

By 1932, bank robbery in the United States had become big business. Large and small, banks were being knocked off at the rate of 12 to 16 each month. Hard-pressed local and state police officers and sheriffs could expect no help from the Federal Bureau of Investigation in the bank heists because of the crazy inconsistencies of federal laws.

A federal bank employee who embezzled $50 or more would violate a federal law. However, if a gang of desperadoes held up a federal bank, killed an employee, took $200,000, and fled to another state, not a single federal statute would have been broken. Once they had crossed a state line after hitting a bank, the robbers could feel reasonably immune from capture because lawmen in pursuit would have to halt at the line between the two states.

Although the FBI did not have jurisdiction, Director J. Edgar Hoover ordered a survey made of banks and bank robberies, anticipating that one day Congress would enact legislation making bank-busting a federal crime. A modus operandi file was begun, and it ballooned into a voluminous collection of data in the months ahead. Among other factors, this file revealed the manner in which various bank jobs were committed. Almost without exception, bank robbers left their "signatures," following a precise course of action. Some gunmen forced employees and customers to flop face-down on the floor; others had them face the wall or locked them in bank vaults. Each gang was convinced that its technique was the best, and doggedly stuck to it.

Although not exactly a signature, one ingenious bank robber in Indiana set fire to a large barn on the outskirts of a small town. Then, while the volunteer firemen and most of the citizens rushed to the scene, the gunman calmly held up the town's bank with no interference.

A hardened criminal named Homer Van Meter was considered by admirers in the underworld to be an ingenious caser of banks. He had a distinctive signature. Putting on an expensive suit, derby hat, pinch-nose spectacles and spats, and assuming the air of a successful businessman, Van Meter would stroll into a targeted bank and hold a pleasant conversation with the president, who envisioned a wealthy new depositor.

All the while, Van Meter would peer through his spectacles and observe the routines and layout of the bank. What details he could not see with his eyes, the bank president usually would provide. A curious fellow, the prospective "customer" wanted to know who among the staff knew the combination of the vault lock. Perhaps within a week, the bank would be cleaned out by an armed gang that seemed to know every facet of the operation.[6]

4

"Ma" Barker and Her Boys

Chief of Police Manley Jackson of Pocahantas, Arkansas, was suspicious of the two strangers seated in a new DeSoto sedan in front of a jewelry store. Their descriptions matched those of a pair of gunmen who had robbed several stores in southern Missouri in recent days. It was November 28, 1931.

Jackson walked toward the DeSoto. When he was about 15 feet away from the vehicle, the chatter of a Tommy gun erupted and the chief crumpled to the pavement with five bullets in his body. He died a few minutes later.

A pair of ex-convicts, 29-year-old Freddie Barker and Alvin "Old Creepy" Karpis, 32 years of age, threw the DeSoto in gear and raced northward into Missouri. There, the two gunmen hooked up with hardened criminals William "Lapland Willie" Weaver and James Wilson to knock off a bank in Mountain View, Missouri, which had a one-man police force. The four robbers fled with a haul of $7,000.

Barker and Karpis split from the others and holed up for a few days. Then, on December 31, 1931—New Year's Eve—the pair held up a store in West Plains, Missouri, a short distance north of the Arkansas line. Eyewitnesses told Sheriff C. R. Kelly that the robbers had driven away in a late-model DeSoto.

A day later, an automobile matching that description was in a West Plains motor company having repair work done on a balky engine. Attendants grew suspicious; the two strangers appeared to be nervous and kept asking the mechanics how much longer the job would take.

Responding to a call, Sheriff Kelly walked into the shop, his gun strapped in its holster. Creepy Karpis and Freddie Barker pulled out concealed pistols and blasted away, and the lawman collapsed on the garage floor, mortally wounded. There was a roar of an engine as the two gunmen sped away.

Now the heat was on. Barker and Karpis headed for a desolate, hilly region outside Thayer, Missouri, where Freddie's domineering mother, Kate "Ma" Barker, was living with a penny-ante hoodlum named Arthur "Old Man" Dunlop, whom she referred to as "my loving man."

Freddie dreaded the scolding he would receive from his dumpy, middle-aged mother, not because he and pal Karpis had murdered two law enforcement officers, but because the customarily obedient son had not followed Ma's tutoring. She had always preached that the car used when pulling a job should be a nondescript model so as not to draw undue attention from policemen. However, her youngest—and favorite—boy couldn't resist going on his latest crime binge while driving a new DeSoto.

Ma Barker was born Arizona Donnie Clark at Ash Grove, in the southwest corner of Missouri, in 1872. It was the hilly region that nurtured the bloodthirsty outlaws Jesse and Frank James. One of her fondest childhood memories was seeing Jesse ride by one day. James was the girl's idea of a real American hero, and she shed bitter tears when "the dirty coward" Bob Ford killed Jesse by shooting him in the back in 1882.

Kate (as she began calling herself early on) was Ozark Mountains tough and grew into a hard young woman, even though her Scotch-Irish parents were devout Presbyterians and she herself was an avid church-goer and always said "praise the Lord" at meals.

In 1892, when she was 20, Kate married George Barker, an itinerant farm laborer originally from Lebanon, Missouri. George was a mild, inoffensive, quiet man who seemed bewildered by his wife; Kate dominated him, and when he dared make a suggestion, she dismissed his view with a curt wave of her hand.

Shortly after their marriage, Kate and George settled in Aurora, Missouri, where their four sons were born—Herman, Lloyd, Arthur, and Freddie.

Just before the two oldest boys, Herman and Lloyd, reached school age, the Barker family moved to Webb City, a mining town in western Missouri, and lived in a tarpaper-covered house. George had a menial job in the zinc mines, while Kate tended to their four sons. She went to church each Sunday, dragging her reluctant brood along, and sang hymns with the same lustiness as the rest of the congregation.

While in their early teens, the Barker boys became known as ruffians—window breakers and petty thieves. When neighbors complained to meek George, they were told that "you'll have to talk to Kate, she handles the boys."

When they reached their late teens, all of the sons had been charged with some law infraction. Each time one of her boys got into trouble, Kate would become furious, not at her wayward offspring but at the accusers, usually merchants and the police. "My boys are being persecuted!" she complained bitterly.

In 1915, Herman, the oldest boy, now 22, got into serious trouble: he was charged with armed robbery. His mother called on the local prosecutor and tearfully pleaded that the case be dropped. Impressed by this seemingly heartbroken mother's grief over her son's misbehavior, the prosecutor freed Herman.

However, Ma had made up her mind: she would leave Webb City to get her boys away from their "persecutors." Her husband mildly protested the move, but she shouted him into silence.

Ma took husband George and her brood to Tulsa, Oklahoma, and the family settled into an old, rundown house near the Santa Fe Railroad tracks. There Ma went into business for herself, operating a "cooling-off service" in her home. Anyone on the lam and any ex-convict seeking a sanctuary could find it with Mrs. Barker. For a hefty daily fee she provided each "guest" with food, a bed, and a heavy dose of advice on how the crook had botched his most recent endeavor so he would not repeat his blunder.

One of Ma's house guests, an ex-con named Al Spencer, was so inspired by her lectures that he collected a gang and held up the *Katy Limited* passenger train, stealing $22,000 in cash and Liberty Bonds.[1]

Soon after moving to Tulsa, the Barker boys formed the Central Park Gang, a band of young toughs who played in the park in the daytime, then sallied forth at night to commit burglaries. As the years rolled by, the Barker boys blossomed into full-fledged outlaws.

On reaching manhood, all the boys were diminutive, each standing five feet three or five feet four inches tall and weighing between 119 and 125 pounds. But they were muscular and agile—as well as being ruthless and cold-blooded, ready to kill at the slightest provocation.

Inexorably, Ma Barker saw in her sons a means to wealth and power. She kept an even closer watch over her brood—guiding, counseling, and cautioning. The cardinal crime principle she kept hammering into her boys' heads was: "Don't get caught—but if you do get caught, keep you mouth shut!"

While the Barker boys were away on capers, Ma occupied herself with working crossword puzzles, knitting, and preparing hot biscuits to serve on their return.

Tulsa police kept the Barker house under surveillance. When officers called, Ma would meet them at the door, welcome them effusively, and invite them in, talking in rapid-fire fashion all the while. Nothing incriminating was ever found. Loot was never allowed in the house, and the ex-cons using her cooling-off service were shooed away at the first hint of a police visit.

Eventually, Ma decided that her husband, mild-mannered George, was as useless as a fifth wheel to her pursuit of riches. So with no ado, she booted him out of the house. For his part, George was delighted to leave; he had always been frightened by the criminals that were usually roaming the house.

Then Ma's world began to shatter. Arthur "Doc" Barker was caught stealing a government automobile and put in jail. He escaped, was recaptured, and escaped again. A few years later, Doc was arrested and charged with the murder of a night watchman while attempting to hijack a drug shipment at St. John's Hospital in Tulsa.

Doc Barker denied any involvement in the murder and screamed that he was being framed, but he was convicted and sentenced to life in the Oklahoma State Penitentiary at McAlester.[2]

Lloyd Barker's budding crime career also struck a snag. In 1922 he was apprehended while robbing a post office in rural Oklahoma, and was sent to Leavenworth Federal Penitentiary for 25 years.[3]

Freddie, meanwhile, robbed the bank of Windfield, Kansas, and was captured by a sheriff's posse. Ma Barker's tearful pleas to prosecutors were fruitless this time, and her favorite son was sentenced to a five- to ten-year term in the Kansas State Penitentiary at Lansing, at the age of 23.

Now Herman was the only Barker offspring not in jail. In early 1927, Herman and a big-time heistman named Ray Terrill were knocking off banks in Oklahoma, Missouri, and Texas, using a new technique that Terrill had invented. Under the veil of night, the two men merely backed up a truck and winch to a small bank, stole the safe, muscled it into the truckbed, and carted it away, to be cracked at their leisure in some remote locale.

While robbing a bank in western Missouri, Herman Barker and Terrill were captured. Herman was removed to a jail in Washington County, Arkansas, to be tried on other charges. Both men escaped from their jails, and soon teamed up again.

On August 19, 1927, Barker and Terrill held up a store in Newton, Kansas, and police officer J. C. Marshall and another lawman flagged down their getaway car. Barker, at the wheel, braked hard. Both men poked Tommy guns out open windows and blazed away, killing Officer Marshall.

Barker quickly threw the car in gear and drove away in a cloud of dust as the surviving policeman fired several shots at the fleeing vehicle. Within minutes, Barker and Terrill lurched to a halt at another roadblock that was manned by several heavily armed lawmen. A blistering shootout erupted, but the outlaws managed to escape once more.

A day later, Herman Barker's lifeless body was found in a weed patch on the outskirts of Wichita, Kansas. An autopsy disclosed that he had been killed by a single bullet. A coroner's jury ruled his death a suicide.

When Ma Barker heard about her oldest son's violent end, she grew hysterical and screamed: "The police murdered Herman—a Barker doesn't commit suicide!"

In early 1933, Freddie Barker was released from the Kansas prison after serving five years for robbing the Windfield bank, and hurried to Old Man Dunlop's cottage near Thayer, Missouri, for a tearful reunion with his mother. When his long-time cellmate, Alvin Karpis, was discharged on May 2, 1931, he also headed for the Thayer home. Freddie was delighted to see his pal, and introduced him to his mother as Old Creepy, a nickname Karpis was known by because of his cold, piercing eyes, glum expression, and angular, scarecrow frame. Ma took a shine to Karpis and he to her. Creepy liked her homespun sayings: "Remember, crime *does* pay—if you're careful!" and "Cops is lousy!"

Born Alvin Karpowicz in Montreal to Lithuanian immigrant parents in 1907, Karpis got an early start in crime. When he was only ten years of age, he burglarized a few stores in Topeka, Kansas, where his father worked as a car painter with the Santa Fe Railroad. A thin, scrawny youngster with a tendency to be sickly, Alvin had an expert tutor: 18-year-old Arthur Witchey, who passed along the crime tips he had learned while confined in a reformatory and as a freelancer.

When Alvin was 17 years of age, his family moved to Chicago, where the youth and a crony went into business for themselves. They opened a roadhouse where hot merchandise and illegal booze were sold. Two years later Karpis got wanderlust and hopped freight trains throughout the Midwest and South. In Florida, he was roughly dragged out of a boxcar by railroad detectives and was given 30 days on a chain gang as a vagrant.

After his release, 19-year-old Alvin returned to Kansas, where he broke into a warehouse, was caught, and received a five- to ten-year term in the Kansas State Reformatory at Hutchinson. Karpis didn't stay long. His next-door cellmate, a hardened tough named Larry DeVol, and Karpis smuggled hacksaws out of the workshop, hacked through a barred door, and fled from the reformatory.

Karpis and DeVol (alias Larry O'Keefe) began marauding throughout the Midwest, pulling off a few dozen burglaries of stores and warehouses. A year after his escape, DeVol was arrested in Chicago and sent to the Kansas State Penitentiary to complete his reformatory term.

Paroled within a few months, Larry DeVol hooked up with his sidekick Alvin Karpis, and the pair committed numerous burglaries in Missouri and Oklahoma. In Perry, Oklahoma, one night, DeVol, working alone, was interrupted by a policeman while looting a drugstore. DeVol fired his pistol and killed the officer.

A few weeks later in another town, DeVol shot and killed a policeman who had caught him leaving a burglarized restaurant with his haul.

While Larry DeVol—described in wanted posters as a "mad-dog killer"— was on the loose, Alvin Karpis was laying low over in Kansas City. One day, two policemen were suspicious of a parked car with one occupant. Investigating, they found a few weapons and an array of burglary tools in the vehicle. Karpis's protests that he used the guns merely for target practice failed to impress the law officers, nor did his explanation that the car belonged to a friend, when actually it had been stolen. Back Karpis went to the reformatory as an escaped prisoner, and within a month he was transferred to the state prison at Lansing.

Alvin was put to work in a coal mine, where time was knocked off a prisoner's sentence if he mined over a certain amount. Now Karpis's devious mind went into gear. A large number of convicts were in for life stretches, and Karpis agreed to pay them retail price for all the extra coal they would mine for him. Although confined, the lifers could always use money. So Karpis was soon back on the street, way ahead of the originally scheduled time.

A week after Freddie Barker and Creepy Karpis returned to Arthur Dunlop's house after their rampage into southern Missouri and northern Arkansas that left two lawmen murdered, a sheriff's posse, acting on a tip, surrounded the hideout at dawn. They shouted for the occupants to come out with their hands in the air, but there was only silence. When the officers barged inside, no one was at home, but there was evidence of a hasty departure. Ma Barker had contacts in the underworld—and in law enforcement agencies also. Presumably she had been tipped off about the raid in the nick of time.

Ma, Freddie, Karpis, and Dunlop drove to St. Paul, which, like numerous large cities in the nation, was held in warm regard by the traveling men (and a few women) of the illegal trades. It was widely known in the underworld that St. Paul was a "good town," one where crooks could reside relatively unmolested.

In St. Paul, as with Chicago, Kansas City, and other major centers, the underworld was happy to toss a few crumbs from their enormous feasts to lawmen who were willing to look the other way at the right time.

When the Barker gang reached St. Paul in January 1932, its members checked in with flamboyant Harry Sawyer (real name Sandlovich), who ran the free-wheeling Green Lantern speakeasy. Sawyer was the chief "fixer" for the St. Paul-Minneapolis underworld, and every hooligan who came to town was expected to check in with him at the Green Lantern.

Sawyer operated a sort of underworld employment agency. Once he knew a criminal had arrived in St. Paul for an indefinite layover (usually until the heat cooled somewhere else), the newcomer was free to pull off freelance jobs. But Sawyer built up a reserve force of specialists that could be tapped by "employers" for specific assignments—hitmen, safe-crackers, burglars, getaway-car drivers, stickup artists, bank robbers.

Strutting around Sawyer's smoky Green Lantern were the old pros of the Midwest. The clientele included Harvey Bailey, pegged by newspapers as the Dean of America's Bank Robbers; Homer "Big Potatoes" Wilson, who won fame among his peers by knocking off two banks in a single day; Vern Miller, a former South Dakota sheriff-turned-badman; Frank "Jelly" Nash, a noted train robber and murderer; Francis Keating and Thomas Holden, who were ex-convicts, escaped murderers, and high-powered bank robbers; and George Ziegler, known as Shotgun George.

Ziegler (real name Fred Goetz) may have been the best educated, smoothest, and brainiest of the era's gangsters. His character was one of infinite contradictions. Well-mannered and always polite, he was capable of enormous kindness and conscienceless cruelty.

Ziegler had a fine record during World War I, having been a lieutenant and aviator. In 1922 he graduated from the University of Illinois, where he played varsity football and excelled as a golfer.

A few years later, George, a ruggedly handsome young man, was arrested and charged with rape. He jumped bond and, not wanting his parents to lose the money, hatched a scheme to repay them.

George knew that a certain physician was in the habit of carrying large sums of money on his person, so the youth waylaid him, stuck a shotgun muzzle in his face, and demanded money. The doctor, apparently valuing his money more than his life, tried to whip out a pistol that he had a permit to carry, and Ziegler nearly tore the man's head off with a shotgun blast. That bloody caper earned George his nickname in the underworld.

When law enforcement officers next heard of Shotgun George Ziegler, he was a member of the Al Capone mob in Chicago as a torpedo (hitman). Besides reputedly taking part in the 1929 St. Valentine's Day massacre of seven members of Capone's rival George "Bugs" Moran's gang on Chicago's North Side, Shotgun George would be credited with six to ten other murders.

Intermittently, Ziegler would vanish from the Chicago gangland scene when struck by fits of conscience. On those occasions, George, under an alias, worked as a civil engineer, the profession he had studied at the University of Illinois. Fellow engineers at adjacent drawing boards would never know that the pleasant, articulate young man was a hardened criminal and an Al Capone hired gun.

Eventually, Ziegler moved to St. Paul, where he hooked up with a brutal gang of killers and bank robbers known in the underworld as the St. Paul Outfit. Leaders of the Outfit were Francis Keating and Tommy Holden, who had been holdup men in Chicago before moving their base to the Minnesota city.

When Vern Miller wanted to join the St. Paul Outfit, Keating and Holden were suspicious. Even though Miller had served a prison term in South Dakota for embezzling public funds, he had once been a sheriff there. So the gang leaders put Miller to the litmus test.

At random, Keating and Holden singled out a small-time hood they despised and told Miller to "work him over." Miller kidnapped the target, drove him to a secluded spot outside the city and, one by one, broke all the man's fingers. Hard-bitten as they were, Holden and Keating were duly impressed, and Vern Miller was accepted into the St. Paul Outfit.

Such was St. Paul's reputation that when the wife of a renowned Hollywood producer was robbed of her expensive jewels in Chicago, FBI agents and police promptly focused on St. Paul, convinced that the thieves would go there to make contact with buyers of stolen goods. Certain telephones were tapped in St. Paul, and information obtained resulted in the recovery of the jewels and the arrest of the robbers.

One day Francis Keating and Tommy Holden were caught after pulling off a daring robbery of a railway postal car that netted them $135,000. Sentenced to the federal penitentiary at Leavenworth for 25 years, Keating and Holden were short-term guests of the government. Through a clever ruse (using stolen trustees' passes), the two convicts walked away on February 28, 1930, and hurried back to their St. Paul sanctuary.

Once Ma and Freddie Barker and Creepy Karpis had reported to gangland overlord Harry Sawyer in the Green Lantern after fleeing from the police trap at Thayer, Missouri, they took up residence in a house on Roberts Avenue in west St. Paul. Arthur Dunlop, Ma's boyfriend, harped constantly about being confined to the house and threatened to return to Missouri.

Periodically, Freddie and Creepy would be gone for a day or two pulling jobs. One of these was a daring heist of a branch of the Northwestern National Bank of Minneapolis. They returned to Ma with one of their largest hauls: $81,000 in cash and $185,000 in negotiable bonds.

Meanwhile, the son of a nearby apartment landlady had grown suspicious of Ma Barker's house. He noticed that each time two of the occupants (Freddie and Creepy) left on a short trip, they always carried violin cases. Perhaps they were musicians, he reflected, although neighbors told him that they never heard the sounds of a violin being played in the house.[4]

Then, on April 25, 1932, the landlady's son spotted the photographs of Alvin Karpis and Freddie Barker in a detective magazine. An accompanying article said the two gunmen were wanted for the murder of a sheriff at West Plains, Missouri.

The landlady's son immediately notified law enforcement officers, but when the suspect house was raided, no one was at home. Apparently, the fugitives had been alerted, perhaps by one of Harry Sawyer's moles on the police force.

Again the flight was on. Taking a roundabout course, Ma, Freddie, and Creepy drove to Kansas City and holed up in a luxury apartment in an exclusive residential neighborhood. Ma signed the lease as "Mrs. A. F. Hunter." "My boys are in the insurance business," she proudly told the landlord.

A day after Ma, Freddie, and Creepy had high-tailed it out of St. Paul, the naked body of Arthur Dunlop was found sprawled face down on the shore of isolated Lake Freasted in Wisconsin. Eighteen bullets had been pumped into Ma's boyfriend. Nearby was a woman's glove, saturated with blood.

Hardly had Ma, Freddie, and Creepy settled in their plush Kansas City apartment than they began planning to replenish the gang's dwindling treasury. They recruited four members of the St. Paul Outfit—Harvey Bailey, James Clark, Edward Davis, and Frank Sawyer—to help rob the Citizens National Bank of Fort Scott, Kansas. Clark, Davis, and Sawyer were escapees from the Oklahoma State Penitentiary. On June 17, 1932, the gang hit the Fort Scott bank and rushed back to Kansas City to split the $32,000 loot, a disappointing amount.

During the years that the Barker boys had been on rampages, they had committed only state offenses—bank robbery, burglary, theft, armed stickups, and murder—and the FBI was powerless to intervene. But in the course of other criminal investigations, the G-Men had collected an enormous amount of information on the Barkers.

Three of the Barkers' associates—Creepy Karpis and the leaders of the St. Paul Outfit, Thomas Holden and Francis Keating—were escaped federal prisoners, however, and the FBI had been tracking them. Nowhere was the search for Keating and Holden more intense than it was in Chicago, where the two outlaws had first won their crime spurs and had many underworld contacts.

One night two G-Men entered the Minuet Club, a popular spot known as a haunt for Chicago crime figures, in pursuit of Holden and Keating. Dimly lighted and smoke-filled, the club provided privacy for customers by means of booths that had drawn curtains. While one G-Man lounged at the bar to keep an eye on the room, the other agent feigned being drunk and staggered from booth to booth, throwing back the curtains to get an eyeful of the patrons.

At the last booth, a heavyset man with a young blonde woman resented having his seclusion disturbed. Drawing back his fist, the man smashed the agent in the nose. Had the G-Man retaliated, it would have blown his cover and hindered the search for Keating and Holden. So he stumbled out of the Minuet Club with his slightly bemused partner and went home to nurse two black eyes.[5]

In mid-1932, Hoover's persistent bloodhounds dug up a hot lead in their pursuit of Holden and Keating. They traced a telephone call made a year earlier by Charlie Harmon, a big-time bank robber, who had since been rubbed out by his friends because he talked too much. The FBI men discovered that Harmon's call had gone to a manufacturer of golf clubs in Kansas City. Investigating at the business firm, agents discovered that the late Charlie Harmon's old friends, Tommy Holden and Francis Keating, were fond of playing golf at the exclusive Old Mission Country Club, where they rubbed elbows and exchanged pleasantries with Kansas City millionaires and top political figures.

On the afternoon of July 7, 1932, Keating, Holden, and Harvey Bailey, stylishly garbed in white caps, knickers, and plaid stockings, were on a green getting ready to putt. Suddenly, just as Bailey addressed the ball, the three looked up into the muzzles of weapons focused on them by FBI agents and a few Kansas City policemen.

Collaring Harvey Bailey had been a bonus: the lawmen had not been aware that he would be one of the golfers. Later, underworld rumors circulated that the FBI had barely missed hauling in another big fish—Jelly Nash, the train robber and murderer. Nash was such a horrendous golfer that he couldn't keep up with the others in the foursome. So he was a hundred yards behind them, hacking futilely at the little white ball, when his cronies were apprehended.

No doubt when Jelly Nash finally completed his round and returned to the clubhouse, he was puzzled over the disappearance of his three partners.

Under heavy guard, Tommy Holden and Francis Keating were returned to the Leavenworth penitentiary, from which they had escaped in the trustees'-passes ruse, to finish their sentences. Harvey Bailey was put on trial at Fort Scott for the robbery of the Citizens National Bank. Bailey was defended by a Tulsa lawyer, J. Earl Smith, whose hefty fee was allegedly put up by Ma Barker, currently holed up with Freddie Barker and Alvin Karpis at a cottage on White Bear Lake, Minnesota.

One of the witnesses at the trial, E. H. Luikhart, former executive vice president of the Lincoln (Nebraska) Bank and Trust Company, identified Bailey as the leader of the gang that robbed that institution of $3 million a year earlier. Luikhart viewed Bailey in the courtroom and in the sheriff's office. "I'm positive he's the one," the former bank executive declared.[6]

A Liberty Bond from the Fort Scott bank found in his possession was the most damaging piece of evidence against Bailey, and he was sentenced to serve ten to 50 years at the Kansas State Penitentiary at Lansing.[7]

Defense attorney J. Earl Smith promptly issued a motion for a new trial and the judge denied it. Smith announced that he would appeal the conviction to the State Supreme Court.

Meanwhile, Harvey Bailey, manacled at the wrists and ankles, was taken to prison by a heavily armed posse of sheriff's deputies and Fort Scott policemen. "No prison can hold me," Bailey boasted.

J. Earl Smith returned to Tulsa and the next night received a telephone call at his home. Telling his wife and two children that he would be gone for 20 minutes, the native of Jackson, Tennessee, drove away at 8:30 P.M.

Smith's body was found beside his motor car on a lonely road near the Indian Hills Country Club. There was a bullet in his head and he had been badly battered by a blunt instrument. The lawyer's car, parked near his body, had a bullet hole in the windshield and another in the roof. Investigators found inside the car a woman's handkerchief (which did not belong to Mrs. Smith) and a suitcase filled with letters and other papers, most of which were related to Harvey Bailey's trial in Fort Scott.[8]

Meanwhile, Ma and Freddie Barker and Creepy Karpis left their Minnesota hideout and moved back to St. Paul, where Ma bought an expensive house under the name of Mrs. Elton Johnson. Joined by Jelly Nash, an escapee from Leavenworth, and Jess Doyle, who had recently been paroled from prison, Freddie and Creepy drove to Kansas and the gang knocked off the Cloud City Bank in Concordia, returning to St. Paul with a whopping $240,000 in loot.

On September 10, 1932, Oklahoma Governor William "Alfalfa Bill" Murray signed a "banishment pardon" for Arthur "Doc" Barker, who was doing life for murdering a night watchman in Tulsa. Conditions of Barker's release were that he leave Oklahoma and never return. After a brief visit to his mild-mannered father George in southwestern Missouri, Doc rejoined the Barker-Karpis gang in St. Paul.[9]

Shortly after Doc Barker had been handed his prison walking papers, Volney Davis, Freddie Barker's boyhood pal and partner in crime, also strolled out of the Oklahoma prison. Davis was in jail for murdering two policemen and had gained a reputation as an incorrigible prisoner, but Governor Murray granted him a two-year "leave of absence" from the penitentiary. Davis would never return.

In Washington, D.C., FBI Director J. Edgar Hoover was furious about the "banishment pardon" and the "leave of absence" granted to the two murderers. Mincing no words, Hoover hammered at the "political liberals and other sentimental moo-cows" who "believed in lightening the sentences of criminal jackals."

Suddenly alarmed by the epidemic of lawlessness, Americans began taking a look at their "federal police force" and its chief. Although the FBI had been in existence for a quarter century, many within America's rank-and-file had never heard of it.

John Edgar Hoover, they found, was a 37-year-old, robust, iron-jawed super-sleuth. Nearly six feet tall with wavy, coal-black hair, he walked briskly and when he spoke, his words emerged in crisp, staccato bursts. The Director, one of Washington's most eligible bachelors, was sensitive about having spent his entire life in the nation's capital, and he winced when shown newspaper profile stories that inevitably had the theme "home town boy makes good." He told aides: "It sounds like I didn't have enough of what it takes to get out of town and find a job."

Few Boy Scouts or Trappist monks ever had fewer vices than the FBI chief. He drank moderately and only on special occasions, hardly ever smoked, and was never known to tell an off-color joke.

When a big case broke, such as the Lindbergh kidnapping, Hoover's office took on the trappings of a military command post. He fought crime with a vitality that bordered on passion. On occasion, he would tackle several fast-breaking investigations at once, shooting out a barrage of teletyped instructions and inquiries to the 24 FBI field offices strategically sprinkled around the nation or barking orders on the telephone to his far-flung investigative domain, which included all 48 states and U.S. territories and possessions.

His reputation as a fire-eating, two-fisted crime-buster, gained from a flood of media articles, resulted in those who called on Hoover for the first time to expect to be confronted by some sort of ogre.

"I thought when I entered the Director's office for the first time that I'd meet an awe-inspiring figure who immediately would jolt me into wondering if I had paid that overdue parking ticket," a *Washington Herald* reporter exclaimed. "Instead, I held a pleasant discussion with a calm, courteous man who seemed to have nothing better to do than to talk to me."

Hoover's two assistant directors were Harold Nathan, who was in charge of investigations, and Clyde A. Tolson, head of personnel and administration. Both were hard working, dedicated, and deeply loyal to their boss. They were the mystery men of the FBI. Little mention of them was made in the print media. Even those in the official Washington whirl seldom heard of Hoover's two indispensable aides. That suited Nathan and Tolson fine: they made it their business to stay out of the limelight and to doggedly devote their skills and energies to keeping the wheels of the Bureau spinning smoothly at all times.

Nathan and Tolson were direct opposites in appearance and demeanor. Nathan was calm, almost detached, while Tolson was mercurial and animated.

Born in 1881, fatherly Harold Nathan was a rarity in the Hoover regime—a holdover from the previous corrupt Bureau of Harry Daugherty and William Burns. That, in itself, was a tribute to his integrity and ability. A graduate of the City College of New York, Nathan had earned his FBI spurs as an agent in most of the field offices in the east, so he was acutely aware of the problems, limitations, and capabilities of the Bureau men fighting in the trenches. After surviving the mighty swipes of J. Edgar Hoover's housecleaning broom, Nathan was appointed assistant director on May 1, 1925.[10]

Clyde Tolson was born in Laredo, Missouri, in 1900, and graduated from George Washington University, Director Hoover's alma mater. Like his boss, Tolson held a reserve commission in the Intelligence division of the War Department. Before he joined the FBI on April 2, 1928, Tolson had served as confidential secretary to Secretaries of War John Weeks and Dwight Davis.[11]

Tolson had never planned to make the FBI his career, only to remain in it for a year or two to gain experience and save enough money to open a private law practice at Cedar Rapids, Iowa. Starting as an agent in the field, he was soon brought in to FBI headquarters as chief clerk. Hoover appointed him assistant director on January 26, 1931.[12]

In the meantime, far to the west, kidnappers had struck again.

5

The Man Who Planned to Kidnap Babe Ruth

Shortly before midnight on February 12, 1933, Denver lay under a blanket of fresh snow as 31-year-old Charles Boettcher II and his attractive wife Anna Lou rolled in their sleek Cadillac along the deserted streets on their way home from dinner and the theater. The couple lived three blocks from the stone mansion of his parents, Mr. and Mrs. Claude Boettcher, who were among Colorado's most prominent and wealthy families. Seventy-eight-year-old Claude had immigrated from Germany to the Old West as a youth and amassed a fortune in cement and sugar.

Young Boettcher, in the vernacular of the era, had the world by the tail. A 1924 graduate of Yale University, he was president of Boettcher, Newton & Company, a Denver investment firm, and was described in the press as a sportsman and a clubman. Handsome and personable, Boettcher was an aviation enthusiast, and two years earlier he had played host in his palatial home to famed aviator Charles Lindbergh, the first man to fly alone across the Atlantic Ocean. Boettcher and Anna Lou, age 26, were the parents of a five-year-old daughter and Anna Lou was nine months pregnant.

Young Boettcher drove into the driveway of the couple's home and halted to open the overhead garage door. Just then, two masked men, clad in dark clothing and brandishing pistols, leaped from behind shrubbery and one called out, "Come here, Charlie, and throw up your hands!"

Boettcher stepped from the car. The gunmen hustled him across the lawn to a waiting sedan and shoved him inside, and adhesive tape was drawn tightly across his eyes. Then, calmly, one of his captors returned to the Boettcher auto and handed an envelope to the shocked and frightened Anna Lou. A roar of an engine, and the kidnappers and their victim were swallowed by the darkness.[1]

Hurrying inside her home, the distraught wife ripped open the envelope and read a note typewritten on plain white paper:

> Don't notify the police. Tell Claude Boettcher he had better get $60,000 ransom. Follow instructions. Remember the Lindbergh baby would still be alive if ransom had been paid. Notify us through a personal ad stating, "Please write. I am ready to return. Mabel."

Frantically, Anna Boettcher telephoned her father-in-law Claude, and he notified the Denver police department. Chief Albert T. Clark then contacted J. Edgar Hoover, the Director of the Federal Bureau of Investigation in Washington, who ordered Agents Val C. Zimmer and A. R. Gere, in the Bureau's Salt Lake City field office, to fly immediately to Denver to join in the kidnapping investigation.

During the past two years, kidnappings had reached epidemic proportions in the United States. So the square-jawed, black-haired Hoover, a bundle of dedicated energy, had installed in Washington's FBI headquarters a special "kidnap number" (NAtional 8-7117), over which any citizen could directly report an abduction. Director Hoover had standing orders that even when a kidnap call arrived in the middle of the night, it was to be forwarded directly to his Washington home.[2]

Back in Denver on the morning after the Boettcher abduction, the elderly father of the victim complied with the instructions of the kidnappers and inserted the advertisement in the *Denver Post,* indicating his willingness to meet ransom demands.

Meanwhile, Charles Boettcher, his eyes securely taped, had been riding in the back seat of the getaway car as one captor drove and the other sat beside him in the front. The journey continued through the next day and into Monday night, when the car halted at what the victim thought was a farm house.

Boettcher, still blindfolded, was led inside and put into a room with a narrow bed. If he did anything to thwart their efforts to obtain ransom, the kidnappers warned, he would be killed. Despite the threats, Boettcher kept his wits, and set about making certain that the hideout could be identified one day—in the event he lived to tell about his ordeal. He left his fingerprints at many places on the walls of the room and burned a tiny hole with a lighted cigarette at a certain point in the carpet.

Only hours after the kidnapping, Claude Boettcher posted a $5,000 reward for the safe return of his son, triggering a rash of sleuthing by instant amateur detectives. Denver streets were far more crowded than usual, and there was an air of excitement as police cars, with sirens screaming, dashed about the city.

Colorado Governor Howard Johnson released an official proclamation declaring an emergency and calling on citizens in the state to be on the lookout for strangers recently coming to their neighborhoods. Law officers, augmented by 4,000 volunteers from the American Legion and service clubs, by the precinct workers of the Republican and Democratic organizations, by off-duty firemen, and by citizens, began reconnoitering houses and apartments in greater Denver.

Two airplanes were made ready at Denver's Lowry Field in the event contact with the kidnappers would be made in some remote locale elsewhere in Colorado or out of state. The Denver City Council offered a $500 reward for the capture of the kidnappers.

Forty-eight hours passed with no further word from the abductors. Seventy-two hours. A week. Still only silence. Claude Boettcher, who had pulled himself up by his own bootstraps from poverty to riches, was widely known as a man of honor. So he released a statement to the *Denver Post,* guaranteeing that he would pay the $60,000 ransom.

Then the Reverend Benjamin D. Dagwell, dean of fashionable St. John's Episcopal Cathedral and the Boettcher clan's pastor, broadcast over the radio that he, as a man of the cloth, was giving his solemn pledge that the ransom would be paid.

The Reverend Dagwell's broadcast got quick results. In the mail, he received three ransom notes which he immediately delivered to the elder Boettcher. After examining their contents, Claude was convinced that the notes were from the genuine kidnappers and not like the ransom demands that had been pouring in from anonymous individuals who were in no way involved in the abduction.

Boettcher, concerned about his son's safety, refused to divulge to the FBI and Denver police the contents of the notes except that they contained instructions for delivering the $60,000. He turned a deaf ear to the plea of Chief Albert Clark that "our investigators might find in them an overlooked clue to solving the kidnapping."

"I expect to have definite word from those holding my son by tomorrow morning," was all that the elder Boettcher would tell investigators.

All the while, the search for the kidnappers spread throughout Colorado and elsewhere in the Midwest. FBI agents working on the case conjectured that some of the contacts young Boettcher had made in shady gambling halls and nightclubs while on business trips might have been involved in the abduction.

In Chicago, FBI agents questioned a man who, six months earlier, allegedly pulled a gun on Charles Boettcher in a Chicago nightclub and demanded that the heir to a fortune dance with the gun-wielder's wife.

Officers at Colorado Springs arrested a man named O. E. Stevens, alias Charles Belmont, who operated a gambling house. Stevens claimed that young Boettcher had given him an IOU for $1,200 to cover gambling losses a year earlier, but that the money never had been paid.

Ten days after the kidnapping, investigators in Denver learned from a confidential source that the elder Boettcher had secretly made arrangements with his son's captors to pay the ransom that night. Despite his 78 years, Boettcher drove off alone from his home in the darkness, bound for nearby Derby, Colorado, and a rendezvous with the kidnappers.

It was the policy of the FBI not to become involved in ransom negotiations and payments until the victim had been returned safely. However, Denver Detectives J. S. Turner and M. D. Corney tailed Claude Boettcher in an unmarked squad car.

Peering through the rear-view mirror, Boettcher could tell by a car's headlights that he was being followed. Shortly before reaching the spot where he would meet the kidnappers, he slammed on the brakes, climbed out of his auto and walked back to accost the detectives who had not had time to conduct evasive action.

Boettcher was furious and demanded to know, "Why won't you let me handle this my way?" Then he returned to his car with the $60,000 ransom in a container on the front seat and drove back home.

"My excursion failed because I was followed," the elderly tycoon angrily told reporters the next morning. "As long as that police car was on my trail, I knew my efforts to carry out instructions were useless."[3]

Frantic because of his thwarted attempt to contact the kidnappers, the father announced that he had posted at his home and at his son's home the $60,000 demanded.

Claude Boettcher broke with the investigators entirely. "I feel I must and I will act independently," he told newsmen.

Chief Albert Clark rebuked the elder Boettcher. "If the Boettcher family concedes to the demands of the kidnappers and pays the $60,000," Clark declared, "it will have a bad effect on law enforcement, not only in Denver but throughout the nation. We can do very little without the cooperation of the Boettcher family."[4]

Press conferences, which had been held twice daily at the elder Boettcher's home, were suddenly discontinued, leading to speculation that the father again had been in contact with the kidnappers and was preparing to pay the ransom.

On the following night, Claude Boettcher drove away and meandered through the streets of Denver until he was certain that investigators were not trailing him. Then he began traveling along a road on the outskirts of Denver as instructed by another note the Reverend Dagwell had received. Boettcher strained to catch a glimpse of the prearranged signal. Then headlights on a parked car flashed twice. Boettcher pitched out a bundle holding the $60,000 in small bills and kept driving without looking back.

Meanwhile, Charles Boettcher II had been confined to his basement prison for 16 days. Once he was permitted to shave, but the lathered brush and razor were handed to him and he was not allowed to remove his blindfold. His diet was sandwiches along with coffee and milk.

Just before midnight on February 29, the captive was put in the back seat of a car and his kidnappers drove through the night, the next day, and into the following night. Suddenly, the car halted and the heir to millions was told to get out. Then the engine roared and the vehicle disappeared into the blackness.

Boettcher ripped the tape off of his eyes and found that he was at 34th Street near York Avenue in a modest residential area of Denver. He went to a nearby drug store and called his father, who was eating a late supper.

"Dad, I'm free and okay," the son said in a voice cracking with emotion.

Then young Boettcher telephoned a friend who sent a car for him, and he spent the remainder of the night at the friend's home. Word of Boettcher's release was flashed across the United States. When the son reached the father's mansion after daybreak, he had to nimbly leap a low fence to avoid a jostling, shouting horde of reporters and photographers.

Two minutes later, the elder Boettcher threw open the front door and charged onto the porch, brandishing a pistol. "Stand back," he yelled at the milling crowd. "I'm sick and tired of being pestered."[5]

Now Denver became an armed camp and police scoured the region even more intensely, trying to intercept the kidnappers as they fled with their loot. At ten o'clock that night, deputy sheriffs were patrolling the roads near Brighton, Colorado, 20 miles north of Denver, when they spotted a small sedan that answered the description of the one in which the abductors had carried off young Boettcher 17 days earlier.

Turning on their siren, the deputies gave chase. When the fleeing car refused to stop, the officers began shooting. The fire was returned, and for several miles, occupants of the two vehicles conducted a running gun battle with bullets hissing through the blackness in both directions. Steadily, the small sedan pulled away and eluded the pursuers. However, the officers were convinced that some of their shots had hit the other vehicle.

In the meantime, Charles Boettcher provided officers with a red-hot lead. While being driven back to Denver, he had briefly slipped the tape off his eyes and spotted a depot sign at Torrington, Wyoming. Sheriff George Carroll was contacted at Cheyenne, and a posse was formed to scour the region for the hideout where the captive had been held.

Then, in Denver, undercover Patrolman J. H. Wells received a tip that a Burlington, Colorado, insurance salesman, Carl W. Pearce, had been talking about the Boettcher snatch. Acting on his own volition, Wells cultivated an acquaintanceship with the 36-year-old Pearce and gained sufficient information to arrest him.

Pearce confessed that he had copied the Boettcher ransom notes on a typewriter from penciled messages written by an acquaintance, Vern Sankey, who had come to Denver from Canada a few months earlier with Mrs. Sankey to put the couple's two children in school.

Mrs. Sankey was promptly arrested in Denver, and the FBI and police officers found $1,400 of marked ransom money in her possession. Investigators also found Sankey's original drafts of the ransom notes that had been sent to Claude Boettcher. Also taken into custody in Denver was Mrs. Ruth Kohler, age 39, who was Carl Pearce's girlfriend and the sister of Mrs. Sankey.

Now a manhunt was launched for the actual kidnappers, 41-year-old Vern

Sankey and Gordon Alcorn, 33. Also being sought was Arthur Youngberg, 37, who had guarded young Boettcher at a hideaway.

In Washington, a records search at FBI headquarters disclosed that Sankey, Alcorn, and Youngberg all had been employees of the Canadian National Railways, where Sankey had been the engineer and Youngberg the fireman on the same locomotive. Sankey was also wanted as a participant in the robbery of the Regina, Saskatchewan, branch of the Royal Bank in February 1931, in which $13,000 had been taken.

In Denver, Chief of Police Albert Clark sent a group of officers to Wyoming to join in the search for the hideout. The lawmen forced their way though waist-high snowdrifts to a small town where they were telephoned by Clark.

"We've got some new dope," the chief told his men. "Get over to Mitchell, South Dakota, as rapidly as possible. I'm sending an airplane with more officers and machine guns to meet you there."

"There's eight feet of snow in the hills, Chief, but we'll get through," an officer replied.

Abandoning their automobile, the Denver police posse set out on a trek reminiscent of derring-do Hollywood movies in which mounties of the Royal Canadian Police braved the ravages of winter in cross-country pursuits of the bad guys. Traveling on snowshoes and hopping freight cars for 63 miles, the officers arrived at a town in Nebraska on the main railroad line, and there they caught a train to Mitchell.

At dawn the next morning, only five days after Charles Boettcher had been released, a combined force of law enforcement officers from Colorado, Wyoming, and South Dakota, armed with Tommy guns, rifles, and shotguns, swooped down on a ranch house in a wild, isolated region near Chamberlain, South Dakota, and arrested Arthur Youngberg. The officers just missed nabbing Vern Sankey and his crony Gordon Alcorn, who had left the previous evening to try to dispose of some of the hot ransom money.

Youngberg was brought back to Denver and confronted by Charles Boettcher in the office of Chief Albert Clark. Boettcher was in a highly agitated mood, having just come from the hospital where his wife Anna Lou had given birth to the couple's second child. About eight feet separated Boettcher and Youngberg, who held his head down.

"Have you ever seen this man before," Clark asked the suspect. Boettcher, who had been blindfolded while a captive and never saw his kidnappers, knew them only by the sound of their voices. He tightly closed his eyes.

"No, I never seen him in my life," Youngberg declared firmly. With that, Boettcher leaped from his chair toward the suspect.

"You're a lying son of a bitch," he exploded, his fists clenched. An officer clamped a bear-hug on the young investment broker and Chief Clark grabbed Youngberg.

As the months rolled past, Vern Sankey and Gordon Alcorn seemed to have vanished. Meanwhile, in Denver on May 27, 1933, Federal Judge J. F. Symes sentenced Carl Pearce to 26 years in the Leavenworth Federal Penitentiary and Arthur Youngberg to 16 years in prison. A conspiracy to kidnap charge against Mrs. Vern Sankey was dismissed, but she was immediately arrested as a participant in the kidnapping of Haskell Bohn of St. Paul a year earlier. Bohn had been freed after $12,000 was paid to his kidnappers.

Sankey's wife and an ex-convict named Ray Robinson were tried for the Bohn snatch. She was acquitted but Robinson, who fingered Sankey as the leader of the gang that abducted the St. Paul businessman, was sentenced to 25 years in prison.

All the while, Vern Sankey, one of the nation's most-wanted criminals, and Gordon Alcorn were living quietly in a blue-collar neighborhood of Chicago. They exchanged ransom bills at Wrigley Field and Comiskey Park (major league baseball stadiums) and at horse racing tracks in the suburban areas.

One day Sankey and Alcorn got into a bitter dispute, and that night Sankey caught his pal in the act of digging up the bulk of the Boettcher ransom money, which they had buried in a remote field. Harsh words and threats were exchanged. The next night, Sankey sneaked back to the site and dug up the loot for himself.

In early January 1934, Melvin Purvis, special agent in charge of the FBI office in Chicago, received a tip from an underworld informant that Vern Sankey was hiding out in the Windy City.

Locating a fugitive in a metropolis of some three million people is a tedious and frustrating task. In the FBI search for Sankey, there were countless false alarms and futile raids. Then one day agents learned that Sankey may have been living under the assumed name W. E. Clark in a modest house on the outskirts of Chicago.

Sankey no longer lived there, but G-Men learned that a man of his description had been a tenant and that he usually got his mail and haircuts at a small barber shop at 4823 North Damen Avenue, a few blocks away. Bureau men sensed they were hot on the fugitive's trail. Why would a home resident pick up his mail at a barber shop?

When approached by FBI agents, John Mueller, owner of the shop, was apprehensive but willing to cooperate. A buzzer was placed beneath the shelf where the barbers kept their shaving mugs and razors. Three FBI men and three detectives took up a vigil in a rear room of an undertaking establishment next door.

As the days rolled by, it appeared that the neatly planned trap would not be sprung. "Mr. Clark" failed to appear, even though the barber said he came to the shop every two or three days for a shave. What the officers didn't know was that "Mr. Clark" had three moles removed from his face with an electric needle and was unable to shave because of soreness.

Finally, on January 31, "Mr. Clark," with a heavy growth of beard and wearing a baggy brown suit and stained shirt, sauntered into Mueller's barber shop. Greeting the nervous Mueller with a smile and a wave, he slid into a chair.

Hoping that his trembling hands didn't betray him, the barber lathered the customer's face and slapped on a hot towel, which covered his eyes. Then, with a quaking finger, Mueller pressed the buzzer, which sounded next door.

FBI agents and detectives charged out of the mortuary and into the barber shop. Hearing the shuffling of feet, the customer slowly removed the hot towel and found himself staring at the muzzles of six pistols.

Vern Sankey seemed almost happy that his months of dodging law-men were over. When searching the fugitive, the G-Men found poison pills in a pocket.

"Those were to beat the law," he explained. As he was being led from the shop, Sankey told his captors, "I wish I'd made a break for it and been killed."

Sankey was taken to the FBI office on the seventeenth floor of the Bankers Building in downtown Chicago. Eager to talk, he readily confessed to the Charles Boettcher kidnapping. However, he explained that the Denver man was actually his second choice—he had hoped to kidnap Babe Ruth, the New York Yankee slugger and one of America's most popular idols.

Although nearing the end of his career, the Bambino, as Babe Ruth was called, was making the astronomical salary of $80,000 per year at a time the average major league player's pay was around $3,000 annually. Sankey said he had changed his mind about abducting Ruth because it would be too difficult to transport him to a hiding place without someone recognizing the captive. The Babe's moon-shaped, flat-nosed face was as well known as that of President Franklin Roosevelt.

Sankey also informed Melvin Purvis of the location of his Chicago apartment. Agents rushed there and arrested 28-year-old Helen Mattern, with whom he had been living while his wife and two children remained in Denver. Wadded in a tin box in a trunk, G-Men found $3,450 in 100-, 20- and one-dollar bills. Nearby were a shotgun, two revolvers, and several boxes of cartridges.

Escorted by a heavily armed contingent of FBI men and Chicago detectives, Sankey was taken to Sioux Falls, South Dakota, by rail in a private car furnished by the Milwaukee Road and locked in a cell in the state penitentiary. He planned to plead guilty in federal court the next morning to kidnapping Charles Boettcher.

Deputy Marshal Frank Gilmore was guarding Sankey, since the poison pills had indicated that the prisoner might try to commit suicide. In a nearby cell, Gordon Alcorn, who had been arrested separately in Chicago, asked Gilmore for some headache tablets. When Gilmore returned five minutes later, Vern Sankey was dead, hanging by two neckties, knotted into a noose, from a crossbar. He had stuffed a handkerchief into his mouth to stifle sounds of strangulation.[6]

Alcorn grimly told the guards, "I ain't goin' to kill myself. I'd rather take my chances in court." A few weeks later he took his chances—and was sentenced to 25 years in prison for kidnapping Charles Boettcher II.

6

The Great Prison Breakout

All through the month tension hovered over the bleak Kansas State Penitentiary at Lansing. Warden Kirk Prather had been aware of unrest in the crowded facility and instructed officials and guards to exercise special vigilance and take precautionary measures to prevent a mass breakout.

Inmates suspected of rebellious plans were shifted frequently from one cell block to another, work assignments were changed, and visitors were watched with intense care. A convict had told Warden Prather that guns were being sneaked into the prison, but a close inspection of incoming provisions failed to turn up any weapons. It was May 1933.

One report that reached the warden indicated that a mass breakout was to be tried through his office and that a bomb had already been hidden near the entrance door. The infernal device would be timed to explode and kill Prather when the escape was launched.

Prather was not unduly concerned about the rumors. In the prior two years, one or two convicts had tried to escape a few times, and each effort had been thwarted. An elaborate plot for a mass escape had been frustrated in September 1931 when a life-term convict tipped off the warden.

Early in the morning of Memorial Day 1933, Warden Prather, along with 1,861 inmates, was watching a baseball game between American Legion teams from Topeka and Leavenworth in the prison yard. Among the convicts idly milling around near the warden were 32-year-old Wilbur "Lone Wolf" Underhill and 49-year-old Harvey Bailey, both the toughest of the tough.

Underhill was serving a life sentence for murdering Merle Colver, a Wichita policeman. Two years earlier, Underhill had escaped from the Oklahoma State Penitentiary, where he was incarcerated for two other murders. Three of his four years at the Oklahoma prison had been spent in solitary confinement because of repeated rebellious and violent behavior.

Bailey had been convicted for the Fort Scott, Kansas, bank robbery. His rap-sheet was three feet long.[1]

Now Underhill and Bailey slipped behind Warden Prather who was seated in the back row of the low wooden stands. In a flash, Underhill stuck a pistol in the warden's ribs. A third convict pinned the official's arms behind him.

At the same moment, other convicts pulled pistols from their prison garb and forced three nearby guards to join Warden Prather, Underhill, and Bailey. Moving as a group, the four prison officials, covered by six armed convicts, headed across the yard to Watchtower Post 3, where they were joined by five other inmates.[2]

Kirk Prather's thoughts flashed back to December 31, 1931, when seven inmates at the Leavenworth Federal Penitentiary (only a few miles away) had kidnapped and shot Warden T. B. White. Was he to meet the same fate? Prather recognized the 11 armed convicts as desperate men with little or nothing to lose—murderers, bank robbers, habitual criminals—all serving life or long terms of up to 100 years.

Lone Wolf Underhill halted the group and told the warden: "Here's our plan. We'll kill all 14 guards within range of our guns, then kill you, unless you do what I say."

Prather, remarkably cool under the circumstances, nodded. It was a tension-packed moment. Overhead, a guard on the wall had his Tommy gun pointed down toward the knot of 15 persons. A few long bursts could kill or wound the entire lot, including the warden and the three guards.

Just then the eerie wail of a siren pierced the cloudless blue sky and ricocheted off the thick gray walls of the prison—a signal that an escape was in progress. "Okay, if that's the way they want to play," Underhill snarled to Harvey Bailey, nodding toward captive guard John Sherman, "Then kill the bastard!"

Bailey lifted his pistol, but before he could fire, Warden Prather shouted to the guard with the Tommy gun on the wall: "Put down your weapon and don't fire under any circumstances!"

Hundreds of other inmates gawked at the spectacular escape unfolding in the prison yard, but none chose to join Underhill and his ten comrades in the break-out.[3]

Acting on Underhill's orders, Prather shouted for the guards in the watchtower to open the small door near the bottom and, one by one, the group climbed a ladder to the top. Underhill fastened the end of the wire noose around the warden's neck to his own wrist, forming a leash and enabling the convict to strangle Prather at will.

A coil of rope, used for lifting fuel and provisions, was thrown down the outside of the wall. Underhill instructed the warden to slide down the rope and he followed, still clinging to the wire leash. Guards John Laws and John Sherman, along with the other ten inmates, took turns lowering themselves to the ground.

It had been a swift operation: less than ten minutes had expired since Warden Prather had been grabbed. While the convicts huddled to decide their next move, John Stewart, a guard stationed 100 yards down the wall, fired a rifle shot. Convict Harvey Bailey let out a yelp and fell with a bullet wound in his leg. Writhing on the ground and grimacing, Bailey cursed and told Prather he was going to kill him. The warden waved both arms frantically for all shooting to stop.

Moments later, a small car driven by 15-year-old Virginia Woodson, daughter of the prison farm superintendent, approached. Wilbur Underhill, brandishing a pistol, leaped into the road and halted the car. The girl, terrified by the unexpected encounter with 11 hardened desperadoes, was pulled roughly from the vehicle.

James Clark, who was serving up to 100 years for the Fort Scott bank heist, took the wheel and six other inmates crammed themselves into the car. The remaining escapees, along with Prather and the two guards, stood on the running boards or clung to every available space on the outside of the auto.

Clark began driving down the dirt road skirting the prison farm as the 14 men inside and clinging to the outside gasped for breath and held on for dear life. Wedged inside, Underhill held onto the leash around the neck of Warden Prather, who was standing on the running board.

"You show us how to keep out of the mud," the convict ringleader told the warden, "Or I'll blow your goddamned head off! Understand?"

Prather nodded and replied that he would direct the driver to a good road.

While heading south toward Highway 5, Underhill got his pistol tangled with his clothing and accidentally fired a shot that caused everyone on board to duck instinctively. No one was hit as the bullet tore through the rear window.

"Be careful with that goddamned thing!" Harvey Bailey snapped.

About 20 miles from the prison, Wilbur Underhill decided that the 11 convicts should split up. So when an automobile approached from the opposite direction, the getaway car halted and three convicts stood in the middle of the road with their weapons.

At the wheel of the other car was M. J. Woods, a railroad employee, and beside him was his 38-year-old, partially paralyzed wife, Alberta. In the back seat were two 17-year-old girls, the Woods's daughter Louise and her friend Clarice Wears. Twenty minutes earlier, the carefree group had left the Woods's home in Kansas City, Kansas, to drive to the town of Leavenworth to place flowers on the grave of Woods's grandfather, a Civil War veteran, at the National Military Home.

Seeing the convicts pointing their weapons in his direction, Woods braked hard and got out of the car as ordered. Alvin Payton, serving 20 years for bank robbery, climbed in behind the wheel, and four convicts got in after him. Eight people were wedged in the vehicle.

One escapee said to teenager Louise Woods: "Sit on my lap."

Despite the frightening situation, the girl replied, "You can shoot me if you want to, but I'll not sit on your lap." She sat on Clarice Wears's lap and the crowded automobile sped away, leaving M. J. Woods standing beside the road.

Payton, the driver, made Louise give him her white sports coat and another convict put on Clarice's coat.

"We ain't goin' to harm you gals," one man said. "You're lucky. Those six other guys we left back there are 'hard babies,' and you'd be in big trouble if they had you."[4]

In the meantime, the car with Wilbur Underhill, five other convicts, Warden Prather, and the two prison guards drove off in another direction. When the vehicle developed engine trouble, the convicts halted a Chevrolet and forced the terrified occupants to get out, and the eight men climbed into and onto the vehicle. Edward Davis, a habitual criminal who had been sentenced to a term of up to 100 years for the Fort Scott bank job, took the wheel.

A short distance south of Ottawa, Kansas, Lone Wolf Underhill spotted a police car coming toward them. From his vantage point on the running board, prison guard John Sherman thought the vehicle held two officers and was carrying a machine gun. A shootout loomed.

The getaway car halted and four convicts with drawn pistols leaped out to do battle. After coming within shooting range, the police car stopped, went into reverse, quickly turned around and raced off in the opposite direction.

Ten minutes later, a dairy employee, Ed Clum, his wife, and son were riding in their car a mile east of Galesburg, Kansas. None of them had heard about the big prison breakout at Lansing. Suddenly, Clum's car was brought to a halt when the Chevrolet packed with men cut it off. Convicts Frank Sawyer, serving 20 years to life for bank robbery, and Bob "Big Boy" Brady, in prison with a life term as a habitual criminal, robbed Clum of $2 at gunpoint, then forced the family out of their car. Taking captive guard John Laws with them, Sawyer and Brady drove off in the Clum car.

Underhill, three other convicts, Warden Prather, and guard Sherman continued in the Chevrolet. One escapee produced a pint of whiskey, an act greeted with loud cheers, and passed the bottle to all but the warden and the guard.

Now the convicts' tongues were loosened by the booze and they began to chat with their captives. "Well, you boys sure pulled a clever job," Warden Prather remarked. "We suspected two weeks ago that you were smuggling guns, but we couldn't find them."

Harvey Bailey, grimacing from his wound, replied, "You boobs never looked in the right places."[5]

At twilight, the Underhill group reached the rugged Cookson Hills of northeastern Oklahoma, a region that had been a hideout for criminals since before statehood in 1907. The convicts and their two hostages had traveled unchallenged for some 200 miles. Underhill turned to Kirk Prather and said, "Warden, here's where we're going to bump you off. We've been waiting all day to get to these hills.''

Knowing that the hard-bitten ringleader had already been charged with or convicted of murdering three men, Prather was convinced that his time on earth would be measured in minutes.

"On the other hand, Warden, you've been a pretty decent guy," Underhill said. "Don't think I've ever met a better warden—and I've met a lot of 'em. You've handled the joint pretty well."

At a secluded spot, the Chevrolet stopped and Underhill said, "Here's where you boys get out." Prather and the two guards stepped out of the car, expecting to be riddled with bullets at any moment. All of the convicts, even the limping Harvey Bailey, followed.

"Got any dough?" Underhill asked. The warden had 30 cents, Laws had 18 cents, and Sherman had 25 cents.

"A bunch of cheap bastards, aren't they?" Underhill exclaimed. His companions laughed uproariously.[6]

Reaching into his pocket, Underhill handed the warden a dollar bill. "Here, take this," he said. "You may want something to eat or smoke—if you can ever find a town in these hills."

Then the convicts returned to the Chevy and drove away. Kirk Prather and the two guards couldn't believe their good fortune. They made their way to Welch, Oklahoma, where the warden telephoned the Kansas State Penitentiary to report that he and the guards had been released unharmed.[7]

One of the largest manhunts in United States history had been launched. Since stolen cars had been taken across state lines, the FBI joined in the search, but the 11 desperate convicts seemed to have vanished into the rugged hills where Kansas, Missouri, Oklahoma, and Arkansas converge. Posses hunted the heavily timbered badlands to no avail. Squads of police and deputy sheriffs guarded the highways, halted cars, and looked into their trunks. They were ready to shoot to kill.

On the night of May 31—some 36 hours after the mass escape—residents of Chetopa, Kansas, heard a shot. Knowing that escaped desperadoes were loose in the region, a few armed civilians went to investigate and found the body of Night Policeman Otto L. Durkee in an automobile accessory shop. Durkee, a decorated veteran of World War I, had been killed instantly by a bullet through the head.

Since Chetopa is only 15 miles from the point where Warden Prather and his guards had been released earlier that night, authorities were convinced that Wilbur Underhill and his cohorts were stealing a tire to replace one that had gone flat when they were confronted by Officer Durkee.

At about the same time that Otto Durkee had been gunned down, Mrs. Alberta Woods, her daughter Louise, and Clarice Wears were eating a midnight supper with their captors at the farm home of William New, near Pleasenton, Kansas, about 100 miles south of the Kansas State Penitentiary. An hour earlier, the escapees had pulled up to the home, brandished their weapons at the frightened New and his wife, and ordered Mrs. New to prepare a meal.

After eating the meal, the convicts took five pairs of overalls, five shirts, and five hats from New's closet, along with a shotgun and shells. Then the men transferred New's license plates to their own car, cut the telephone lines leading to the house, got into their vehicle, and drove off into the night.

Despite her harrowing ordeal, teenaged Clarice Wears could find a ray of humor. "I think I'll spend Memorial Day working in my garden," she told her companions.

Moments later shock set in. Mrs. Woods and the two girls began to tremble, and they spent the remainder of the night alert for a sound that would herald the return of their captors to the isolated farm.

That same night in northwest Arkansas, Siloam Springs Chief of Police Bob La Follette received a report that an automobile had just been stolen in town. A short time later, while patrolling in his squad car, the chief spotted the stolen vehicle, which was occupied by three men. Turning on his siren and red light, La Follette gave chase and, when the driver failed to stop, the chief opened fire.

Escapee Wilbur Underhill and two pals shot back and the running gun battle raged along a blacktop highway until Chief La Follette lost track of the other car's red tail lights and gave up the pursuit.

After daylight, the car stolen in Siloam Springs was found abandoned at the end of a country road in northeastern Oklahoma. Graphic testimony to Chief La Follette's marksmanship were the five bullet holes in the automobile.

Early the next morning (May 31) in southwestern Missouri, two disheveled men hitchhiking on Route 66 near Joplin were picked up by a young couple, B. K. Blair and Alice Braithwaite, both of Joplin. A minute after the hitchhikers got in the car, they pulled a gun on their benefactors and ordered them to "keep driving 'til we tell you to stop."

The talkative hitchhikers told the couple that their names were Jim Clark and Clifford Dopson, that they and nine others had "blown" the Kansas penitentiary and that they had separated from their companions a short time before.

"We had to kill a bull (policeman) last night," one convict remarked in a casual tone. The "bull" may have been the World War I hero policeman Otto Durkee at Chetopa, Kansas.

At a point near Neosho, Missouri, Clark and Dopson released the couple and took over their car.

That same day in the Kansas capital of Topeka, newly inaugurated Governor Alfred M. Landon was sputtering with rage. He described the mass break of 11 hardened convicts and the kidnapping of Warden Prather and two guards as "outrageous and a blot on our state." Landon then announced a reward of $350 for the apprehension of each of the convicts, "dead or alive."[8]

People in four states were living in terror. All over the nation, the desperate and sometimes bloody escape saga was the focus of millions. An editorial in *The New York Times* said:

> It is in Jesse James country that the adventure of the eleven fugitive Kansas convicts is working itself out. The professors say that the American frontier passed away in the year 1890, but the spirit of the "Wild West" is in this entire episode—the amazing boldness of the escape from prison, the taking of hostages, the flight across country, down to the disappearance of the fugitives in the wilds of the Ozarks.

Two days after the big breakout, a pair of armed men charged into the Bank of Chelsea in Chelsea, Oklahoma, and shouted, "This is a holdup—get your hands in the air!" Customers and bank clerks were gruffly ordered to lie on the floor or "we'll blow your brains out!"

Then the gunmen leaped the counter, hurried into the cages, and scooped up $2,500 in currency. There was much more cash in sight, but just then gunfire erupted outside. Across the street, City Marshall Ed Chiles had opened fire on four of the robbers' companions who were waiting outside the bank in two automobiles.

From inside the getaway cars, the four men fired back. After their two comrades ran out of the bank, the cars roared off with Marshal Ed Chiles still blazing away at them. Near the end of the main street a citizen, who had heard that the bank had been robbed, whipped out a pistol and took several potshots at the robbers' automobiles as they raced past and on out of town.

Shown a rogue's gallery of mug shots, eyewitnesses identified one of the bank robbers as Wilbur Underhill.

Along their trail of terror in four states, the 11 Kansas escapees had added bank robbery to charges of kidnapping, car theft, and murder.

Early the next morning, Sheriff Carl Curtis of Delaware County, Oklahoma, and his posse got into a blistering gunfight with three men trying to flee in an automobile 20 miles outside of Jay. Abandoning their vehicle, the three men fled on foot into thick woods.

Three hours later Sheriff Curtis received a tip that a suspicious stranger had entered a farm home near Dripping Springs, Oklahoma. Curtis and his posse rushed to the locale, surrounded the house, and ordered the stranger to come out.

Inside, escapee Lewis Bechtel, who was serving a long term for bank robbery, was eating lunch as the farmer and his wife fearfully stood by. Bechtel set his pistol on the table and emerged with his hands in the air. "I'm glad it's over," he told the sheriff. Bechtel was the first of the 11 escapees to be captured.

That night in Pine Bluff, Arkansas, a young couple, Austin Adams and Beatrice Garner, were seated in a car waiting for Adams's brother to return from a nearby photography shop. Suddenly, two Kansas escapees came up to the vehicle, one on each side, and drew pistols. One man took the wheel of the car while the other held his weapon on Adams and Garner.

The convicts drove out of Pine Bluff and began a wild, 12-hour meandering ride over large portions of southern Arkansas. Several times they stopped for gasoline and oil, using money taken from Adams. At each stop, the kidnapped couple was threatened with death if they tried to signal the attendant.

Finally, Adams persuaded the men to release him and his girlfriend, and the couple was dropped off at the Malvern, Arkansas, railroad station. The abductors gave them money for train fare back to Pine Bluff.

From a newspaper picture, Austin Adams and Beatrice Garner identified one of their abductors as Kenneth Conn.

Meanwhile, Frank Sawyer, who had been serving a term of up to 100 years for bank robbery, was on a kidnapping binge in central Oklahoma. At about 7:30 A.M. he abducted two boys near Norman, home of the University of Oklahoma. A few minutes later, Sawyer released them and kidnapped Mr. and Mrs. Fred Gray of Lawton, Oklahoma, and took their car, forcing the terrified couple to go with him.

Sawyer drove toward Middleburg, where the car had a flat tire. The convict stole another vehicle from a man and his wife and ordered them to accompany him and the Grays. When a steering rod on that machine went bad, the convict drove to the farm home of Mr. and Mrs. J. H. Strongfield, took their car at gunpoint, and forced them to go with him and the four others.

With six hostages packed in the car, Sawyer continued to the home of Olin Morris. There he released Gray and his wife and ordered Morris and his son to go with him and the other kidnap victims. After driving the Morris car to a farm near Gracemont, the convict got out and told his captives to drive on.

Then Sawyer walked to a farm home where Bob Goodfellow, Caddo County Clerk, was visiting a young woman, and compelled the couple to drive him north in Goodfellow's automobile. East of Binger, the driver lost control and ran off the road, and the car was stuck in a ditch. Sawyer, Goodfellow, and the woman stepped out. Less than a minute later, Sheriff Horace Crisp and Deputy Al Marlow drove up and got out of their squad car. Recognizing Bob Goodfellow, Crisp asked if he wanted his car pulled out of the ditch.

Suddenly, Sawyer grabbed Goodfellow and, using him as a shield, opened fire. The officers whipped out their revolvers and shot back. A bullet struck Goodfellow in the groin and he and Sawyer fell to the ground with arms and legs tangled.

Goodfellow's girlfriend pounced on the convict and pulled his hair. Crisp and Marlow also leaped on Sawyer and subdued him. Taken to the jail at Chickasha, Oklahoma, Frank Sawyer admitted his identity.

Thirteen days after the Kansas prison breakout, U.S. Customs Officers W. K. Kilborn and J. A. Tilley were routinely checking titles and bills of sale of vehicles approaching the Rio Grande River, the border of Mexico. Tilley leaned over to talk with the occupants of an automobile carrying two men, two women, and a baby.

In a flash, Officer Tilley pulled out his revolver and pointed it at the two men. From wanted bulletins, he had recognized them as Billy Woods and Clifford Dopson, escapees from the Kansas prison. Along with their girlfriends, the convicts had been heading for Mexico in the stolen car.

Four months passed, and seven of the 11 escapees had eluded the massive dragnet. Then, on October 6, 1933, Sheriff Ira Allen and Deputy Ed Jackson halted a car on a highway east of Tucumcari, New Mexico. When the officers walked toward the vehicle, the driver stuck a pistol out of the open window and fired. Allen and Jackson responded with two blasts from their shotguns. Pellets struck the driver, Bob "Big Boy" Brady. Bleeding but not seriously wounded, the Kansas escapee surrendered.

Inside Brady's stolen car the officers found a small arsenal of weapons and about $3,500 in currency, which was traced to an armed holdup of the First National Bank of Frederick, Oklahoma.

In the weeks ahead all the remaining escapees, except for the ringleader, Wilbur Underhill, were captured or killed. Underhill, billed in the press as "The Tri-State Terror," was thought to have fled to Mexico. Then, on December 30, 1933, R. H. Colvin, special agent in charge of the Federal Bureau of Investigation office in Oklahoma City, received a tip from an informant that Underhill was holed up in a house in Shawnee, Oklahoma.

At midnight on New Year's Eve, G-Men Colvin and Frank Smith, along with several Oklahoma City policemen and deputy sheriffs, reconnoitered the suspected hideout but it was dark and appeared to be empty. Not wanting to tip their hand, the lawmen left and returned three hours later. At 2:30 A.M., lights were on in two rooms, and the posse surrounded the bungalow.

Colvin and Policeman Clarence Hurt sneaked up to a window where a light was burning. Despite the cold weather, the window was half open—presumably to expedite a sudden flight. Colvin recognized Wilbur Underhill. With pistol in hand, the G-Man shouted through the open window, "Stick 'em up, Wilbur!"

Underhill was standing and his 37-year-old wife, whom he had married a few weeks earlier in Coalgate, Oklahoma, was sitting on the edge of a bed. Whirling, the Lone Wolf grabbed a weapon from a small table and fired through the window, the bullet hissing past Agent Colvin's head.

Colvin ducked for cover and the posse of officers around the house began blazing away with Tommy guns, rifles, and shotguns. Bullets streamed into the bedroom and into an adjoining room where Raymond Roe (alias Ralph Rowe) and a female beautician were in bed.

Roe was wounded in the right shoulder and his girlfriend was hit in the stomach by a pellet. Underhill dashed into another room and his wife fainted.

Moments later the ear-splitting gunfire ceased and an eerie silence descended over the neighborhood. Suddenly, Underhill threw open the front door and, firing with pistols held in each hand, darted across open ground as the lawmen sprayed him with a torrent of bullets. The shadowy figure went down, then got up and kept running until disappearing behind a house.

G-Men Colvin and Smith and other officers cautiously edged into the hideout and arrested Raymond Roe, Mrs. Underhill (after she revived), and Roe's wounded girlfriend, who was rushed to a hospital where she died a few hours later.

Found in Underhill's clothing was $5,300 in bonds that had been part of the loot taken when two gunmen held up the State National Bank of Frankfort, Kentucky, a few days earlier. The robbers had also stolen $9,515 in currency.

In the meantime, Underhill, leaving a trail of blood, made his way for 16 blocks, broke into a furniture store, and hid under the covers on a bed. A small group of lawmen stormed into the store and took the escaped ringleader into custody.

"His body was riddled by 13 bullets," Sheriff Stanley Rogers of Oklahoma City told reporters. "How he managed to keep going through all the machine gun fire and how he managed to get 16 blocks to the store is beyond understanding."[9]

Later that morning, Mrs. Underhill was escorted by guards to Municipal Hospital to see her husband. She was expensively clothed and wore several large diamonds. Sobbing at her husband's bedside, Mrs. Underhill said in a choked voice, "Wilbur's a good man and he's been trying to go straight, but they just won't let him."[10]

Five days after Wilbur Underhill was brought to the Shawnee hospital, the FBI picked up reports from underworld informants that a plan was afoot to "deliver" him. So late on the afternoon of January 5, 1934, the fugitive was placed in an ambulance and G-Men rushed him to the Oklahoma State Penitentiary at McAlester, 70 miles away.[11]

Three and a half years earlier, on July 14, 1931, Underhill had escaped from that same prison where he was serving a life term for killing an Okmulgee, Oklahoma, drug store clerk in a robbery. Now, as his stretcher was being carried through the gates, the Lone Wolf smiled weakly at Warden Sam Brown and whispered, "I'm ready to come back home."[12]

Two hours later, Wilbur Underhill died.

The "Texas Rattlesnake" and His Moll

Residents in a respectable neighborhood of Joplin, Missouri, had grown suspicious of the hard-featured young woman and two men who had moved into a rented apartment three weeks earlier in March 1933. One nervous citizen telephoned the police and complained that "they're darting in and out of the apartment at night like frightened animals."

Joplin police dismissed the call as that of a paranoic woman with nothing better to do than to spy on her neighbors. Actually, the persons in the apartment were two of the Great Depression era's most kill-crazy desperadoes, Clyde Barrow and Bonnie Parker. Holed up with them was 19-year-old William Daniel Jones, whom the couple had kidnapped while robbing a gasoline station in Dallas. After finding out who his captors were, young Jones joined them willingly. Clyde needed the youth to be his accomplice in robberies—and to help try to cope with Bonnie's insatiable craving for sex.

Neighbors became more alarmed when a new couple joined the three persons in the apartment. They were Clyde's older brother, Ivan M. "Buck" Barrow, and Buck's black-haired, attractive wife, Blanche. Buck had been serving a long term in a Texas prison for a string of armed robberies, but had just been granted a full pardon by Governor Miriam A. "Ma" Ferguson, who had handed out pardons to 2,000 convicts during her first term in office in the 1920s.

Joplin police headquarters now dispatched officers to investigate. Peeking from behind curtains, Clyde and Buck Barrow saw three policemen step out of their cars and walk toward the apartment. A burst of gunfire erupted, and officers Harry L. McGinnis and Wes Harryman were shot dead and the other was wounded.

Clyde Barrow and teenager Bill Jones received grazing wounds in the shootout, but all five members of the gang slipped out the back door and fled in a car that had been parked for just such an emergency.

Born on a farm near Telice, Texas, on March 24, 1909, Clyde Barrow was one of eight children. His older brother Buck had always been his idol, and the boys got into repeated trouble. In 1918, Clyde was committed to the Harris County School for Boys as an incorrigible thief and truant. Released in his teens, he went to Houston, where he began rolling drunks and stealing high-powered automobiles. Then he joined the Square Root Gang, a group of youthful petty thieves and penny-ante burglars.

During the late 1920s, Clyde returned to Dallas, where he and Buck teamed up to rob Mom and Pop grocery stores and gasoline stations. In 1928, the brothers decided to expand their zone of operations and held up a gasoline station in Denton, Texas. Fleeing from the scene with Clyde at the wheel, the Barrows were jumped by police in a squad car. A wild chase ensued at speeds up to 55 or 60 miles per hour.

The pursuing officers opened fire, and Buck was slightly wounded. Then Clyde lost control of the car on a sharp turn and crashed into a ditch. Abandoning his brother to the police, Clyde scrambled from the disabled vehicle and fled. Charged with robbery, Buck received a five-year term at the Eastham State Prison at Waldo, Texas.

In January 1930, Clyde was living in West Dallas when he met 19-year-old Bonnie Parker, who resided with her devout Baptist parents in Cement City, a short distance from Dallas. Five feet, three inches tall and slender (99 pounds), Bonnie had bobbed auburn hair, blue eyes, and a fair complexion. She walked with a peculiar gait, both knees slightly buckled.

When she was sixteen years of age, Bonnie married her childhood sweetheart, Roy Thornton, who soon began serving a 99-year term in Eastham for murder. His young wife began "dating" her men friends, of which there was no shortage. Bonnie complained to her mother that she was "bored crapless," and then Clyde Barrow came into her life. Clyde was 20 years old at the time, five feet, seven inches tall, and weighed about 150 pounds. Bonnie was fascinated with his tattoos, an anchor and shield on one forearm and the bosom of a woman on the other forearm.

Less than a week after Clyde and Bonnie first laid eyes on one another, they began living together. Even though Clyde was homosexual, he tried mightily to satisfy his nymphomaniac paramour, a nearly impossible task.[1]

Shortly after the odd couple linked up, Clyde burglarized a small store in Waco, Texas, and his fingerprints were discovered. Later, Dallas policemen broke into Clyde's and Bonnie's small apartment while the couple was engaged in a passionate interlude on a sofa. Pulling on his trousers, Barrow was hauled off to jail and faced seven charges of car theft, burglary, and robbery. After pleading guilty to three counts, he was given a two-year sentence in the Waco jail.

Bonnie was nearly hysterical. "It was such a shock to learn that Clyde was a criminal," she tearfully lied to her mother.

Bonnie soon recovered from her shock, and visited Clyde in the Waco jail. She slipped him a loaded pistol (which had been taped to the inside of her thigh) and within a few hours, Barrow was out of jail and on the run.

Five days later, Clyde held up a railway office at Middleton, Ohio, but was captured by police before he could flee. Returned to Texas, Barrow was sentenced to the full term of 14 years for his earlier crimes and for jailbreaking. This time he was sent to the state prison at Eastham.

Eastham was no country club. Convicts had to work all day in the hot sun picking cotton as guards on horseback kept close watch. In the evening, the inmates had to run all the way back to the prison. It was not uncommon for convicts to sever their heel tendons to make themselves unfit for work. Clyde persuaded a cellmate to chop off two of his (Barrow's) toes with an axe.[2]

An Eastham convict, Ed Crowder, informed police officials that Clyde Barrow had been gambling, and he was put in isolation for several days. Three days after Barrow was returned to his cell block, Crowder was found dead in a remote part of the prison, his head beaten to a pulp by a heavy metal pipe.

After serving 20 months of his 14-year sentence at Eastham, Barrow was paroled after his mother made a tearful plea to Governor Ross Sterling. "I'll die before I ever see the insides of a prison again," Clyde prophetically told a cellmate on leaving.[3]

In March 1932, Clyde and Bonnie linked up again, stole a car, and were overtaken at Mabank, Texas, by police after a wild chase. Bonnie was captured and spent three months in jail at Kaufman, Texas. Clyde eluded the police.

With Bonnie in jail, Barrow recruited a hardened young criminal, 19-year-old Ray Hamilton, to be his accomplice. The two men had long known each other, both having been in the Square Root Gang in Houston and later cellmates at Eastham.

On April 17, Barrow and Hamilton entered a jewelry store at Hillsboro, Texas, drew their weapons, and demanded that owner John W. Bucher hand over the firm's money. When 65-year-old Bucher seemed to be stalling, a shot rang out and the jeweler toppled over dead. The bandits fled with a take of $40 they grabbed from the cash register.

Governor Ross Sterling put a $250 bounty on Clyde's head, but that gesture failed to impede the outlaw. He and Hamilton knocked off a string of gasoline stations in the Dallas and Lufkin, Texas, areas, with their biggest haul in any one job being $76. Then Hamilton and Barrow, looking for a good time, paid a visit to a barn dance in the little town of Atoka, Oklahoma.

Outside the dancehall the two gunmen, who had been drinking heavily, struck up a conversation with a group of men. When Clyde pulled out a bottle of booze and began taking a drink, Sheriff C. G. Maxwell and Deputy Eugene Moore happened to appear.

"Cut that out!" Maxwell called out. "We don't permit that here."

Prohibition laws were in force. Moments later two guns barked. Deputy Moore, shot through the head and heart, was killed instantly. Sheriff Maxwell slumped to the ground, mortally wounded.

By now, Bonnie Parker had been released from the Kaufman jail, and she quickly hooked up again with Barrow and Hamilton. That same day, August 12, 1932, the three desperadoes held up the Neuhoff Packing Company in Texas, and escaped with their biggest bundle of loot, $1,100.

With Bonnie remaining in the getaway car as a lookout, Barrow and Hamilton raided the Texas National Guard Armory at Fort Worth and stole machine guns, automatic rifles, and shotguns. Two weeks later, on October 8, the gang knocked off the bank at Abilene, Texas, and fled with $1,400.

Forty-eight hours afterward, three people entered a grocery store in Sherman, Texas, and a ''blond girl'' (later identified as Bonnie Parker) pumped three bullets into 67-year-old butcher Howard Hall. The gang raced out of town with the $50 they had taken in the robbery. Hall died a few hours later.

Between crimes, Bonnie, Clyde, and Ray Hamilton had been living the good life. They splurged on new clothes, dined at fancy restaurants, and relaxed in ornate hotels. Bonnie was a stickler about her appearance and paid frequent visits to beauty shops, where she enjoyed engaging in conversation with the hair stylists about the horrible Bonnie and Clyde who were frightening residents in several states.[4]

Within a few weeks, the gang's bankroll had shrunk to $20, so they pulled off several stickups and hit a bank at Carthage, Missouri, for $200.

In December 1932, the Federal Bureau of Investigation became involved in the widespread search for the Barrow gang when a Ford automobile was found abandoned near Jackson, Michigan. Investigation disclosed that the car had been stolen in Pawhuska, Oklahoma. Murder, kidnapping, and jailbreaks were state crimes, but the interstate transportation of a stolen vehicle was a federal offense and brought in the FBI.

At Pawhuska, G-Men learned that another Ford car, stolen in Illinois, had been abandoned there, and a search of this vehicle revealed that it had been occupied by a man and a woman, indicated by articles found inside it. Also discovered in the Illinois Ford was a prescription bottle that led FBI agents to a drug store in Nacogdoches, Texas, where it was learned that the person for whom the prescription had been filled was Clyde Barrow's aunt.

FBI men questioned the aunt, who told them that she had been visited recently by Clyde Barrow and Bonnie Parker, and that they had obtained the prescription bottle from her.

Now the search for the two desperadoes and Ray Hamilton shifted to Michigan where, a few days earlier, Bonnie and Clyde had dropped off Hamilton, who wanted to visit his father. Then Bonnie and Clyde drove back south, and on December 5, 1932, they tried to steal a Ford V–8 in Temple, Texas. Doyle Johnson, the owner, saw the couple and dashed up to the car, and a pistol shot rang out. Johnson collapsed and died within minutes.

A month later, on January 6, 1933, Clyde Barrow shot and killed Deputy Sheriff Malcolm Davis after the outlaw and Bonnie had walked into a trap at a Dallas bank that had been set for another bank robber, Odell Chandless.

Suddenly, Clyde Barrow, the bloodthirsty killer, and his tattooed, cigar-smoking, equally ruthless paramour became the darlings of segments of the nation's press. Lavish Page 1 stories related in detail the couple's most trivial exploits. Sticking a pistol in a frightened gasoline station attendant's face and stealing $30 had become big news in New York City, Los Angeles, Chicago, and elsewhere. Brutal crime had been gilded with a sheen of glamour.

Clyde, whom the press had dubbed "The Texas Rattlesnake," received most of the ink, a condition that irked Bonnie, who enjoyed publicity. She was delighted when an enterprising editor pegged her with the nickname "Suicide Sal."

Bonnie had a knack for promoting herself. She and Clyde would often take pictures of one another, posing with drawn pistols, grinning and smoking cigars. These creative works were mailed to major newspapers and often were splashed over front pages.

The female gunslinger also liked to write poems about her adventures with Clyde, and print media published them, even though they were 25 to 30 stanzas long. In April 1933, when the Barrow gang (Clyde, Bonnie, teenager William Jones, and Buck and Blanche Barrow) had escaped from their Joplin hideout after killing two policemen and wounding another in a blazing gun battle, lawmen found one of Bonnie's lengthy poems on the kitchen table.

Bonnie liked the nickname the newspapers had given her, and the poem was entitled, *The Story of Suicide Sal*. Three of the 25 stanzas read:

> You have heard the story of Jesse James,
> Of how he lived and died.
> If you still are in need of something to read,
> Here is the story of Bonnie and Clyde.

> Now Bonnie and Clyde are the Barrow gang,
> I'm sure you all have read
> How they rob and steal,
> And how those who squeal,
> Are usually found dying or dead.

> There are lots of untruths to their write-ups,
> They are not so merciless as that;
> They hate all the laws,
> The stool-pigeons, spotters and rats.

In mid-1933, the Barrow Gang (as the press labeled the three men and two women) began a crime rampage that terrorized the Midwest. They robbed banks at Lucerne, Indiana; Okabena, Minnesota; and Alma, Texas. After sticking up the Alma bank, they were intercepted by newly elected City Marshal Henry

Humphrey, who was riddled with bullets and killed. The gang fled in Humphrey's squad car.

On a blistering hot July afternoon in Oklahoma City, a black Ford sedan pulled up beside a traffic officer. A well-dressed young woman leaned out the open window on the passenger's side and asked in a pleasant voice, "How do we get to Sixth and Main?"

Pointing with his hand, the officer gave the directions.

"Thank you," Bonnie Parker replied. Then she lifted the shotgun that had been concealed on the seat between her and Clyde Barrow and fired both barrels, blowing off the policeman's head. Stunned pedestrians heard the woman squeal in delight as the Ford raced off.

After that brutal and senseless murder, the Barrow gang drove to Iowa, pulled off a few stickups when they needed money, and checked into a seedy tourist camp near Platte City, Iowa. The manner in which they sneaked out of their two cabins at night and kept shades drawn in the day drew suspicions. A posse of officers surrounded the cabins, and a shootout erupted. Buck Barrow received a grazing head wound and his wife Blanche was temporarily blinded by splinters of flying glass, but the gang managed to leap into their stolen Buick sedan and make a getaway.

Now hundreds of law officers in Iowa were searching for the Barrow Gang, which had made camp along a river and in thick woods near Dexter, Iowa. William Jones was sent to bring back five chicken dinners. After he had returned, the camp site was surrounded by 20 officers and a raging gun battle broke out.

Bonnie and Clyde, who led charmed lives, and young Jones waded the river and escaped through a fusillade of bullets, even though all three had received minor wounds. Buck Barrow had been shot five times. Police found Blanche kneeling over him and crying hysterically: "Don't die, Daddy, don't die!" Five days later, he succumbed at a nearby hospital.[5]

William Jones left them, and Bonnie and Clyde returned to Dallas, where they hid out during the final months of 1933, pulling stickups to keep themselves in money. They slept in a string of stolen automobiles, and held secret rendezvous with family members in remote rural areas.[6]

The couple avoided detection because of a scheme hatched by Bonnie. "The cops are looking for a man and a blonde woman," she told Clyde. "Not *two* blonde women." So she acquired a blonde wig, a dress, silk stockings, and high heels for Clyde, and he moved freely around the Dallas area disguised as a woman.

While the FBI and other law agencies were hunting desperately for Bonnie and Clyde, William A. Hamm, Jr., the 39-year-old president of the Theodore Hamm Brewing Company in St. Paul and owner of a string of movie houses, was walking the short distance from the brewery to his home for lunch at about 12:45 in the afternoon of June 15, 1933. Three men climbed out of a black

Buick parked at the curb and approached him. One stuck out his hand, smiled and said, "Hello, Mr. Hamm." Then the two other strangers grabbed the wealthy executive and hustled him into the car.

Hamm was ordered to lie on the floorboard in back and a white hood was pulled over his head. After going for what seemed to Hamm to be about 30 miles, the car stopped next to another automobile holding four men. Hamm's hood was removed long enough for him to sign four ransom notes while still flat on the floorboard.

Then goggles with cotton stuffed behind the lenses were placed over his eyes and the kidnappers drove on for what Hamm estimated was about eight hours. When the car stopped, the victim was taken into a house with boarded windows and put on a small bed in a second floor room.

When Hamm's goggles were removed briefly on occasion, he saw that his prison looked like a farm house. It might have been on the outskirts of a large city, for he could regularly hear heavy traffic in the background. Because the weather was cooler at night than it had been in St. Paul of late, he thought that he was somewhere in far north Minnesota. Actually, he was in the Chicago suburb of Bensonville.

At 2:40 that afternoon, about two hours after the abduction, William W. Dunn, sales manager for the brewery and a close friend of Hamm, received a telephone call in his office.

"Is this Mr. Dunn?" a voice asked. Speaking in a rough tone, the man said, "I want you to listen to what I have to say. And don't butt in. We have Hamm. We want you to get $100,000 in twenty, ten and five dollar bills." Punctuating his demands with a barrage of profanity, the caller added:

"You'd better be sure that the money is not marked or you're dead and so is Hamm!"

"Say, what's going on?" Dunn asked. "Is this some kind of a joke?"

"Shut up and listen," the caller broke in. "We'll phone you tomorrow." Then he slammed down the phone.

Bill Dunn was slightly annoyed. He was far too busy to have a friend pulling a gag on him. However, when Hamm had not returned to his office by 4:00 P.M., Dunn grew extremely worried and advised other executives of the anonymous telephone call. St. Paul Police Chief Thomas Dahill was notified.

At 2:05 A.M., Dunn was awakened by a telephone jangling in his bedroom. "Well, Dunn, you know now this is no joke," the voice said. "If you fail to carry out our instructions, Hamm will die."

After Dunn reached his office later that morning, a taxi driver delivered a note from the kidnappers. The driver told police that a man he didn't know had paid him $2 for the job. Delivery of the $100,000 ransom would be made in a brewery truck, the note said. One man was to drive the truck, which was to be entirely open so that the interior would be clearly visible from a passing automobile.

The next day the truck drove away from the Hamm brewery with one man standing in the open back with a box containing the $100,000 and took the route designated by the kidnappers. A few blocks from the brewery, a large black sedan with three men in it pulled along side and motioned for the man in the truck to pitch out the container with the ransom money.

A few hours later, several men entered the room where William Hamm had been confined and guarded for four days. "We've got some good news for you," one man said. "The dough's been paid, and we're goin' to take you back."

After dark, three men and Hamm climbed into a car and they drove for about seven hours. The captive was blindfolded throughout the trip, and the abductors hardly spoke a word. Just at daybreak the car stopped and Hamm was told to get out. "If there's anything we can do to help you, Mr. Hamm, just let us know," one man said.[7]

Hamm, near exhaustion from his ordeal, staggered into the yard of a farmer and learned that he was in Wyoming, Minnesota, about 45 miles from St. Paul. The brewery executive telephoned his wife from the farmer's home, and two St. Paul policemen came to bring him back.

A few weeks after the Hamm kidnapping, Melvin Purvis, special agent in charge of the Chicago FBI office, arrested a local gangster, Roger "The Terrible" Touhy, and three of his henchmen and charged them with the crime. "We have an iron-clad case," Purvis told the press.

Touhy was one of eight children, the son of a Chicago policeman. He attended a Catholic grade school and was an altar boy in his church. When the United States entered World War I in 1917, 18-year-old Roger enlisted in the navy and spent two years teaching code to naval officers at Harvard University.

Settling in Des Plaines, a northwestern suburb of Chicago, Touhy established a trucking business, which was well on its way to going broke in 1926. Then the enterprising young man hit on an idea to rescue his floundering firm: he would use his trucks to haul illegal beer (it was the Prohibition era).

Soon Touhy became a big-time bootlegger. He hired a chemist and began making his own brew, which discriminating buyers claimed was the finest in the Midwest. He bought his own cooperage to make leak-proof barrels and disguised his beer shipments by buying several oil trucks and painting them so they resembled Texaco Oil Company trucks.

By the early 1930s, Touhy's business was booming. His drivers were selling 1,000 barrels per week at $55 a barrel (it cost him $4.50 a barrel to produce the brew). Barrels of his premium brew were shipped with Touhy's compliments to certain politicians and policemen.

Roger was not as "terrible" as his nickname implied to many citizens in the Des Plaines area. He filled an important need (beer) and he kept warehouses from moving into the neighborhood. Whenever a group of mobsters set up a roadside brothel, Touhy would relieve local law enforcement officers from trying to handle the situation. The bootleg king merely sent some of his boys to, in Touhy's words, "wreck the joint."

When Touhy heard rumblings of rival gangsters planning to invade his turf with booze, whores, or slot machines, he would invite them or their representatives to his headquarters for a friendly visit. There they gaped at walls lined with Tommy guns (borrowed for the occasions from cooperative police departments).

Touhy earlier paid a young man in a nearby gasoline station to telephone him at his headquarters every three or four minutes during these visits by gangsters, and told him to pay no attention to what the bootlegger said into the mouthpiece. With his potential rivals sitting across the desk from him, Touhy would regularly pick up the phone when it rang.

"Yeah, yeah," he would snap. "Why, the dirty bastard! Bump him off."

On any given visit from rival mobsters, Touhy would order at least five enemies to be killed—leaving the puzzled gasoline station attendant on the other end of the line wondering if Touhy was playing with a full deck of cards.

Even two of Al Capone's top torpedoes, Frank "The Enforcer" Nitti and Murray "The Camel" Humphreys, returned from Touhy's base to convince Capone that it would be folly to try to move in on Des Plaines.

In August 1933, Roger Touhy and his three henchmen were taken from Chicago to St. Paul to stand trial for the William Hamm kidnapping. The government's case was weak, and all four defendants were found not guilty.[8]

A few weeks later, the FBI had one of its most embarrassing moments when it announced that the Barker-Karpis gang was now the principal suspect in the Hamm abduction.[9]

8

"We Just Wanted an Easy Pay-Off"

Shortly before 11:00 A.M. on May 27, 1933, the doorbell rang at the home of City Manager Henry F. McElroy in the fashionable Milburn Golf Club district of Kansas City. Housekeeper Heda Christensen answered through a latched screen.

"I'm from Katz," one of two men said pleasantly. "I've got some face creams and lotions for the judge's (McElroy's) little girl."

The housekeeper left the two at the door to inform the daughter, 25-year-old Mary McElroy, that "a man is here with some face creams." Mary was taking a bath, and she yelled downstairs that she had ordered no face creams and needed none.

Returning with the message, the housekeeper was confronted by a sawed-off shotgun and the threat:

"Open the door or I'll blow your head off!"

Terrified, the woman unlatched the door. "Do as I say and you won't get hurt," one of the gunmen snarled.

"Where's the little girl?"

"She's taking a bath," was the reply.[1]

The men brushed past her, went to the second floor bathroom, knocked on the door and demanded that Mary dress immediately. She let loose with a long scream, and was told to "shut up, or I'll shoot through the door."

Mary left the bathroom by a door leading to her bedroom and dressed in a brightly colored dress and a tan coat. When she finally came out, the gunmen expressed surprise when they realized that their intended victim was not a child but a young woman. They demanded that she change her clothes into less noticeable garb, but she refused.

"I'm going to the horse races later," she told the men. "I've got some hot tips."

"We'll bet those for you," one man replied with a grin.

They now mentioned a ransom of $60,000, and the city manager's daughter laughingly declared: "I'm worth more than that. Why, that's not as much as they got for Mike Katz."

She referred to a prominent Kansas City drug chain owner for whose release kidnappers obtained a ransom of a reported $100,000.

As the captors prepared to leave with their victim, they told the housekeeper to tell Henry McElroy that his daughter had been kidnapped and would be killed if he refused to comply with their demands or permitted newspapers to learn of the abduction.[2]

The housekeeper pleaded with them to bring her back safely, and one of the gunmen, his eyes shielded by dark glasses, replied, "We'll have her back all right. You tell Judge McElroy that we'll get in touch with him this evening." (McElroy was widely known as "Judge.")

Shifting a sawed-off shotgun in his hands, he and his partner departed with their captive. McElroy was notified and he hurried home, where he and his 23-year-old son, Henry F. McElroy, Jr., began a lonely vigil. Just past 7:15 P.M., the gloomy silence was broken when a special delivery letter was delivered. Written on soiled white paper of a cheap grade, it had Mary's thumb print at the top. The letter read:

Dead Dad:

I have been kidnapped. They are demanding $60,000. If this is reported to the police or the newspapers, they will ask $100,000, and I may not be returned. You will hear later where to send it. Any letter without my thumb print is counterfeit. We are off the gold standard, so send used currency.

I will be released six hours after you send it. They want $20,000 in twenties, $20,000 in tens and $20,000 in fives.

If this money is marked they will harm you or Henry. So be careful. They have treated me with great consideration, and I am not frightened. My love,

Mary

Three hours after receipt of this letter, a second was received. It had been mailed at 9:30 P.M. and bore a thumb print in the left-hand corner. The letter said:

Dear Dad:

Stay at home Sunday. They will get in touch with you. They want the money done up in thousand-dollar packages. They want nothing but used currency. When you receive information where to go, go alone in your car. If any detectives follow you, you won't be met.

The money will be checked for counterfeit and marks before I am released. If any trouble comes up after I am released they will try to avenge it. I love you.

Mary

At about 8:30 in the morning, Judge McElroy received a telephone call and a voice said: "This is the gang calling. Can you get the $60,000?"

McElroy pleaded that he was unable to pay that amount. As city manager his salary was $10,000 per year, he explained, but he said he had independent means, having engaged in the Kansas City real estate business for many years.

"I can get $30,000," said McElroy.

"Do better than that," was the abrupt answer.

"Be reasonable," McElroy pleaded. "Men who were worth $100,000 now are worth only $10,000. There is reason to everything."

"Raise it ten," come back the voice.

"I don't see how I can," said the father. "It is difficult to explain the distress you have put me to. Do this for me—please try to do this—let's not have a long wait until I see my daughter."

"I'll see what I can do. I'll give my word that your daughter is alright."

A second conversation two hours later resulted in an agreement to release the girl for $30,000.

"How do I know you will be square with us?" the kidnapper demanded.

"Say, you don't know me, do you?" McElroy answered. "Do you know that I never made a promise I didn't keep? When I give my word, you are safe."

After hesitating, the kidnappers gave him instructions for delivering the $30,000. McElroy drove across the state line to a vacant shack in Kansas City, Kansas, and felt in a mailbox for a typewritten note. The message told him to travel certain streets until he reached a cement post near which he would find a tin can buried. It contained instructions on how to find a second can. McElroy then drove to a spot overlooking the Kaw River and got out of his car, as directed.

Two masked men, wearing overalls and carrying sawed-off shotguns, came forward. The $30,000, wrapped in newspaper, was handed to them. McElroy, although nervous, could see that there were four other persons in the masked men's motor car.

The kidnappers balked over accepting the ransom because it included five $1,000 bills. Seeing their displeasure, McElroy said;

"I wish you would appreciate what I have been up against. My friends have gone together to raise this money for me. You understand we can't have just the denominations you want on such short notice."

While the men mulled over the situation for a few moments, the judge added:

"I swear to you that these bills have not been recorded and no preparations for following them up have been made."

Clutching the ransom package, the kidnappers returned to their car and drove away.

In the meantime, Mary McElroy was being held in a dingy basement. She was never blindfolded. After threatening to kill her should she hinder their efforts to gain the ransom money, Mary's captors were amiable and attentive. They showed her how a Tommy gun worked, and gave her roses and a detective magazine with which to while away the time. The kidnappers even provided her with an electric fan and a small radio.

However, a handcuff was locked about her left wrist and chained to the wall, permitting her to move in a radius of only five or six feet.

Less than two hours after Judge McElroy had paid the ransom, the kidnappers entered the basement. While removing Mary's chains, the man who appeared to be the leader said:

"Your old man coughed up the dough, although not in the right denominations, but we're going to release you anyhow."

The two men praised Mary's father on the way he handled Kansas City affairs and complimented her on her light-hearted attitude while in captivity.

"We'll be glad to recommend you as a victim to other kidnappers," one man quipped.[3]

Then the captors ordered Mary to remove her clothes, intending to search her for concealed evidence that could be used against the gang. Misreading their purpose, she thought that they were going to perpetrate a second crime against her.

"I'd rather die than take my clothes off," she exclaimed.

Shrugging, the men continued to unchain her, then placed a bandanna handkerchief over her eyes and led her toward a car.

"Here's a little token to remember us by," one kidnapper said as he handed her a bouquet of fresh-cut roses.

After a drive of about two hours, the abductors released Mary at the gate of the Milburn Golf Club grounds. Holding the rose bouquet in one hand, she ripped off the blindfold with the other and waved at the car as the kidnappers drove away. They waved back.

When Mary talked to reporters that afternoon, two roses from the bouquet were pinned to her frock. "I didn't break," were her first words. "I didn't break once." Smiling, she added: "It did me good to get away. I had a good rest. I needed it."[4]

Once it had been established that Mary McElroy probably had been taken across a state line, the Federal Bureau of Investigation joined in the search for the kidnappers. For days, the G-Men and Kansas City lawmen tracked down leads and tediously sifted through clues in an effort to identify the kidnappers. Then the investigators intercepted what appeared to be a routine telegram from an Amarillo, Texas motor car agency to a junk dealer in Leavenworth, Kansas. It read:

Walter H. McGee trading in 1932 Oldsmobile eight sedan, motor number 5998. States he purchased from you. You wire us verifying your serial, and is car clear.

In itself, the telegram signified only a minor car transaction. But one investigator telephoned the Amarillo car dealer and learned that Walter McGee's description matched that given of one kidnapper by Mary McElroy. It was a long shot at best, but the Amarillo police were contacted and they arrested McGee and two couples.

McGee, a 37-year-old ex-convict from the Oregon penitentiary, carried a .38-caliber revolver in a holster and a money pouch containing $3,000. Searching the car, officers found five $1,000 bills in a suitcase and $1,290 under the seat.

Reed E. Vetterli, special agent in charge of the Kansas City office of the FBI, and two Kansas City detectives flew to Amarillo to grill Walter McGee. The suspect vehemently denied knowing anything about the McElroy kidnapping until his arrest in Amarillo.

The two couples apprehended with McGee, Wendell and Hazel Johnson and L. R. and Hazel Gilbert, insisted that they had never known McGee until he picked them up in Oklahoma City after he promised to give them an all-expenses paid pleasure trip.[5]

Walter McGee was flown to Kansas City and questioned at police headquarters. He was defiant and sullen, claiming that he was in the East when Mary McElroy was abducted. Then the G-Men and detectives sprung a surprise on him—a signed confession by his former wife, Lucille Cates, in which she identified him as the ringleader.

Cates had been arrested a day earlier on a tip from an informant. She admitted that she had been forced to serve as a cook for the kidnap gang and Mary McElroy at the Shawnee, Kansas, hideout. Cates had $840 in her purse when arrested, and said that the money had been given to her by McGee for buying food and cooking meals.

Lawmen asked McGee to explain the roughly $9,000 in currency that had been found in his possession in Amarillo, pointing out that the bills corresponded with serial numbers listed by Judge McElroy's friends in making up the ransom fund. McGee merely shrugged.

An hour later, Henry McElroy confronted Walter McGee. "We've met before, McGee, haven't we?" the father of the victim declared evenly, looking intently into the suspect's eyes.

In a bizarre scenario, McGee arose from his chair and shook hands with McElroy. "Yes, we've met before (on the lonely Kansas road)," McGee said, breaking out in tears.

Wiping his eyes, McGee turned to the law officers and said, "I want to tell everything and get it over with."

He disclosed that he and three companions had planned originally to snatch Judge McElroy's 23-year-old son, Henry, Jr. Learning that the young man was fond of dancing, they plotted to grab him at a dance. But the gang had trouble identifying the intended victim, so they targeted who they thought was the city manager's "little girl."

"We didn't intend to harm her," McGee declared. "We just wanted an easy pay-off."

McGee identified the man who had broken into the McElroy home with him only a week earlier as Clarence Stevens.

"About a month ago, Stevens and I were in a bootleg joint and someone— there were several guys there—mentioned all the kidnappings that were taking place," the prisoner said. "Somebody said they wondered why McElroy's son hadn't been snatched."

Right afterward, the plot took form, McGee added. "Me and Stevens tailed Mr. McElroy for several days, and when we never seen his son, we decided to kidnap his daughter," he said.

McGee said the actual kidnappers were himself, his brother George McGee, Clarence Stevens, and Clarence Click. When Click was arrested near Kansas City, he admitted that he had received $4,700 as his share of the ransom money. Twenty-one-year-old George McGee and Clarence Stevens were at large.

On June 2, four days after her release, Mary McElroy, her father, and brother were escorted by officers to the Shawnee bungalow owned by Clarence Click where she had been held captive. Walking hesitantly into her basement jail, Mary fainted.

Charged with kidnapping under the Missouri law that provided death by hanging as the maximum penalty, Walter McGee and Clarence Click were held without bond.

"We've nailed the gang," FBI Agent Reed Vetterli declared in a joint statement with Kansas City Director of Police Eugene C. Reppert. Solving the case in less than a week from the time Mary McElroy was taken from her home may have been the fastest such achievement for a major kidnapping case in U.S. crime annals.

Two weeks later, on June 18, police at Roanoke, Virginia, arrested a young man who gave his name as George L. Jackson on charges of drunkenness and carrying a concealed weapon. Jackson had in his possession an automobile bearing Kansas license plates. Police found on him $130 in travelers' checks, a $100 bill, and three $20 bills. When confronted with a circular from the FBI, George Jackson admitted that he was Walter McGee's younger brother George McGee.

On July 27, two months after the McElroy abduction, Walter McGee was found guilty by a jury in Kansas City and was given a death verdict, the nation's first for a kidnapping. McGee heard the verdict with no show of emotion.

"I don't see why anyone should be hanged for a thing like that," he told reporters later.[6]

Taken back to his cell, McGee erupted in an outburst of profanity and had to be subdued by guards.

A few weeks later, George McGee went on trial in the same courthouse. Although identified from the witness stand by Mary McElroy and her father, he denied any involvement in the kidnapping. However, prosecutors read a signed confession that George McGee had made to Roanoke officers in which he had said that his job was to go back and kill Mary McElroy should the ransom payoff go awry.

After deliberating for three hours, a jury found him guilty and recommended life imprisonment.

When 27-year-old Clarence Click stood trial, he was portrayed by his lawyers as the unwilling tool of leaders of the kidnap gang. Joseph Keenan, who had been sent to Kansas City by the U.S. Department of Justice to aid the prosecution of the three men, contended that Click had knowingly rented his bungalow to Walter McGee as a place to hold Mary McElroy and that he received more than $4,000 of the ransom money.

The prosecution asked for the death penalty for Click, but a jury found him guilty and fixed his sentence at eight years in the Missouri State Penitentiary at Jefferson City. Click greeted the verdict with a broad smile.

Nervous and distraught over the prosecution of her kidnappers, Mary McElroy suffered an emotional breakdown during Click's trial and had to be hospitalized. A few weeks later, she disappeared from her home and was located by police on a Chicago-bound Greyhound bus at Normal, Illinois, the next day. She was returned home in an airplane.

Judge McElroy explained to newsmen that his daughter had been "extremely upset" as a result of a rash of anonymous threatening telephone calls and letters.

"I know it sounds kind of silly, but I felt as though I had committed murder in testifying against those men," Mary said. In the weeks ahead, the kidnap victim paid several visits to Walter McGee at the Missouri penitentiary where he was waiting to be hanged. Four days before the kidnapper was to go to the gallows, Mary McElroy called on Missouri Governor Guy B. Park and made an emotional, tearful plea, urging him to commute the death sentence. A day later, Park reduced McGee's penalty to life imprisonment.

"I had no desire for revenge," Mary told reporters on learning of the governor's commutation. "Now maybe I can enjoy a good night's sleep."

In 1933, kidnappings and extortion threats were rampant, creating an aura of apprehension among the rich and the not-so-rich alike.

In Madison, Illinois, August Leur, a 78-year-old banker, was abducted by two men and held in a cold, damp cave for five days. Leur, a bachelor, was released without payment of a ransom when the kidnappers could not locate any of his relatives.

In Harwichport, Massachusetts, Peggy McMath was returned safely after her kidnappers were paid $60,000.

In San Jose, California, ten-year-old Brooke Hart was murdered by his two kidnappers, who were lynched when citizens broke into the jail where they were being held.

In Albany, New York, John J. O'Connell was released after being held for 23 days when a $40,000 ransom was paid.

In Boston, Theodore C. Haffenreffer, head of New England's largest brewery, was threatened with kidnapping if he did not appear at a certain Boston hotel on a specified night and turn over $15,000. Haffenreffer contacted the police, who sent a detective posing as the wealthy brewer, but the extortionist failed to keep the appointment.

In Paterson, New Jersey, four men kidnapped 18-year-old Herman Miller, messenger for a dental laboratory, as he emerged from the Law Building. He was driven to a wooded area near Coytesville, New Jersey, bound, gagged, and abandoned. The abductors had mistaken the dental messenger for a bank messenger who was to leave the same building with $5,000 in collections from the Prudential Insurance Company.[7]

In St. Louis, 32-year-old August A. "Gussie" Busch, Jr., heir to Anheuser-Busch brewery millions, had a police guard for months after being threatened with kidnapping if he failed to leave $50,000 at a designated spot.

In San Francisco, D. J. Will, a wealthy businessman, received an extortion note that said his nine-year-old daughter Mary would be abducted unless he left $20,000 in a cemetery. Will thought he recognized the handwriting and called police who arrested little Mary's nursemaid. The mousey, gray-haired woman confessed that she was the culprit.[8]

In Winston-Salem, North Carolina, R. J. "Dick" Reynolds, who would inherit $25 million of his father's tobacco-built estate on his 28th birthday in a few months, was threatened by mail. Unless he paid a $10,000 ransom, his wife Elizabeth would be kidnapped.

Written on cheap ruled paper and printed with a pencil, the extortionist demanded that the money be left at the corner of Dunleith Avenue and First Street in Winston-Salem, an hour after midnight on a certain day.

Recalling the FBI "kidnap number," Dick Reynolds telephoned Washington and was put through to J. Edgar Hoover. After making several suggestions on how Reynolds should proceed, the Director ordered FBI agents from Charlotte, North Carolina, to rush to Winston-Salem and take charge of the investigation, working with state and local lawmen.

A decoy package of money was placed at the point designated by the extortionist, and the FBI men and two Winston-Salem detectives hid nearby. Just as dawn was starting to break, at 6:05 A.M., a man was seen strolling toward the package. He walked on past, turned around and walked past again, then came back for a third time. Finally, the man reached down and picked up the package, and the officers pounced on him.

Taken in for questioning, the man said his name was John Lanier, an un-employed textile worker. Claiming he knew nothing about an extortion note, he said he had been merely waiting on the corner for his father, and when he happened to see the package, curiosity compelled him to pick it up.

Later, the 35-year-old suspect confessed that he had written the extortion note, saying he was in deep financial trouble. Dick Reynolds pleaded for leniency, and John Lanier received a light sentence.

Despite the string of successes scored by the Federal Bureau of Investigation under J. Edgar Hoover, some politicians were obsessed with tinkering with the organization. In late 1933, Senator Royal S. Copeland of New York put forward a proposal that would plunge the Bureau back into a reservoir for paying off political hacks.

Copeland's scheme was to expand the FBI by having each governor of a state nominate men who would become agents. The governors' appointees would be trained by the FBI and then given "roving commissions" within their own states. Director Hoover would be put in the position of trying to issue orders to FBI agents who owed their primary allegiance to the governors who had given them the jobs.

Hoover argued that the Copeland plan would demolish the foundation of the FBI's success—nonpolitical selection and centralized administrative control of the agents. Copeland's proposal withered, then died, due to lack of nourishment from Congress and the public.

Another scheme emerging from the hallowed halls of Congress was that mar-tial law be declared and the U.S. Army sent into action. That proposal was also shot down by J. Edgar Hoover, who doubted if the marauding gangsters would array themselves in battalions and regiments to do battle with Uncle Sam's army. Nor did the FBI boss look kindly upon a possible scenario in which tens of thousands of armed soldiers, none of them trained in law enforcement or the collection of evidence, would be sent out in small packs to roam the nation in search of kidnappers, bank robbers, stickup artists, and murderers.

9

A Hit-and-Run Raid

Early on the bright morning of Friday, June 16, 1933, three law enforcement officers were motoring through the heavily wooded hills of central Arkansas toward Hot Springs. Federal Bureau of Investigation Agents F. Joseph Lackey and Frank Smith were accompanied by McAlester, Oklahoma, Chief of Police Otto Reed, one of the toughest and most respected lawmen in that part of the country.

They were embarked upon what could be a perilous mission. A few days earlier, a mobster collared by the FBI had told agents about the whereabouts of Frank "Jelly" Nash, an escapee from the federal penitentiary at Leavenworth. Nash, the tipster disclosed, was holed up in Hot Springs, a haven for the kingpins and the small fry in American's crime empire.[1]

Amidst the tens of thousands of legitimate tourists who invaded the resort city each year, gangsters and their molls, secure in the knowledge that the Hot Springs chief of detectives would alert them should the FBI be closing in, relaxed in the luxury hotels and restaurants.[2]

The turncoat detective chief not only closed his eyes to the presence of mobsters in the city of 20,000 permanent residents, but he was working a few rackets of his own—such as selling hot diamonds to the patrons of Hot Springs whorehouses.

Knowing that the underworld had a mole or two in the Hot Springs police department, Joe Lackey, Frank Smith, and Otto Reed would not inform local officers of their arrival. They planned to slip into Hot Springs, grab Jelly Nash, and hightail it out of town and back to Kansas City. From there Nash would be taken 16 miles up the Missouri River to Leavenworth to finish his 25-year term for armed robbery.

Nash was a hardened criminal with widespread connections in the underworld—a killer, a thief, a bigamist, and a talented liar. He had been involved in crime for 20 years, since 1913, when he and a young crony robbed a bank at Sapulpa, Oklahoma. Although barely out of his teens, Nash was ruthless: he killed his pal by shooting him in the back and ran off with all of the bank loot. Nash was captured and sentenced to life in the Oklahoma State Penitentiary at McAlester.

Jelly was a smooth talker and a consummate actor. Had he not launched a career in crime, he might have done well on the stage. Projecting extreme remorse for his wayward life, Nash humbly told an Oklahoma parole board that he wanted to go straight, and pleaded for a chance to join the army and fight for his country in the World War.

Jelly's performance was magnificent. Five years after he had murdered his pal in cold blood, Nash was paroled from prison. Outside the gray walls at McAlester, his patriotism vanished. Army recruiters would never even see him.

Two years later, Jelly was back in the same gloomy prison, this time to serve a 25-year term for safe-cracking. Again he adopted his repentant sinner role, and after serving two years, he was given a gubernatorial pardon.

Nash wasn't free for long. In early 1924 he was convicted with members of the notorious Al Spencer gang of robbing the *Katy Limited*, a crack passenger train, in Oklahoma and making off with $20,000, a hefty haul. This time, Jelly was given a change of scenery—the federal penitentiary at Leavenworth—on a 25-year sentence.

Ensconced behind walls, Nash became a model prisoner. No doubt aware that his conning of dewy-eyed parole boards would no longer work, he hatched another scheme for springing himself. Soft-spoken, friendly, always willing to do any task asked of him by prison authorities, Nash became a trusted handyman for the warden, who may have been impressed by the fact that the convict haunted the library and was an avid reader of Shakespeare.

On October 19, 1924, Jelly was sent on an errand outside the penitentiary. This was his chance. He simply kept going and scurried back to the desolate Cookson Hills in eastern Oklahoma, established old connections in gangland, and hid out until the heat was off.

Through the nationwide underworld grapevine, Nash promoted the Cookson Hills as an ideal cooling-off spot for those on the lam.

"The police never come here," he declared. Another prime feature of the Cooksons was that it was easily accessible to the Hot Springs hoodlum haven.

While laying low in the desolate Cookson Hills, Jelly Nash cooked up a scheme to aid a number of his pals at Leavenworth to escape. On the morning of December 31, 1931, seven hard-core convicts, each one armed, kidnapped and shot the warden and fled. Evidence collected by the FBI pointed to Nash as the one who had arranged to slip the weapons inside the prison.

Now, as FBI agents Lackey and Smith and Chief Reed drove into Hot Springs in pursuit of Nash, they grew more alert, aware that this was largely hostile territory. From informants, the lawmen knew that the bald Jelly was wearing a red wig, had grown a mustache, and had had his Roman nose bobbed by a surgeon.

They had been in town for less than an hour when a local informant whom Frank Smith knew furnished them with a description of Nash's automobile and its Oklahoma license number. While Smith waited at the Como Hotel for more information, Joe Lackey and Otto Reed spotted the fugitive's car parked on Hot Springs' main street.

Chief Reed remained to keep an eye open should Nash return to his car and Joe Lackey rushed back to the hotel for Smith. It was now midmorning and the sidewalks and streets were starting to fill with carefree tourists. Within minutes, Lackey and Smith were back. Nash, it was now learned, was inside the White Front Pool Hall, a special hoodlum hangout that was owned and operated by the city's rackets kingpin, Richard Tallman Galatas.

Leaving their Chevrolet sedan parked in the middle of the street in front of the pool hall, the three officers sauntered inside. Lackey casually bought a cigar at a counter near the front door. Glancing about nonchalantly, the lawmen spotted a red mop of hair. Under it was Jelly Nash, seated at a table with two men and drinking a bottle of beer.

Ten or 12 other men were loitering about the room, and the officers were unable to tell how many more might be at pool tables behind a partition.

For a few minutes, Lackey, Smith, and Reed, finding themselves in the lair of the enemy, pondered their next move. Were they to go to the table where Nash was seated, a shootout could erupt if the patrons in the smoke-filled pool room were criminal types and armed—a distinct possibility.

Then Jelly Nash got up, brushed past the three officers, and started to open the front door. "Okay, Nash," Smith said evenly as the lawmen drew their weapons. "Stop right there and raise your hands!" Jelly appeared to be terrorized. His hands shot up and he called out that he had no gun.

Joe Lackey and Otto Reed had not turned around. Their revolvers were leveled at the crowd of pool players and loafers, who glared menacingly at the officers. With their prisoner in tow and guns still pointed at the crowd, the three lawmen backed out through the door.

Hurrying to their Chevrolet, the officers bundled Nash into the front passenger seat. Smith and Reed scrambled into the back and Lackey leaped in behind the wheel. As the car sped off toward the city limits, the two officers in the back covered Nash and were ready to fire at any pursuing vehicles.

A few miles out of Hot Springs, the raiders relaxed slightly. They had made a clean getaway. It had been an incredible scenario: law enforcement officers fleeing from the vengeance of the underworld, which, in Hot Springs, far outnumbered and outgunned them.

Reaching out playfully, Chief Reed yanked the thick red wig off Jelly Nash's head. "We knew you were bald, Frank," Reed said. "Who in the hell do you think you're fooling?"

Nash's underworld confederates reacted swiftly to the hit-and-run raid. Within minutes, Richard Galatas, the Hot Springs rackets boss, heard of the episode at his White Front Pool Hall and rushed to contact his man, the chief of detectives. Galatas and the crooked detective hatched a clever scheme. Neighboring police departments were notified by the Hot Springs police that "a man has been kidnapped here" and asked that the getaway car be halted, the "kidnappers" arrested and their "captive" released.

Meanwhile, Joe Lackey continued to push down on the accelerator. Thirty-two miles from Hot Springs, on the outskirts of Benton, Arkansas, he braked hard at a roadblock manned by several men armed with shotguns and rifles. Several tense, silent moments passed. Were the grim-faced men at the roadblock gangsters or policemen? Finally Lackey stuck his head out the open window and called out:

"FBI! We've got a federal prisoner!"

"Hot Springs (police) said you was kidnappers," a deputy sheriff explained.

Back in Hot Springs, Richard Galatas went to the home of a woman friend and launched a barrage of long-distance telephone calls throughout the Midwest underworld. It was the beginning of a monstrous criminal power plan to free Jelly Nash from the FBI.

His first call was to 40-year-old Louis "Doc" Stacci, who owned the O. P. Inn, a popular gangland hangout in Melrose Park, a suburb of Chicago. Stacci, an old pal of Jelly Nash, agreed to help by trying to recruit a few gunmen to pull the job.

Stacci telephoned Vern Miller, a friend of his and Nash's, who was laying low in a modest house at 6612 Edgevale Road in a residential section of Kansas City. Miller agreed to take on the task of snatching Jelly Nash from the feds.

Thirty-seven-year-old Vern Miller grew up in White Lake, South Dakota, where his father was a prominent civic leader. After graduation from high school, Vern became a wanderer. He was a rough-and-tumble fist fighter, a migratory laborer, a parachute jumper at county fairs, bailing out from balloons puffed up with smoke before airplane barnstorming became popular.

During World War I, Miller received training as a machine gunner and fought in France as an infantry sergeant. Returning to Huron, South Dakota, he told eye-popping stories of his heroism in combat and demonstrated that he was a crack shot with a pistol. Based largely on his war record, he was elected sheriff of his native county.

Vern Miller was a hero to most citizens and soon earned a sterling reputation as a manhunter. He feared no one. It was said that he delighted, purely for sport, in chasing bootleggers' cars and shooting his pistol into their rear gasoline tanks. However, the young sheriff had one horrendous character flaw: he was a prodigious spender, and his modest salary could not nearly provide him with the luxuries he craved.

Suddenly, Miller was in big trouble: he was arrested and charged with embezzling public funds. Tried before a local jury of former admirers, he was convicted, fined $5,200, and sentenced to serve a two- to ten-year term in the South Dakota Penitentiary. After his release two years later, the discredited sheriff moved to Chicago where he established gangland ties and then relocated to St. Paul where he joined the Keating-Holden mob before he reached the age of 30.

Vern had all the tools to make it big in the underworld. He was courageous, a crack shot with several weapons, and he had brains and imagination. What's more, he did not look, talk, or act like a criminal. He dressed conservatively, much as would a Chicago banker, and was so gifted in speech and appearance that he gained membership in respectable country clubs in Asheville, North Carolina and Kansas City. While on resort vacations he posed as a wealthy Oklahoma oilman, and guests with whom he held amiable conversations, including legitimate oil millionaires, never knew the difference.

Cool and calculating, Vern Miller was a professional killer, never letting emotions interfere with his mission.[3]

Next, Richard Galatas in Hot Springs put in a call to Herbert "Deafy" Farmer, who lived on a small farm on the outskirts of Joplin, Missouri, through which G-Men Lackey and Smith and Chief Reed would be taking Jelly Nash en route to Kansas City. Farmer and Nash had once done time together.

Deafy's farm had long served the underworld as a hideout, medical center, and communications hub. Wounded or ill criminals were cared for by a shady doctor who practiced nearby. Gangsters' cars were hidden in his garages and barns. Neighbors had long been aware of the strange activities around the place, but were too frightened to notify police.

Deafy Farmer agreed to help in the conspiracy by concealing Jelly Nash on his farm once Vern Miller and his gunmen had freed the fugitive.

Late on the afternoon of June 16—the same day that the lawmen had whisked Nash out of Hot Springs—a monoplane bounced to a landing on a grassy meadow at Deafy Farmer's place. Out hopped Richard Galatas, Jelly's wife Frances, and the Nash couple's seven-year-old daughter. Whether Mrs. Nash had been drawn into the plot (as she would claim) or was a willing participant (as the government would charge), her role was to wait at Deafy Farmer's sanctuary, and Jelly would join her there after being freed from his captors.[4]

In the meantime, FBI Agents Joe Lackey and Frank Smith, Chief Otto Reed, and their prisoner were barreling along the hilly, winding Arkansas road at speeds as high as 55 miles per hour. Outside Little Rock, the car screeched to a halt at a roadblock that had been set up to intercept the "kidnappers."

When Lackey and Smith identified themselves, Little Rock police escorted their automobile through the city and dropped off on the northern outskirts.

"Where you going?" a police lieutenant asked.

"Joplin," Lackey lied.

A few miles outside Little Rock, the road divided. One branch led to Joplin, the other to Fort Smith, Arkansas. The lawmen took the Fort Smith branch. At Russellville, the group halted to eat, and Agent Smith telephoned R. H. Colvin, the special agent in charge of the Oklahoma City FBI office.

Colvin told Smith to continue to Fort Smith and take a train for the rest of the trek to Kansas City. The lawmen reached Fort Smith at about 6:00 P.M. and locked Jelly Nash in the county jail. Frank Smith was an old friend of the sheriff and the jailer, knew that they could be trusted, and told them who Nash was. "Don't tell anyone that Jelly's in town," Smith cautioned.

Again Frank Smith called Colvin in Oklahoma City. "It's all set," Colvin said. "Get on the Missouri Pacific *Flyer* for Kansas City tonight. I've called Reed Vetterli (special agent in charge of the Kansas City FBI office) and he'll meet you at Union Station with a car and take you on to Leavenworth."

At 8:15 P.M., only minutes before the speeding passenger train was due to arrive, Nash was taken from the jail. However, the *Flyer* was late and the lawmen and their handcuffed prisoner had to wait on the platform for 15 minutes. "An ideal spot for an ambush!" Lackey reflected.

While waiting for the train, Lackey was approached by a young Fort Smith newspaper reporter who asked for details concerning the prisoner, which the G-Man refused to give. Then Lackey was given a shock: the reporter already knew that the prisoner was the notorious Jelly Nash. "It came over the press wires that you're taking Nash to Joplin, but Joplin newsmen had been unable to locate you," the reporter said.

The lawmen grew edgy. It seemed that the entire world now knew that they were taking Jelly Nash to Kansas City and then to Leavenworth penitentiary.

Everyone, except for Jelly, felt relief when the train arrived. The party scrambled aboard and settled down in drawing room A, car 11. Nash was given the upper berth and handcuffed to a sturdy railing. Exhausted from their long and strenuous day, the lawmen would take turns grabbing brief periods of sleep in the lower berth.

Nash was an affable and glib traveling companion. When the officers joked about his red wig, Jelly grinned. "You do what you can (to avoid detection)," he said. "I paid a hunnert bucks fer it in Chicago."[5]

At the time that the *Flyer* was rolling northward to Kansas City from Arkansas, two killers and bank robbers were driving westward across central Missouri, also bound for Kansas City. Behind the wheel was 31-year-old Charles "Pretty Boy" Floyd, who had reached such heights in his crime profession that the press labeled him Public Enemy Number 1.

Riding with Floyd was his close pal Adam Richetti, who was almost as vicious as Pretty Boy. Despite the closeness of their ages (Floyd was the elder by two years), Richetti idolized Pretty Boy and even tried to mock his mannerisms.

Near Columbia, home of the University of Missouri, two members of the Missouri State Police, Sergeants Ben Booth and Roger Wilson, turned on the siren of their cruiser and halted the car carrying Floyd and Richetti for a routine check of the occupants. As the two officers approached the parked vehicle, a Tommy-gun burst ripped into Booth and Wilson, killing them almost instantly.

Floyd and Richetti roared away and continued their flight to Kansas City. Within minutes, law enforcement officers radioed word that the two outlaws were the main suspects in the murder of Sergeants Booth and Wilson.

10

Cutting a Deal in "Tom's Town"

Pretty Boy Floyd and Adam Richetti were eager to reach the sanctuary of Kansas City before law enforcement officers all over Missouri learned that they had gunned down the two State Police sergeants in cold blood. Kansas City was a cesspool of corruption where gangsters and crooked politicians shared control.

The underworld called Kansas City "Tom's Town" after Thomas J. Pendergast, the Big Boss. Years earlier, the rotund Pendergast had opened his city to vice lords and racketeers whom he could shake down for hefty payoffs to support his extravagant lifestyle, which included horse racing bets of $10,000 or more.[1]

When Floyd and Richetti approached the small town of Bolivar, Missouri, in their flight to Tom's Town, their car's engine began to chug and clank. Luck was with the outlaws, for Richetti's brother Joe operated an auto repair shop in Bolivar.

Having nursed their balky engine for the last two miles, the men pulled into Joe Richetti's shop. Joe was far from happy to see his brother and Floyd, especially after he peeked into the back seat and spotted an arsenal of Tommy guns, pistols, sawed-off shotguns, and stacks of ammunition.

Joe began repairing the car; he knew better than to ask questions. A few minutes later, Joe glanced up and his heart skipped a beat: Polk County Sheriff John Killingsworth had walked into the garage. Joking and laughing, the sheriff was in fine fettle. Adam Richetti recognized Killingsworth, seized a Tommy gun from the car, and pointed it at the sheriff. Pretty Boy, a tall, heavyset man, whipped out a pair of .45-caliber pistols and covered Joe Richetti and three other mechanics.

"If you bastards know what's good for you, you'll shutup!" Floyd snarled.

Sheriff Killingsworth felt that he was on the brink of sudden death, now recognizing Pretty Boy Floyd and Adam Richetti as the vicious killers who were wanted for the deaths of the two policemen at Columbia a few hours earlier. Moreover, Killingsworth had seen the two gunmen's pictures on wanted posters many times.

Joe Richetti, an honest and God-fearing man, ignored the menacing weapons and leaped between Sheriff Killingsworth and the gunmen.

"If you kill him, you'll have to kill me," he told his brother. For one of the few times in his life, Adam Richetti backed down.

Rapidly, the fugitives' arsenal was switched to another car and the sheriff, after being disarmed, was ordered to get into the back seat. Again he felt he was on the verge of meeting his Creator. Pretty Boy and Adam climbed into the front seat and they raced off.

Near Deepwater, Missouri, Floyd braked the car to a stop, turned around and told Killingsworth, "Get the hell out!" This is it, the law officer concluded. However, once he was standing on the roadside, the car sped off.

Floyd and Richetti arrived in Kansas City at about 9:00 P.M. They had no way of knowing that in less than 12 hours they would be key figures in one of the most flamboyant and bloody crimes of the 1930s.

A day after his release, Sheriff Killingsworth told the press about his wild ride with the two notorious gunmen:

> I was in the back seat with Floyd. Richetti drove for about 35 miles and I was afraid because he was drinking. Then Floyd took the wheel. He sure is a good driver.
>
> What worried me from the start was that the boys [other officers] would try to help me out. Floyd, I saw right away, would kill a man, but not unless he had to.
>
> They told me I would be safe if I would direct them to safety. We wandered over roads I knew would be hard to follow. Then the highway patrol got right behind us. They stuck a gun in my side and told me to wave them back. I was more than willing.

Adam Richetti and Pretty Boy Floyd (he despised the nickname) were only in their late 20s, but each had a long career in violent crime. Richetti's began on August 7, 1928, when he was arrested in Hammond, Indiana, and charged with a holdup. He was sentenced to from one to ten years in the State Reformatory at Pendleton, Indiana, and was paroled less than two years later.

Richetti promptly set his sights on bigger game, and he was apprehended at Sulphur, Oklahoma, on March 9, 1932, while robbing a bank. Sentenced to the Oklahoma State Penitentiary at McAlester, Richetti served less than five months when he managed to put up a $1,500 bond and was paroled. Jumping bail, he got his hands on a revolver and robbed a store at Tishomingo, Oklahoma.

In early 1933, Adam Richetti teamed up with Pretty Boy Floyd to knock off several banks in the Midwest. Richetti was an alcoholic, and sobered up only when he and Floyd pulled off a bank job.

Charles Arthur Floyd was born and reared at Akins, Oklahoma, where he worked on his father's small, dirt-poor farm, trying to eke out a living as did the other hardscrabble folks in that Cookson Hills region. At night, young Charles would often go "hell raisin' " in Akins and nearby Sallisaw, where he consumed so much of a local beverage called Choctaw Beer that he was given the nickname Chock.

In 1924, things were bad for the Floyd family and other sharecroppers in eastern Oklahoma. Chárles married a 16-year-old local girl, and a year later, she was pregnant. Desperate for money, Charles rode the rails to St. Louis and was caught after pulling a $5,000 payroll robbery.

Floyd was sentenced to the Missouri State Penitentiary in Jefferson City for five years, and was paroled after serving half of that time. While he was locked up, his teenaged wife gave birth to their son.

Charles returned home, happy to see his wife and new son. However, he was bitter, and swore to himself that he'd never be locked up again.

In 1929, Charles, now 27 years of age, went to Kansas City where he hooked up with Red Lovett, who had been a cellmate in Jefferson City, and through him met two professional bank robbers, Jack Atkins and Tom Bradley. Together the four-man gang set out for Ohio and rented an Akron cottage as a base of operations.

Floyd and his three cohorts knocked over a series of small-town banks, the last one at Sylvania, Ohio, on March 11, 1930. Speeding back into Akron, the gunmen drove through a red traffic light and Policeman Harlan F. Manes gave chase in his car.

Punching out a back window, the desperadoes sent a torrent of bullets hissing toward Officer Manes, killing him almost instantly. Then the driver of the bank robbers' car lost control and the vehicle smashed into a telephone pole.

With sirens blaring, police cars roared up and pried the dazed gunmen out of the wrecked car. Three of them were tried for the murder of the Akron policeman. In a curious verdict, Tom Bradley was sent to the electric chair, Jack Atkins was given life in prison, and Pretty Boy Floyd was acquitted.

Before Floyd could be released, it was discovered that he had been one of the Sylvania bank robbers, so he was tried on that charge and sentenced to 15 years in the Ohio State Penitentiary. Two deputies taking Floyd to prison fell asleep while their train was speeding cross-country. Floyd sprang forward, kicked out a window and leaped through the opening, hitting the ground with enormous impact. Agile for a big man, Floyd bounced to his feet and fled through a cornfield. By the time the train could be halted, it was a half-mile away and the prisoner was long gone. Floyd would never stop running for the remainder of his life.

Pretty Boy headed for Toledo, Ohio, where he joined up with a young Missouri man named Bill "the Killer" Miller, who had been credited with murdering five men at the last count. Bill the Killer regarded Floyd as a young punk who needed seasoning. So the two men drove into northern Michigan and held up lone farmers and small stores.[2]

Bill the Killer (no kin to Vern Miller) and Floyd then went to Kansas City, where they blew much of their loot on wild drinking parties and floozy women. At a whorehouse called Mother Ash's, Floyd was said to have gotten the Pretty Boy nickname. When the tall, muscular young man first walked into the place, the madam, who was usually the chief administrator and cashier, called out, "Well, Pretty Boy, I'm going to take care of you personally!"

In the days ahead, Floyd was smitten by the madam's daughter-in-law Rose, and Bill the Killer took a liking to Rose's sister Beulah. This amorous development created an awkward situation: Rose and Beulah were married to William and Wallace Ash, sons of the madam.

Hard feelings sprouted among the four men. The Ash boys, who were small-time gangsters and doubled as bouncers in their mother's whorehouse, let it be known in the underworld of Kansas City that they were going to kill Pretty Boy and Bill Miller.

One day Wallace Ash received a telephone call from his wife requesting that he and his brother William rendezvous with the women. Perhaps eager for a reconciliation, the brothers left for the engagement.

Two days later, on March 25, 1931, Wallace and William Ash were found sprawled in a ditch, each with a bullet in the back of his head. Next to them was their burnt out automobile.

With Rose and Beulah in tow, Floyd and Bill Miller went on a wild fling of bank robberies in Kentucky, then holed up in a tourist court (motel) in Bowling Green, Ohio, to wait for the heat to cool. Bowling Green is not a large town, so merchants and other locals became suspicious of the two couples who were flashing large rolls of bills on a buying spree.

Bowling Green Chief of Police Carl Galliher was notified about the big-spending strangers and, taking along Patrolman Ralph Castner, went to investigate. The two officers approached Bill Miller, Rose, and Beulah as they were about to enter a store.

"Hold it right there!" Chief Galliher called out.

From across the street came the booming voice of Pretty Boy Floyd, who had been acting as a lookout: "Duck, Bill!"

Miller flopped down and Floyd, a pistol in each hand, opened fire. Officer Castner toppled over, dead. Galliher leaped behind a car and shot at Bill Miller, who had drawn his gun and was ready to sprint across the street to Floyd. A bullet ripped away much of Killer Bill's neck, and he crumpled to the pavement and died moments later.

Beulah, seeing her boyfriend cut down, screamed hysterically, picked up the dying man's gun, and aimed it at the police chief. Galliher got off the first shot and his bullet grazed Beulah's head. Floyd continued to blaze away at Galliher, the bullets making eerie noises as they ricocheted on the street of the customarily peaceful college town. Moments later a slug, probably from Pretty Boy's smoking pistols, nicked Rose in the leg, causing it to bleed profusely.

Pretty Boy knew that the Battle of Bowling Green was lost. He ran madly down the street, whirling occasionally to squeeze off a wild shot, leaped into the gang's car, and roared out of town.

The bloody shootout catapulted Pretty Boy Floyd into national ill-fame, and forced him to live like a hunted animal. After hiding out in Toledo for a few weeks he drove to Kansas City and took refuge in a secret room above a floral shop, which was a front for a local booze-running operation.

Prohibition agents learned that the cop killer might be hiding above the floral shop. On July 21, 1931, several officers raided the place and broke into the room where Pretty Boy was crouched behind a bed with a gun in each hand. Weapons roared. Prohibition Agent Curtis C. Burks's head was nearly blown away by a burst from Floyd's powerful .45 revolver. Then the fugitive leaped out of a window and fled amidst a hail of bullets.

Knowing that he was extremely "hot," Floyd scampered back to his home stomping grounds in eastern Oklahoma's Cookson Hills. Legend had it that a few months earlier, after Pretty Boy gained wide notoriety as a cop killer, he wrote to the sheriff of his home county:

"I'm coming to visit Mother. If you're smart, you won't try to stop me." The sheriff was *very* smart.

Many of the folks in Cookson Hills looked sympathetically upon Pretty Boy, regarding him as a modern-day Robin Hood who stole from rich bankers and gave to the poor. All over America, bankers had been foreclosing on farmers who, gripped by the Great Depression, could not meet their mortgage payments. Many of the hardscrabble people in eastern Oklahoma were often delighted to hear that one of their own had knocked off yet another greedy bank.

On one occasion, possibly on a dare, Floyd returned to his home territory to rob the bank at Sallisaw, the small town where he had often gone "hell-raisin' " as a youth. Most of the town folks knew Pretty Boy. So when he casually stepped from his car clutching a Tommy gun, he saw a few Sallisaw men idling outside the nearby barber shop.

"How do, Charles," one of them called to Floyd. "What'er ya doin' back in town?"

"How you, Clem?" Pretty Boy replied. "Came to rob this here bank!"

"Give 'em hell!" a second admirer yelled.

Using the friendly confines of Cookson Hills as a base, Floyd teamed with 40-year-old George Birdwell, a former preacher who had "lost the callin'." One local explained Birdwell's switch in occupations:

"George figured as how there's a heap more money in robbin' banks than in preachin'."

Floyd and Birdwell robbed so many banks that the insurance rates in Oklahoma doubled in one year. The governor took to the radio airwaves to denounce Pretty Boy and put a $6,000 bounty on the outlaw's head—dead or alive, no questions asked.

Floyd was miffed at the governor. From a rural Oklahoma post office, he mailed a letter to a Tulsa newspaper, complaining about the "measly size" of the governor's bounty.

A year later, George Birdwell was shot to death while pulling off a bank heist by himself.[3]

Three hours before Pretty Boy Floyd and his new partner Adam Richetti drove into Kansas City on the night of June 16, 1933, the telephone jangled at Deafy Farmer's place outside Joplin. As was often the habit with neighbors on rural party lines, a man down the road picked up his telephone to eavesdrop. He heard a deep voice tell Deafy:

"We watched them from three different angles, but they got through with the papers."

The eavesdropping neighbor had no way of knowing that the double-talk meant that FBI agents Smith and Lackey and Chief Reed had gotten through the roadblocks to Fort Smith with Jelly Nash.

In Kansas City at the same time, Vern Miller, the South Dakota sheriff-turned-badman, contacted Johnny Lazia, a politician reputed to have extensive underworld ties. Late that night—only 13 hours after Jelly Nash had been spirited out of Hot Springs—Miller and Lazia rendezvoused in Union Station.

"The 'briefcase boys' (FBI agents) grabbed Jelly Nash at the Springs and are bringing him here on the train," Miller told Lazia. "I'm going to snatch him back, but I need some local talent (hired gunmen)."

Lazia blanched. That scheme would mean tangling with the FBI. So he refused to suggest any locals for the job, but told Miller that "the right boys for you just got into town."[4]

Vern Miller and Johnny Lazia left Union Station and drove to a high-class whorehouse on Holmes Street. As Lazia expected, Pretty Boy Floyd, a habitué of brothels, was there, even though he had murdered two police sergeants at Columbia earlier in the day and was the target of a statewide manhunt.

After introducing Vern Miller to Floyd, John Lazia departed. Miller and Pretty Boy went into a room and cut a deal, although it would never be known if Floyd was primarily interested in the big money he and Adam Richetti would be paid as hired guns or if he was eager to snatch a federal prisoner away from the hated FBI.[5]

Hauling a half-drunk Adam Richetti along, Floyd and Miller drove to Miller's Edgevale Road home to drink beer and plan the Jelly Nash caper when the Missouri Pacific *Flyer* arrived at Union Station in about seven hours.

At the FBI office in Kansas City, Special Agent in Charge Reed Vetterli had completed plans for meeting the passenger train and escorting Jelly Nash on the final 16-mile leg of his trek back to Leavenworth. Two Kansas City detectives, W. J. "Red" Grooms and Frank Hermanson, would join Vetterli and a young FBI agent, Raymond S. Caffrey, at Union Station.[6]

The arresting officers (Lackey, Smith, and Reed) and their prisoner would be driven to Leavenworth in Caffrey's Chevrolet sedan. Vetterli would drive his car behind, and Hermanson and Grooms would bring up the rear in the Kansas City Police Department's new "hot shot," an armored car designed mainly for use in riots and shootouts.

11

A Massacre that Outraged America

G-Man Joe Lackey hung from the doorway of the *Flyer* passenger train as it chugged to a halt in Kansas City's cavernous Union Station. It was 7:12 on Saturday morning, June 17, 1933. Lackey quickly swept the platform with his eyes. Nothing looked suspicious. Then he spotted a few fellow FBI agents, Reed Vetterli and Ray Caffrey, and near to them were Kansas City Detectives Frank Hermanson and Red Grooms.

Lackey climbed down to exchange a few words with the officers, then returned to stateroom A, where Jelly Nash had spent the night in an upper berth, handcuffed to a railing.

"Everything looks okay," Lackey told Agent Frank Smith and Chief Otto Reed.

While Reed went out into the corridor to stand guard, Nash was uncuffed, helped down from the berth and then manacled again with his hands in front.

"Well, Jelly," Lackey said, "It won't be long 'til you're back with your pals in the joint!"

After walking up to the main level of the station, the seven officers formed a fan-shaped formation around Nash and started across the broad concourse. Lackey and Reed carried shotguns and the other lawmen kept hands near their holstered weapons. Throngs of curious people gawked at the passing procession, and no doubt wondered about the identity of the prisoner in handcuffs whose red wig kept slipping.

Pushing through Union Station's front door, the officers paused and, squinting in the early morning rays of a bright sun, glanced in each direction. Again, nothing suspicious.

Reaching Agent Caffrey's Chevrolet parked about 100 feet from the station, Lackey, Smith, and Reed climbed into the back seat and Jelly Nash was told to sit in the front passenger seat. Then Caffrey walked around the car to get in on the driver's side, while Agent Vetterli and Detectives Grooms and Hermanson remained standing on the right side of the Chevy.

Suddenly from only a few feet away, a booming voice shouted:

"*Up! Up! Up!*"

Before the law officers could react, a second loud voice thundered: "*Let 'em have it!*"

A terrific racket erupted as three or more Tommy guns began chattering like noisy typewriters. Bullets splattered the Chevrolet. Joe Lackey slumped forward with two .45-caliber slugs lodged in his spine and a third bullet embedded near his pelvic bone. Struggling, Lackey managed to draw his gun and tried to fire out of the open window, but a bullet tore the weapon from his grasp.

Chief Reed took a chest full of slugs and crumbled to the floor, dead. Outside the Chevy, Frank Hermanson was able to whip out his weapon and fire one round before he was killed. Red Grooms, riddled by bullets, toppled over dead onto his comrade. On the other side of the car, Ray Caffrey died from a bullet in the head.

Jelly Nash, with handcuffed wrists, waved frantically and, above the raucous din of gunfire, yelled, "For God's sake, don't shoot *me*!" A split second later, bullets nearly tore off Jelly's head, blowing away his red wig.

Suddenly, an eerie silence fell over Union Station plaza. It had taken less than 30 seconds to murder four law enforcement officers and their federal prisoner and to seriously wound two other FBI agents.

With their Tommy guns still smoking, the three gunmen dashed to Caffrey's Chevrolet and glanced inside.

"They're all dead! Let's get the hell out of here!" one killer was heard to yell.

At that moment, Kansas City Policeman Mike Fanning charged out of the station on hearing the machine-gun fire. Nearby, Mrs. Lottie West, a caseworker for the Travelers Aid Society, had watched the entire bloody scenario in horror. Seeing Officer Fanning, whom she knew, Mrs. West screamed, "They're killing everyone, Mike!"

Fanning pulled out his revolver and fired at the three gunmen who were running toward their getaway car. A tall, heavyset man went down, but Fanning could not tell if a bullet had struck him or he had stumbled. Moments later the big man scrambled to his feet and raced to a dark-colored Chevrolet holding his two partners, and the car roared away.

Mike Fanning, a veteran policeman, rushed to the bullet-punctured Chevrolet and was sickened by the sight that greeted his eyes when he glanced inside. The car was a shambles. Upholstery had been ripped by bullets as though a demented demon had slashed it repeatedly with a razor-sharp blade. Blood was splashed on the inside of the windows, and Fanning spotted bits and pieces that he recognized as bone and flesh. Bodies were sprawled grotesquely in pools of blood.

Agent Joe Lackey, grievously wounded, was removed from the vehicle and rushed to a hospital. Agent Reed Vetterli had been hit in the arm by a bullet. Agent Frank Smith, who had flopped face-down on the floorboard and feigned death when the three killers had glanced inside the car, miraculously survived unscathed by the blizzard of bullets.[1]

Word of the brazen butchery was promptly flashed to J. Edgar Hoover in Washington, D.C. Struggling to control the white-hot fury that welled in him, the FBI chief took personal command of the investigation and dispatched swarms of his agents to Kansas City.

In hours, newspapers across the United States carried blaring headlines that read "Kansas City Massacre." An entire nation was outraged and demanded that the killers be brought to justice. It was a turning point in the FBI's war against crime in America.[2]

Mr. and Mrs. John Q. Public were infuriated by the bloody insolence of the underworld. When gangland dared to openly challenge the power of the law, when it was brazen enough to slaughter law enforcement officers in broad daylight in the heart of a major city, the average citizen demanded a new deal on crime.

During the years of Prohibition, most Americans had yawned over the bloody gang wars. What difference did they make? After all, the gangsters were merely wiping out one another.

America's underworld—in a 30-second time span—had lost its greatest ally: public indifference.

A few days after the Kansas City Massacre, in a speech before the International Chiefs of Police at the Sherman Hotel in Chicago, J. Edgar Hoover paid tribute to the lawmen who had been gunned down.

"These men met death as gallantly as any soldier who ever fell in battle in defense of his country and its ideals," the Director declared. "They lived and died nobly, and their lives and their deaths remain as a never-to-be-forgotten example and inspiration to us all." Hoover made a solemn pledge: "Those jackals who participated in these cold-blooded murders will be hunted down. Sooner or later the penalty which is their due will be paid!"[3]

Meanwhile, in Kansas City the blood had hardly dried that fateful Saturday morning than the town became the "hottest" spot in the United States. Every underworld character, from kingpins to two-bit hoodlums, ducked for a hideout. Gangster haunts looked as though they had suddenly been struck by a pestilence.

One of the FBI agents rushed to Kansas City was Gus T. Jones, a former Texas Ranger and one of Hoover's favorites. Working out of San Antonio, Jones had been hunting down bank robbers and other criminals in the Midwest and South for years. He knew the gangland figures, their ways, and their haunts. Few G-Men had as many stool pigeons in the underworld as did the bespectacled Gus Jones.

Early on, Jones became convinced that big-time criminal Harvey Bailey had been the ringleader in the massacre. Less than three weeks earlier, on Memorial

Day, Bailey had been one of the 11 convicts in the daring escape from the Kansas State Penitentiary, where he had been serving a ten- to 50-year sentence for robbing a bank at Fort Scott, Kansas. Bailey was considered to be highly dangerous and went armed with a Tommy gun and two pistols.

It appeared that Gus Jones was right. Everywhere FBI agents probed they gained evidence that the notorious Harvey Bailey was the main culprit.

His mug shots were shown to workers at Union Station and several of them identified him as having been on the premises shortly before the killings. Photos of Bailey's criminal associates were also brought out, and a few of those figures were identified.

Bailey's face was certainly widely recognized in Kansas City, for his picture had been plastered over the front pages of local newspapers when he broke out of the penitentiary.

What seemed to be the clinching piece of evidence that Harvey Bailey was the ringleader was provided by Samuel E. Link, a Kansas City businessman. Link told FBI agents that when he tried to park his car in front of Union Station on that Saturday morning three men in a four-door Reo automobile drove up and gruffly ordered him to "get your goddamned car out of the way."

Perhaps a minute later, Link added, he heard a loud shout and looked up to see a man he recognized as Harvey Bailey climb out of the left rear door of the Reo. "Moments later, all hell broke loose!" Link stated.

What's more, he said he knew Bailey from past encounters when he had been a deputy constable in Kansas City. "No doubt about it—the guy gettin' out of the Reo was Harvey Bailey," Link declared.

In Washington, D.C., tens of thousands of wanted posters of Harvey Bailey and his cohorts in the Memorial Day prison break in Kansas were prepared at FBI headquarters and flooded the United States. All over the Midwest and South FBI men wore out shoe soles and automobile tires running down reports of Bailey sightings.

The massive manhunt had become so intense that Bailey, while remaining in hiding, took the unique step of confessing by mail to another major crime in order to try to clear himself of the Kansas City murders. The fugitive wrote to the FBI that he had robbed a bank in Arkansas late on the afternoon before the Union Station killings and couldn't have reached Kansas City in time.

"I'm sending along my fingerprints in motor oil," Bailey added, to help authorities solve the "Arkansas bank job."

Harvey Bailey hadn't confessed because of a sudden surge of remorse. Should he be caught—a distinct possibility—he could be given up to 50 years for the Arkansas bank robbery. But should he be convicted of the Kansas City Massacre, Bailey would be hanged in the Missouri State Penitentiary at Jefferson City.

Throughout the investigation of the Union Station murders, Reed Vetterli, who headed the Kansas City FBI office, had been working closely with the local police department. Although still in extreme pain from the gunshot wound received in the ambush, Vetterli had returned to his post, determined to identify and apprehend the perpetrators.

One day Agent Gus Jones, the old Texas Ranger, received a confidential teletype from Special Agent in Charge R. H. Colvin of the Oklahoma City FBI office. Colvin's message said:

> Have apparently reliable information that (a high Kansas City police official) is wrong (crooked) and in the protection in Kansas City. This information comes from high-powered criminals.
>
> Am afraid that (Reed) Vetterli's confidence misplaced. Suggest confer with him on this and govern your actions accordingly.

That disclosure shook FBI confidence in the integrity of the Kansas City Police Department and came at a time when the close-knit cooperation of all law enforcement agencies was crucial. It was yet another classic case of the reputation of hundreds of dedicated, scrupulously honest policemen being tarnished by the alleged dealings of one or two bad apples at the top of the barrel.

As FBI agents continued to run down leads and collect information, it began to appear that Harvey Bailey was not the prime suspect. Mrs. Lottie West, the Travelers Aid Society caseworker who had been an eyewitness to the Union Station murders, identified the big man who had fallen to the pavement when fired on by Policeman Mike Fanning as Charles ''Pretty Boy'' Floyd.

Then D. O. Smith, the special agent in charge of the Chicago FBI, sent an urgent teletype to Reed Vetterli in Kansas City:

> It has been ascertained through a confidential informant that a Kansas City gang is at present harboring Pretty Boy Floyd in the Italian quarters, Kansas City, which district bears a decidedly tough reputation . . .
>
> (Informant) believes that (Vern) Miller, Pretty Boy Floyd and the above-mentioned Italians committed the murders at the Union Station in Kansas City the 17th last.[4]

Now even supersleuth Gus Jones began to have doubts about Harvey Bailey's involvement in the massacre.

Meanwhile, a young FBI agent named Hal Bray was engaged in one of the more mundane pursuits that are so crucial to solving complex crimes. Bray contacted the telephone company in Hot Springs to obtain a record of long-distance calls made from that city on June 16, the day that Jelly Nash had been recaptured, and studied the listings. It was a painstaking chore, for hundreds of long distance calls had gone out of Hot Springs on June 16 and the next day.

Finally, after countless hours, Bray seemed to have struck pay dirt: calls from rackets boss Richard Galatas in Hot Springs had been made to Deafy Farmer's home outside Joplin, Missouri. Further digging disclosed that Deafy was a friend of Jelly Nash, who had holed up on Farmer's premises in the past.

Anxious to follow up on this red-hot lead, Hal Bray promptly asked the Joplin telephone company for its long-distance records, but learned that they already had been shipped to the accounting division of Southwestern Bell Telephone Company in St. Louis. Bray took his problem to Reed Vetterli, who obtained the records from St. Louis.

Again, Bray spent long, tedious hours sifting through the hundreds of Joplin long-distance calls. Then, for some reason he could not define, Bray focused on two particular Joplin telephone numbers. Those numbers linked Deafy Farmer's telephone to a number at 6612 Edgevale Road in Kansas City. Investigation disclosed that a man named Vincent C. Moore lived there with a woman presumed to be his wife.[5]

FBI records at the Washington headquarters had no listing for a Vincent C. Moore. However, Bureau agents, in a carefully coordinated operation, swooped down on the Edgevale residence and burst inside. No one was at home, but there was ample evidence of a hasty departure.

Photos were shown to neighbors, and the G-Men were able to determine that the man known as Vincent Moore was actually Vern Miller, the hired gun. Out of his place came everything that might yield a clue: shoes, papers, empty beer bottles. All of these items were flown to the FBI laboratory in Washington, D.C. for scientific examination.

Years earlier, J. Edgar Hoover recognized that the Bureau had a critical need for its own laboratory and sent agents to study the operation of privately owned facilities that examined evidence in criminal cases. An agent also was assigned to visit universities throughout the United States and report back what they were doing in this field. Nationally known experts in such areas as pathology, bacteriology, photography, and microscopy were consulted. Using borrowed microscopes, ultraviolet light equipment, and other bits and pieces of paraphernalia, the FBI Laboratory began operation on November 24, 1932.[6]

Now, barely eight months later, FBI technicians were minutely inspecting the items that had been hauled out of Vern Miller's house in Kansas City. The beer bottles were assigned to a special section set up to include the single fingerprints of the nation's top criminals. This section was manned by specialists whose job was to identify latent fingerprints—or parts of a fingerprint or palm print—left at the scene of a crime or found on an object used in a crime.

Nearly invisible prints left on a bottle, glass, doorknob, or any smooth surface can be found when dusted with a special powder. Then the prints are "lifted" onto adhesive tape. The powder clings to the adhesive and there reproduces the tiny skin ridges—a fingerprint. Special cameras can photograph the fingerprint.

Centuries earlier, men recognized the distinctive pattern of fingerprints, but the system of identification that came into popular use in the United States and Europe was one created in the 1880s by Alphonse Bertillon, a Frenchman. Bertillon's technique required complicated measurements, such as the length and width of the head, the length and width of the left foot, left forearm, left little finger, and the like. Presumably, no two human bodies had the same precise measurements in all these parts.

Bertillon's system proved to be faulty countless times. However, it was not until 1904 that the city of St. Louis police department became a trailblazer by switching criminal identification procedures from the Bertillon system to fingerprints.

That same year, the United States Department of Justice authorized the installation of a criminal fingerprint system at the federal penitentiary at Leavenworth for an expenditure "not to exceed $60." The work was done with prison labor, resulting in a situation whereby the "employees" on the project on occasion ran across copies of their own fingerprints.

In 1921, the fingerprint records and Bertillon system files at Leavenworth were transferred to the Department of Justice in Washington, D.C., and combined with similar records that had been stored in the national capital by the International Association of Chiefs of Police since 1896.

When J. Edgar Hoover took control of the FBI in 1924, he inherited a monumental mess. Nearly a million fingerprint records and Bertillon files were piled haphazardly in storage. Locating a specific set of prints would have been equivalent to parting the Red Sea. At the urging of Hoover, Congress, within the next few years, provided funds and authorized the establishment of a permanent Division of Identification and Information, which would include fingerprints not only of criminals, but of lawabiding citizens as well. Order was brought out of chaos. Director Hoover called the FBI fingerprint section a "Who's Who in the Field of Crime."[7]

Now, in the Kansas City Massacre investigation, the Who's Who paid off: a fingerprint lifted from a beer bottle at Vern Miller's home in Kansas City matched that of Adam Richetti, whom Hoover labeled "a mad-dog killer."

With Vern Miller and Adam Richetti tied to the Kansas City murders, the FBI concluded that the third gunman had to be Pretty Boy Floyd. As one Bureau agent put it: "Richetti won't go to the toilet unless Pretty Boy is with him."

The intense search now focused on Miller, Richetti, and Floyd. Kansas City, particularly the "Italian quarters," was turned upside down by law enforcement officers. But the scouring of underworld haunts and "safe houses" proved to be fruitless: the three wanted men had fled not long after the massacre.

Vern Miller and his girlfriend Vi Gibson (alias Vi Mathis) drove to the Chicago suburb of Maywood and, cloaked by darkness, slipped into an apartment rented by Volney Davis, an old friend of Miller's, and his eccentric live-in partner Edna "the Kissing Bandit" Murray, an escapee from the Missouri State Penitentiary.

Part Cherokee, Davis, a young, curly-haired tough, had been granted a "two-year leave of absence" from the Oklahoma State Penitentiary, where he was serving a life sentence for murder, and joined the Barker-Karpis gang in the kidnapping of William Hamm. As hardened a criminal as he was, Davis was jittery over holding open house for one of the FBI's most wanted desperadoes who had also earned the wrath of the underworld big-shots for bringing federal heat onto their lucrative operations.

After four days, Davis managed to ease his old pal out of the apartment, and Miller and Vi ran east, first to New York City and then to New Jersey. Old cronies in the East greeted Miller with all the enthusiasm they would muster for the arrival of the Bubonic Plague. Miller was hot—boiling hot. Doors were slammed in his face. No one would take in the fugitive couple, so they had to hide out in flea-bag hotels and tourist courts, constantly fearful of both the FBI and of gangland wrath.

At the same time that Miller and his moll had blown Kansas City, Pretty Boy and Adam Richetti headed to Toledo. Along the way, they were joined by their girlfriends, Rose and Beulah, the widows of the Ash brothers whom Floyd and Bill "the Killer" Miller had murdered in 1931. Two weeks after reaching Toledo, the foursome moved on to Buffalo, New York, where they rented an apartment in a blue-collar neighborhood. Floyd and Rose used the names Mr. and Mrs. George Sanders while Richetti and Beulah adopted the alias Mr. and Mrs. Ed Brennan.[8]

A queer lot, the neighbors soon pegged the newcomers. Why did they never go outside in the daytime? Why did they have no visible means of income? Why did they have no telephone? Neither of the couples talked with neighbors, although the women sometimes tossed money and candy out of the second-floor window to children playing in the yard.

Day after day, the once loquacious Adam Richetti sat with his head in his hands, morose and sullen. Seldom did he speak, and when he did it was usually in a sharp dispute with Floyd.

Floyd was not one to sit still. Night and day, like a caged animal, he paced from one end of the apartment to the other. "That guy up there is driving me loony!" the man in the lower apartment complained to his wife.[9]

Meanwhile, back in Missouri, young FBI agent Hal Bray continued the painstaking digging into long distance telephone call records and developed a pattern of conversations between Hot Springs, Joplin, Chicago, and Kansas City.

In September 1933, only three months after the Union Station murders, a federal grand jury was ready to indict four persons for conspiracy to release a federal prisoner (Jelly Nash). Charged with the crime were Richard Galatas, the Hot Springs rackets kingpin; Vern Miller; Chicago gangster Louis "Doc" Stacci; Herbert "Deafy" Farmer, the Joplin hideout operator, and Frank Mulloy, a Kansas City roadhouse operator who had relayed Stacci's message to Miller. All were taken into custody by the FBI except for Vern Miller who was hiding out, as were Pretty Boy Floyd and Adam Richetti.

On the night of October 31, Melvin Purvis, special agent in charge of the FBI office in Chicago, was playing host in his apartment to an unlikely guest— Gus "Big Mike" Winkler, an overlord in Al Capone's crime empire.

Two weeks earlier, Winkler had been arrested by Chicago police and grilled about his role in a series of major crimes, including murders. Melvin Purvis had also questioned Winkler in the FBI's nineteenth-floor office in a downtown skyscraper and suggested that Big Mike might want to provide him with information on Vern Miller's whereabouts. Winkler had no reply.

Later, Capone's lieutenant had a change of heart. He telephoned Agent Purvis to ask for a secret meeting, and arrangements were made for Winkler to come to Purvis' apartment.

Seated on a sofa and face-to-face with the man who was trying to put him in prison for life or have him executed, Big Mike was nervous and perspiring. He found himself between a rock and a hard place, for there would be gangland vengeance heaped on him should word seep out that he was cuddling up to the G-Men.

Winkler didn't know that a dictaphone concealed in a bookcase next to the sofa was carrying his words to a recording machine manned by two FBI agents in an adjoining room.

For whatever he hoped to gain in this high-wire balancing act, Big Mike told Purvis that Vi Gibson, Vern Miller's mistress, and her friend, Bobbie Moore (alias Mrs. Jake Harris) were living in an apartment hotel on Chicago's North Side. Presumably, Vern Miller was also there or not far away.

Melvin Purvis and his men promptly laid a trap for Miller. Two agents were placed in a rented apartment near the one occupied by Vi Gibson and Bobbie Moore. The agents, who had resided in Huron, South Dakota, when Vern Miller lived there and knew him by sight, peered through a small hole from which they could observe anyone leaving or approaching the suspected apartment. Other FBI agents were placed at strategic points outside the hotel.

After a long and tedious vigil, the two agents at the peephole spotted a man approaching—Vern Miller. Using the sixth sense of a hunted animal, Miller realized something was wrong. He spun around, ran back down the hall and scampered down the steps.

At this point, Murphy's Law took over. When the peephole agents had first seen Miller, they flashed a signal to the other agents. But there was a mixup that resulted in the G-Men outside the hotel not being notified soon enough.

Vern Miller charged madly out the front door and leaped into a waiting Ford automobile with Bobbie Moore at the wheel. With a roar of an engine and the squealing of tires, the car sped away. An FBI agent fired a burst with his Tommy gun at the fleeing Ford, riddling it with 17 bullets. Miller was leading a charmed life: neither he nor Bobbie Moore was hit. A few blocks away, the getaway car was abandoned. Miller fled in one direction; Moore in another.[10]

Seventy-two hours later, Big Mike Winkler walked out of a Chicago restaurant after enjoying a sumptuous meal. A black sedan roared up and braked hard. A Tommy gun was poked out the open window and a burst of fire echoed over the scene. Winkler, his body filled with slugs, crumpled onto the sidewalk, mortally wounded.

Less than a month after Big Mike's demise, a farmer in Michigan was driving along a back road on the bitterly cold night of November 29, 1933. Suddenly the headlights fell onto a large, odd-looking bundle lying beside the road.

Police were notified and came to investigate. They pulled away a pair of dirty old blankets that covered the mutilated body of a dead man. He was nude and his arms and legs were trussed with clothesline. His face had been beaten to a pulp with a heavy instrument, perhaps a hammer. Bruises on his throat indicated that he also might have been strangled.

Michigan police sent the dead man's fingerprints to the FBI laboratory in Washington. The murdered man was Vern Miller, ex-sheriff and World War I hero—and suspect in the Kansas City Massacre.[11]

12

"Machine Gun" Kelly and His Ambitious Wife

"Damn it, George, we've got to snatch some rich bastard. It's the only way to haul in big money!"

Twenty-nine-year-old Kathryn Kelly, a curvaceous, dark-haired beauty, was badgering her husband, George "Machine Gun" Kelly, who had just awakened from a drunken stupor on this afternoon in early June 1933.

As George yawned and scratched the heavy stubble on his face, Kathryn held up the newspaper clippings she had culled. Blaring headlines told about the huge $100,000 ransom paid to the kidnappers of William Hamm, Jr., a St. Paul business tycoon, a few days earlier.

George was far from enthused. "It's too damned risky," he protested.

Refusing to take "no" for an answer, Kathryn launched into a tirade and nagged George until, as usual, he caved in. If ever there was a henpecked man, it was Machine Gun Kelly.[1]

Kathryn and 36-year-old George made an odd couple. Despite his terrifying nickname, Kelly had been merely a bumbling, small-time bootlegger who drank nearly as much of his rotgut as he sold to back-street speakeasies and shady druggists. Until Kathryn came into his life he was content with being a penny-ante crook. Vivacious, ambitious, and ruthless, Kathryn's goal was the big time—stylish clothes and expensive furs, flashy automobiles and precious jewels.

Christened Cleo Coleman Brooks after her 1904 birth in tiny Saltilo, Mississippi, Kathryn grew up in an impoverished family. As a child she fantasized that her tattered garments were actually exquisite dresses befitting the rich and powerful queen that she dreamed of being one day.

When 15 years of age, she changed Cleo to Kathryn (which sounded more glamorous to her), married an Asher, Oklahoma, boy and gave birth to a daughter. A short time later, Kathryn divorced her husband and went to live with her mother Ora, who had abandoned her own husband and was operating a ramshackle hotel outside Fort Worth, Texas.

At the age of 17 Kathryn began hauling illegal booze from Fort Worth to her mother's hotel, where men could buy the liquor and rent women by the hour or by the night.

Later, Ora divorced her husband and married Robert G. ''Boss'' Shannon, a politician of some clout who lived on a ranch near Paradise, Texas, about 40 miles northwest of Fort Worth.

In 1924, the flamboyant Kathryn met and married a moderately successful bootlegger, Charlie Thorne, of Coleman, Texas, 160 miles southwest of Fort Worth. For the new Mrs. Thorne, it was a mighty leap upward. Charlie built her a home on Mulkey Street in Fort Worth and provided her with the luxuries she had dreamed about as an impoverished child in Mississippi.

However, it was not Kathryn's idea of a dream marriage: Charlie Thorne was no Prince Charming. He was fond of the bottle, and Kathryn, a friend would say, ''could gulp down booze like it was water.'' Almost from the day they were married, Kathryn and Charlie, drunk or sober, engaged in shouting, cursing brawls, resulting in a goodly amount of broken furniture and glassware at the couple's homes in Coleman and Fort Worth.

After three years of stormy marriage, Kathryn zipped into a Fort Worth gasoline station behind the wheel of her flashy, 16-cylinder automobile. The attendant, who knew her, said, ''What's wrong, Kathryn? You look mad as hell.''

''I'm heading for Coleman to kill that goddamned son of a bitch Charlie Thorne!'' she snapped, her dark eyes flashing.

Long aware of the Thornes' domestic battles, the attendant merely shrugged and began pumping gasoline. A day later, Charlie Thorne was found dead in his Coleman ranch home, a bullet through the head. Nearby was a typewritten note that read: ''I can't live with her or without her, hence I am departing this life.'' Curiously, even Thorne's signature was typed.

A coroner's jury ruled the death suicide.

A few weeks after Charlie was buried, his widow, now 23 years of age, was in Oklahoma City and making the rounds. At one saloon, she was introduced to George Kelly, who had been known in Memphis as a ''society bootlegger'' before having to high-tail it out of town one night with the police on his heels. Kelly had fled all the way to New Mexico and resumed his penny-ante bootlegging. A short time later he was arrested, convicted, and served three months in the New Mexico State Penitentiary.

Now, George Kelly sought to impress Kathryn, whose flirtatious glances and skin-tight dresses often turned male heads. He bragged about his big-time connections in the underworld and what a tough guy he was. ''No cop'll ever take *me* alive!'' he boasted.[2]

Kate sensed that George was actually a two-bit, low-stakes hood who had picked up his tough-talk routine by watching Hollywood gangster flicks.

It was Kate, not big-mouthed George, who had the underworld connections. She had developed them over the years at the "fugitive farm" operated by her mother Ora and Boss Shannon near Paradise, Texas. There criminals on the run from the law could hide out until the heat was off—for a daily fee of $50.

Kate, somehow, was fascinated with George and determined to mold this heavyset, uncouth, third-rate booze peddler into a big-time bank robber. Her work was cut out for her, however, for George had never robbed a bank. He didn't like guns. And he never hurt people.

"You've got to be able to hurt people, George!" she ranted at him repeatedly. "If you aren't tough, no one'll respect you!"

Kate set out to build up George's image. From a shady arms dealer, she bought a Tommy gun and gave it to George; then she took him to her mother's fugitive farm and had him spend long hours target-practicing with the weapon. Eventually, Kelly became quite adept at handling and firing the automatic weapon.

Now Kate needed a catchy nickname for George, a moniker that editors could splash across their front pages in blaring headlines. So on solo tours of the saloons and other underworld hangouts in Fort Worth and Oklahoma City, she spread the word about Machine Gun Kelly.

Kathryn always carried a large number of .45-caliber cartridges that George had expended while target-shooting on her mother's ranch.

"Here's a souvenir from *Machine Gun* Kelly," she said.

Kelly himself was seldom seen in these underworld haunts.

"Where is Machine Gun?" Kathryn often would be asked when she was handing out the cartridges. She would respond with a sly wink and say: "Up north on some big jobs." Actually, George was usually holed up in a small room at her mother's fugitive farm, sleeping off a drunk.

Kathryn's promotional efforts began to pay off. Machine Gun Kelly's name sped through the underworld grapevine from coast to coast. Hoods who had never laid eyes on the man were loudly boasting of the jobs they had pulled with the desperado.[3]

One facet of George's makeup Kathryn could not alter—his stupidity. He seemed to botch everything he tried to do. In 1931, Kelly drove a truckload of whisky onto an Indian reservation—and directly into the arms of a squad of Prohibition agents. That antic cost Kelly a short term at Leavenworth.[4]

Kathryn wasted no time in grieving over George being back behind bars. "The dumb bastard got just what he asked for," she exclaimed to a woman friend.

Kathryn returned to Fort Worth, where she began consorting with an ex-convict who was working as a "locator" (a person who singles out likely places to be burglarized).

Nearly a year passed during which a series of stores were burglarized in Fort Worth and other cities in the region. Police noted that each heist seemed to be well planned, as though carried out by professionals. Neighbors on Mulkey

Street noticed that Kathryn's clothes became more expensive and they saw her drive up one day in a spiffy new Cadillac convertible.

In Abilene, Texas, detectives gained information that a well-dressed and attractive woman answering Kathryn Thorne's description had been seen in the vicinity shortly before a large fur store was burglarized. They also obtained a description of a man who was thought to have pulled off the heist.

Fort Worth police converged on Kathryn's house on Mulkey Street, and there they found Kathryn, her boyfriend, and the stolen furs.

Taken to the police station, Kathryn wept profusely and pleaded that she was innocent. She projected outrage over learning, to her horror, that the boyfriend she trusted was actually a vile thief. The burglar, following the unwritten code of the underworld, came to her defense. Kathryn, he swore, was a dear, sweet, almost naive young lady who had had no idea that her lover was a professional heister. Kathryn was freed from charges and her boyfriend was carted off to spend five years in the Texas penitentiary.

Kathryn was not lonely for long. Machine Gun Kelly was released from Leavenworth and the pair rendezvoused in Minneapolis, where they were married. The newlyweds moved to her mother's ranch outside Paradise. Shortly after their arrival, Kathryn managed to get George linked with a two-bit bank-robbing gang, whose members were flattered to have the renowned Machine Gun Kelly with them.

After Kathryn had given him his marching orders, Kelly, reluctantly perhaps, hit the road with his new partners. A week later, Kathryn was elated to hear on local radio that the "notorious Machine Gun Kelly gang" had knocked off banks at Tupelo, Mississippi, and Wilmer, Texas. However, when George returned to the ranch, she was furious. The entire loot in the two bank heists had been $2,900, of which Kelly's share came to a puny $1,000.[5]

Worse, Kathryn's bloated ego had been punctured. Gangsters like Pretty Boy Floyd, John Dillinger, and Baby Face Nelson were getting national newspaper headlines, but the loot from the bank holdups at Tupelo and Wilmer was so small that only local media reported them.

If big, humbling George was ever going to be accepted by the aristocrats of the underworld, he would have to make some big hauls. So Kathryn plotted their first kidnapping. She recruited a mysterious figure named Eddie Doll to join with George Kelly to abduct a South Bend, Indiana, manufacturer. Doll, who went by 18 aliases, was a bank robber, holdup, man and leader in an automobile theft ring.

Starting as a 15-year-old car thief in Chicago, Eddie Doll rose swiftly to the pinnacle of the underworld. He was unlike most mobsters, being personable, articulate, and inventive. Old yeggs (bank robbers) gave him the "honor" of having helped to invent innovative techniques for the daylight holdups of banks, an outbreak of which had been sweeping the nation in recent years. Because of his success, Doll and his bank robber partner were dubbed admiringly the "Gold Dust Twins."

Despite his reputation as a sharp operator, Doll tripped himself up while engaged as leader of a gang dealing with the theft and interstate transportation of automobiles, a federal offense. The FBI soon got on his trail and arrested him. Doll gave bond and immediately jumped his bail, resulting in the G-Men again pursuing him.

Eddie Doll was a handsome man: tall and well-proportioned, with deep brown eyes, wavy hair, and a flashing smile. His nickname was Burlington Eddie because of his liking for an Iowa town of that name. He craved beautiful women, and with a hefty bankroll to splurge in luxury hotels and posh dining spots, he had no difficulty in conducting amatory conquests.[6]

Burlington Eddie had ambled through one affair after another, usually one-night stands. At least twice, he had branched off into wedlock. One wife he quickly deserted, another he had married bigamously under an alias.

Then, on St. Patrick's Day of 1931, Doll was cruising in his 16-cylinder car on Michigan Avenue in downtown Chicago when he spotted an attractive young woman waiting for a city bus near the Wrigley Building and offered her a ride home. Dazzled by the sharply dressed, debonair man with a breezy yet innocent style, she accepted. She told Doll that her name was Mary Jones (not her real name) and the smooth-talking crook told her that he was a cattleman from Texas, who also had extensive oil holdings in Oklahoma.

In the weeks ahead, Eddie and Mary were almost inseparable—dinner, the theater, dancing, hockey games, horse races. These were glamorous times for the naive young woman who had come to Chicago from rural Vermont a few months earlier. Then a strange thing struck Burlington Eddie: he fell madly in love with Mary.

Doll now feared that his past might cause him to lose something highly precious; he could not tell her the truth about his background and current career in big-time crime. He needed a plausible reason to explain his lengthy absences and habit of moving from hotel to hotel every few days and registering under a different alias each time.

"I'm keeping my cattle and oil," Eddie explained to Mary one day in his usual, sincere patter. "But I've got great news: the federal government has hired me as a narcotics agent at $750 per month."

Mary was delighted, unaware that such a salary was more than double what legitimate federal agents were drawing.

Mary paid a short visit to her folks back in Vermont and when she returned, yearning to see Eddie, she telephoned him at various hotels under the different names he had said he was using as a government investigator. Her calls were in vain. Then, one day he appeared. "I've been on another big case," Doll explained. "I couldn't break my cover to contact you."

As a federal narcotics agent, Eddie could be gone for extended periods without arousing Mary's curiosity. For nearly a year, most of the wooing was done by telephone and mail as Doll traveled the nation on "secret assignments."

Mary had no way of knowing that a bank happened to be robbed at each locale to which her beloved Eddie had been sent by the "government."

Suddenly, while out on assignment, Eddie telephoned Mary and asked her to meet him in New York where the couple would be married. Mary was ecstatic and was waiting for him when he arrived. They were married by a minister on lower Fifth Avenue.

After spending ten days in Vermont, where Mary proudly showed off her rich cattleman/oilman, Doll got antsy. Perhaps his bankroll was dwindling. At any rate, he told his new bride that he had been assigned some "big jobs," but that she could travel with him.

The first stop was Dallas, where Mary lolled in a luxurious hotel suite while Eddie went out "on business for a few days." While he was gone, it is doubtful if Mary noticed in the newspapers that four men had robbed the bank at Blue Ridge, Texas, during which a young man and woman, both bank employees, had been taken as hostages in the getaway car. (They were released unharmed outside of town.)

Mary, the naive girl from rural Vermont, didn't think it strange when Eddie returned from the business trips and handed her $500 or $1,000 to spend on herself. After all, her husband did have extensive cattle and oil holdings.

Then it was on to Portland, Oregon, where Mary, always the dutiful wife, bided her time in a big hotel while the dedicated narcotics agent was investigating yet another "really big case." Doll, indeed, was "investigating"—the layout and routines at one of Portland's largest banks. A few days later, four heavily armed men robbed the institution and made away with nearly $50,000.

Now Eddie and Mary went back to Chicago. He had to work harder than ever in his crime profession in order to keep playing the big shot to the woman he adored. That critical need for a steady income no doubt resulted in his leaping for the opportunity to join Machine Gun Kelly in kidnapping the South Bend manufacturer.

While Mary remained in Chicago to take in the stage shows and the latest Hollywood movies, Burlington Eddie accompanied Kelly to South Bend, home of Notre Dame University and its great football team coached by the legendary Knute Rockne. The two men constantly shadowed their prey until they had recorded his every action and routine.

Now they were ready to strike. Lurking in the bushes at the target's home one night, Machine Gun and Eddie, wearing masks, leaped out with drawn pistols when the manufacturer and his wife came back late. The victims were driven far into the countryside where the wife was released along a dirt road.

After binding the captive and taping his eyes, the kidnappers headed for a hideout that Burlington Eddie had earlier designated: the home of his own brother.

Eddie had already sold his brother on the federal narcotics agent ploy. "He's a witness in a big bootleg case," he told his brother. "We've got to hide him until the trial's over."

The kidnapper was exposing his own brother to a lengthy prison term by using his house to conceal the captive.

For days the victim was imprisoned in a dark basement while Doll and Machine Gun Kelly haggled with him over the payment of ransom. The captive swore that he had no money with which to pay for his release, which was indeed the case. Although he and his wife continued to outwardly display the trappings of the wealthy, the manufacturer had been wiped out by the Great Depression and may have been hard put to raise $100 ransom.

In a bizarre move, Doll and Kelly finally released the manufacturer after making dire threats to kill him and his wife should he fail to raise and pay a $60,000 ransom.

A conference was called by Eddie and George and Kathryn Kelly. Since the Kelly car had been used to transport the captive, there was the possibility that it might be traced. So the Kellys fled Chicago for Kansas City, from where repeated letters were sent to the South Bend man demanding the ransom payment. Doll and Machine Gun, no doubt with Kathryn's connivance, constantly threatened the manufacturer by long-distance telephone: pay up or else.

New financial demands were made, new meeting spots were named for dropping off the $60,000 ransom. Finally, negotiations dwindled, then vanished. The manufacturer never did pay the demanded amount.

Eddie Doll was embarrassed. He had told Mary that he was expecting a sizeable bonus from the federal government for a great job of investigation he had done on a big case, but when the ransom was never forthcoming, he had no heavy greenbacks to give to his wife.

Burlington Eddie seemed to be losing his criminal magic touch—and his courage. No longer was he a Gold Dust Twin. Perhaps the double life he had been leading, and the fear of Mary discovering the truth about her dashing narcotics agent and cattle king and oil baron, was grinding him down.

In desperation for cash, Doll joined three other men to pull off a daring mail robbery in Illinois. The mail sacks were thought to contain some $50,000, but when Doll and the others rifled them on a desolate country road, the money was not there.

Doll grew jittery and was running short of excuses about why he and Mary were having to cut down so drastically on their extravagant lifestyle. When he learned through underworld contacts that FBI agents were on his trail—interviewing prison inmates and seeking out friends and relatives who had been associated with him—Burlington Eddie nearly panicked.

Finally, the "narcotics investigator" told Mary that he was "tired of it all," that he wanted to give up his job and his cattle and his oil and get a little chicken farm down South, where he could live in peace and quiet in one place and be happy with his beloved wife. Mary, still incredibly naive, happily agreed.

Despite the South Bend debacle, Kathryn Kelly envisioned great potential in kidnapping. After she and Machine Gun returned to her home on Mulkey Street in Fort Worth, she selected a wealthy Texas banker as the next abduction target.

Kathryn threw a lavish party at her home and most of the invited guests were characters in the Fort Worth underworld—along with two local detectives she thought were crooked. She had invited the lawmen, Ed Weatherford and J. S. Swinney, to pick their brains about current law enforcement activities. Weatherford and Swinney, however, were scrupulously honest and were using Kathryn to get information on the underworld.

Kathryn got roaring drunk that night. Her usual sophisticated patter gave way to loud slang, punctuated by language that would have made a mule skinner blush. Her lips loosened by booze, she told her detective friends about the rich rewards from kidnappings.

"Why shouldn't those rich sons of bitches be snatched?" she snapped. "They've got millions—why shouldn't someone else get part of it?"

Swinney and Weatherford, projecting casual interest, drew Kathryn out and learned that her kidnapping target was Guy Waggoner, a wealthy Fort Worth oil operator and sportsman. Making excuses for leaving the party, which by now was going full blast, the detectives hurried away to warn the prospective victim.

Waggoner, who was on vacation at his summer home in Colorado Springs, Colorado, appealed to the FBI and to local police. Armed guards were stationed at the Waggoner home, and J. R. Wright, a former sheriff at Fort Worth, was engaged as a bodyguard.

Later, the FBI would learn that Waggoner was only one of several rich men whom Kathryn and Machine Gun Kelly had been considering as kidnap victims. There was a banker, a brewer, a department store owner, and Charles F. Urschel, an Oklahoma City oil tycoon and one of the state's richest men. Urschel's wife Berneice was also wealthy in her own right, having been the widow of T. B. Slick, an Oklahoma oil baron.

Confident that big money lay on the horizon, the Kellys targeted Charles Urschel for abduction. Then they recruited a middle-aged, small-time swindler and con man named Albert F. Bates to help Machine Gun make the snatch.

Without the cagy Burlington Eddie Doll to contribute his know-how, the plan was flawed. Incredibly, Kelly and Bates neither shadowed Urschel nor checked out his picture in library newspaper files in order to recognize him.

FBI Director J. Edgar Hoover

Department of Justice Building in Washington, D.C., where the FBI was headquartered in the 1930s.

Attorney General Harlan F. Stone
J. Edgar Hoover's first boss

FBI Agent Melvin H. Purvis
Nemesis of Dillinger and Floyd

Swarms of automobiles descended on the Lindbergh mansion (*above*), eradicating car tracks of the kidnapper.
Ransom note (*left*) found in nursery of Charles A. Lindbergh, Jr. The handwriting matched that of Bruno Hauptmann.

Clyde Barrow and cigar-smoking Bonnie
Parker, perhaps the most cold-blooded
murderers of the 1930s desperadoes. They
loved publicity and mailed these photos to
newspapers. Both were killed by a posse
of law officers.

Frank "Jelly" Nash
Bank robber and hired gun

Vern C. Miller
Sheriff-turned-badman

Harvey Bailey
Bank robber given life term

Clarence Shaffer
Murderer trapped and killed

Charles A. "Pretty Boy" Floyd
Killed by FBI in shootout

Adam Richetti
Executed for Kansas City Massacre

Postmaster James A. Farley (*right*), President
Roosevelt's chief dispenser of patronage, tried
to sack Director Hoover and replace him with
a political crony who ran a private detective
agency in New York City.

"Handsome Harry" Pierpont
Executed for sheriff's murder

"Three-Fingered Jack" Hamilton
Died in shootout with FBI

"Fat Charley" Makley
Killed in prison break

Homer Van Meter
Shot dead by lawmen

Fingerprints of "Pretty Boy" Floyd

WANTED

JOHN HERBERT DILLINGER

On June 23, 1934, HOMER S. CUMMINGS, Attorney General of the United States, under the authority vested in him by an Act of Congress approved June 6, 1934, offered a reward of

$10,000.00

for the capture of John Herbert Dillinger or a reward of

$5,000.00

for information leading to the arrest of John Herbert Dillinger.

DESCRIPTION

Age, 32 years; Height, 5 feet 7-1/8 inches; Weight, 153 pounds; Build, medium; Hair, medium chestnut; Eyes, grey; Complexion, medium; Occupation, machinist; Marks and scars, 1/2 inch scar back left hand, scar middle upper lip, brown mole between eyebrows.

All claims to any of the aforesaid rewards and all questions and disputes that may arise as among claimants to the foregoing rewards shall be passed upon by the Attorney General and his decisions shall be final and conclusive. The right is reserved to divide and allocate portions of any of said rewards as between several claimants. No part of the aforesaid rewards shall be paid to any official or employee of the Department of Justice.

If you are in possession of any information concerning the whereabouts of John Herbert Dillinger, communicate immediately by telephone or telegraph collect to the nearest office of the Division of Investigation, United States Department of Justice, the local addresses of which are set forth on the reverse side of this notice.

JOHN EDGAR HOOVER, DIRECTOR,
DIVISION OF INVESTIGATION,
UNITED STATES DEPARTMENT OF JUSTICE,
WASHINGTON, D. C.

June 25, 1934

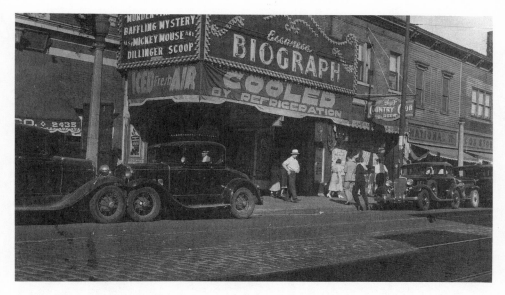

Chicago theater where John Dillinger was killed after choosing to shoot it out with G-Men.

George "Baby Face" Nelson
Murdered three FBI agents

George "Machine Gun" Kelly
Life term in Alcatraz

President Franklin D. Roosevelt signs seven new crime bills that provided the FBI with sweeping new powers in the war against the desperadoes in 1935. Watching on the far left is Attorney General Homer S. Cummings and next to him is FBI Chief J. Edgar Hoover.

FBI Agent Raymond J. Caffrey
Kansas City Massacre victim

FBI Agent W. Carter Baum
Killed by Dillinger Gang

FBI Inspector Samuel O. Cowley
Killed by Baby Face Nelson

FBI Agent Herman E. Hollis
Shot to Death by John Paul Chase

"Now Sap," Machine Gun Kelly wrote when threatening to kill Charles Urschel after the millionaire's release.

Kidnappers forced Charles Ross to pose with current newspaper before the Chicago tycoon was murdered.

Gang leader "Ma" Barker
Killed in shootout with FBI

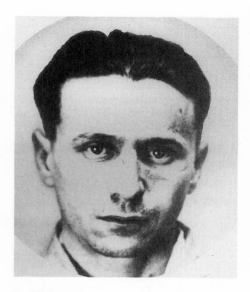

Freddie Barker
Died in gun battle with FBI

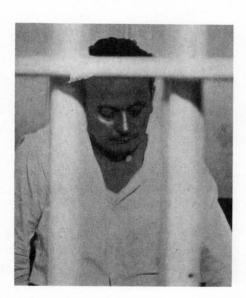

Arthur "Doc" Barker
Life term in Alcatraz

Alvin "Old Creepy" Karpis
J. Edgar Hoover's captive

FBI Agent Truett E. Rowe
Killed by escaped prisoner

FBI Agent Wimberly W. Baker
Killed in Topeka shootout

FBI Agent William R. Ramsey
Shot to death by bank robber

Inspector Earl J. Connelley
Led raid on Barker gang

Hoover died shortly before the FBI moved into this cavernous structure, to be known as the
J. Edgar Hoover Building on Pennsylvania Avenue.

13

An Oil Tycoon with a Photographic Memory

It was 45 minutes before midnight on Saturday, July 22, 1933, when Charles and Berneice Urschel were playing a final rubber of bridge with their good friends Mr. and Mrs. Walter Jarrett on the enclosed sun porch of the Urschel mansion in Oklahoma City. Suddenly there was a loud crash as two men, one armed with a Tommy gun and the other with a pistol, broke through the screen door.

"Stick 'em up!" George Kelly, the big man with the machine gun, barked. "Which one of you guys is Urschel?"

Urschel and Jarrett remain silent. Kelly seemed to be flustered by this unexpected situation.

"All right, we'll take both of you," he finally said.

After warning the badly shaken wives against calling for help, Kelly and his sidekick, con man Albert Bates, hustled Urschel and Jarrett to their Chevrolet sedan, ordered the captives into the back seat, and sped away.

Kelly drove to a point about 12 miles from the city limits, then halted under a dim light at the intersection of two back roads. He ordered the captives to hand him their billfolds, whose contents made it possible to identify Charles Urschel.

After taking $50 from his billfold, the kidnappers ordered Walter Jarrett to get out of the car with a dire warning not to tell police in which direction they had gone.

Immediately after Jarrett's release Urschel was securely blindfolded. Then the kidnappers drove until about 3:30 A.M., when their car ran out of gas. Kelly took Urschel into the underbrush while Bates left to get gasoline. He returned in about 30 minutes and the trek resumed.

About an hour later the kidnappers drove into a structure that Urschel deduced was a garage, judging by the sound of the opening and closing of an overhead door and the oily odor.

From the conversation of the kidnappers and the noises, Urschel concluded that license plates were being transferred from the Chevrolet to another automobile. Still blindfolded, Urschel was put in the second car and ordered to lie flat on the back seat. From the vehicle's roominess, he judged it to be a seven-passenger Cadillac or Buick.

In the meantime, as soon as the kidnappers had driven off with her husband, Mrs. Urschel telephoned the FBI's special "kidnap number"—NAtional 8–7117. When her call arrived at the headquarters communications center in Washington, D.C., it was switched to J. Edgar Hoover's home. The Director spoke with Mrs. Urschel for several minutes, issued her suggestions and instructions, then climbed out of bed, dressed, and rushed to his office. It would be three days before Hoover would be able to grab a short nap.

In keeping with its policy of not becoming involved in ransom negotiations nor directly launching an investigation until the victim was released and safe, the FBI remained under cover.

Two days after the Urschel abduction, Kathryn Kelly drove to Fort Worth in an effort to gain from her sources any indication that she and Machine Gun were being connected to the crime. She telephoned one of the undercover detectives who had attended her party earlier, and invited him to her house on Mulkey Street for a visit. While walking toward her front porch, the detective noticed an Oklahoma City newspaper lying on the front seat of her big new automobile. A blaring headline told of the sensational Urschel abduction.

Kathryn received the officer with typical graciousness, but after 30 minutes of rambling conversation, he realized that she didn't have any specific topic to discuss. It was as though she hoped he would bring up whatever it was that was on her mind.

Kathryn said that she had just arrived home after driving steadily for 500 miles from St. Louis. But she didn't seem to be tired. If she had been on the main highways in Missouri and Oklahoma, how did the red soil of Oklahoma's back roads get on her car's tires?[1]

Minutes after leaving Kathryn's house, the undercover officer telephoned the Fort Worth office of the FBI and told of his suspicions. A search of the five million criminal listings that the FBI stored in the old Southern Railway Building on Pennsylvania Avenue in Washington, D.C. turned up the records and fingerprints of George and Kathryn Kelly.

Now G-Men in Texas and Oklahoma began questioning the Kellys' associates, and as a result of the information obtained, the FBI pegged the couple as the prime suspects in the Urschel kidnapping.

On July 26, four days after the abduction, John C. Catlett, a wealthy Tulsa oil baron and friend of Charles Urschel, received a package delivered by Western Union. Inside the container was a letter to him from Urschel, requesting that Catlett act as the go-between for his release.

There was also a typewritten letter addressed to E. E. Kirkpatrick, another close friend of the kidnap victim, who lived in Oklahoma City. It read in part:

> Immediately upon receipt of this letter you will proceed to obtain the sum of two hundred thousand dollars ($200,000.00) in genuine used Federal Reserve currency in the denomination of twenty dollar ($20.00) Bills.
>
> It will be useless for you to attempt taking notes of serial numbers making up Dummy Package, or anything else in the line of attempted double cross. Bear this in mind, Charles F. Urschel will remain in our custody until money has been inspected and exchanged and furthermore will be at the Scene of contact for pay-off and if there should be any attempt at any double XX it will be he that suffers the consequence.
>
> Run this Ad for one week in *Daily Oklahoman*:
>
> For Sale—160 Acres Land, good five room house, deep well. Also Cows, Tools, Tractor, Corn and Hay. $3750.00 for quick sale . . . Terms . . . Box # ——
>
> You will hear from us as soon as convenient after insertion of Ad.[2]

Kirkpatrick arranged for the advertisement to be inserted and on July 28, an envelope postmarked in Joplin, Missouri, and addressed to the *Daily Oklahoman*, Box H–807, reached the newspaper. The letter to Kirkpatrick read in part:

> You will pack two hundred thousand dollars ($200,000.00) in used genuine Federal Reserve notes of twenty dollar denomination in a suitable light colored Leather Bag and have someone purchase transportation for you, including berth, aboard Train #28 (*The Sooner*) which departs at 10:10 P.M. via the *M. K. & T.* Lines for Kansas City, Mo.
>
> You will ride on the Observation Platform where you may be observed by some-one at some Station along the Line between Okla. City and K.C. Mo. If indication are alright, some-where along the Right-of-Way you will observe a Fire on the Right Side of Track (Facing direction train is bound) that first Fire will be your Cue to be prepared to throw Bag to Track immediately after passing Second Fire.
>
> Remember This—If any Trickery is attempted you will find the remains of Urschel and instead of joy there will be double grief—for, some-one very near and dear to the Urschel family is under constant Surveillaince and will like-wise suffer for *your Error*.
>
> If there is the slightest Hitch in these Plans for any reason what-so-ever, not your fault, you will proceed on into Kansas City, Mo. and register at the Muehlebach Hotel under the name of E. E. Kincaid of Little Rock, Arkansas and await further instructions there.
>
> You are to make this trip (on the night of) Saturday July 29th, 1933.

Since the Urschel family decided to pay the ransom, FBI agents obtained $200,000 in used 20-dollar bills and recorded the serial numbers. Two new, light-colored Gladstone bags were filled. One held the genuine bills and the other identical bag contained old magazines.

When the train pulled out of the Oklahoma City station after dark on July 29, E. E. Kirkpatrick sat on the observation platform at the rear with the bag containing the magazines. This ploy was a safeguard against the possibility that a kidnapper might try to hijack the ransom bag from Kirkpatrick. J. G. Catlett sat just inside the observation platform with the bag holding the $200,000 so it would be handy when needed.

Kirkpatrick remained on the platform all night and was covered with a coat of soot spewed out by the coal-burning locomotive, but no fires along the right-of-way were seen.

Machine Gun Kelly had botched the deal. When driving toward the points where he and Al Bates were to light the two fires, Kelly managed to flood the car's engine. So the two kidnappers were late and roared up to the railroad tracks just in time to watch the train—and their $200,000—speed past and disappear into the black night.

Upon arrival in Kansas City, Kirkpatrick and Catlett, as instructed, went to the Muehlebach Hotel, where Kirkpatrick registered under the name of E. E. Kincaid and waited in his room. Soon a telegram arrived: "Owing to unavoidable incident unable to keep appointment. Will phone you about six.—C. H. Moore."[3] Just past 5:30 P.M., the telephone jangled in Kirkpatrick's room.

"Mr. Kincaid?" a male voice asked. Told that it was he, the caller said, "This is Moore. You got my telegram?"

Yes, he had, acknowledged Kirkpatrick.

"Okay, you take a cab to the LaSalle Hotel and walk a block or two west on Linwood," the voice said. "You'll get more instructions then. No funny stuff!"

A half-hour later, Kirkpatrick, carrying the bag with the $200,000, was walking along Linwood Avenue when he saw a heavyset man get out of a car parked at the curb. Machine Gun Kelly was sharply dressed: an expensive, cream-colored suit, wing-tipped shoes, silk necktie and a Panama hat worn at a rakish angle. Kathryn always insisted that a big-time racketeer should look like one.

Kelly approached Kirkpatrick, reached out and said, "I'll take that bag."

"How do I know you're the man?" Kirkpatrick queried, hoping that his voice did not betray his nervousness.

"Hell, you know goddamned well I am!" the big man barked.

Again Kelly reached to take the bag. Kirkpatrick pulled it back.

"What kind of assurance do I have that Mr. Urschel won't be harmed?" he asked.

Machine Gun was irritated. "Don't argue with me!" he snapped. "Give me that goddamned bag!"

"Not until you give me some definite assurance to give to Mrs. Urschel."

Kelly was perspiring profusely. Kirkpatrick wasn't acting meekly like he was supposed to act. There were several moments of silence. Finally, the kidnapper said, "The title deeds to the farm will be delivered within 12 hours."[4]

Kirkpatrick dropped the bag to the sidewalk, spun around and walked away. Kelly swooped up the Gladstone and hurried to his car where his sidekick Al Bates had been anxiously watching the scenario.

Hours later, Machine Gun was preparing to release Charles Urschel, but Kathryn argued vehemently that they should "kill the bastard to protect ourselves." It was a stormy session. For once, George stood up to his wife, claiming that it would be "bad for future business" if they were to kill Urschel.

After dark on the night of July 31, nine days after he had been kidnapped, Urschel was driven to a secluded point on the outskirts of Norman, Oklahoma, handed a ten dollar bill, and released alongside the road. Exhausted, heavily bearded, disheveled, but otherwise unharmed, the victim reached his Oklahoma City mansion shortly before midnight for a tearful and joyous reunion with his wife.

As soon as Urschel had a sound sleep (he had slept hardly at all for nine days) and recovered from the initial shock of his ordeal, he was interviewed by FBI agents. Considering the peril, Urschel had kept his wits about him at all times and displayed a remarkable memory for even minuscule details. After his abduction, the kidnappers had driven steadily for 12 hours, he said. Although blindfolded continually, Urschel felt that most of the trip had been over back roads due to the absence of sounds from passing traffic.

At one point, the road was made slippery by a heavy cloudburst. Wanting to pinpoint the hour, Urschel casually asked his captors for the time.

"You ain't goin' no place," the voice of Big Man replied. "But it's 9:35 (A.M.)."

A few hours later, the car was driven into what Urschel thought was a garage. He again asked for the time of day, and Big Man replied, "It's 2:30 (P.M.)."[5]

The three men remained in this building until dark, when Urschel was walked outside. They passed through a squeaking narrow gate, onto a boardwalk, and into a house. Urschel was put onto an iron cot in a small room.

A day later, on July 24, Urschel, still blindfolded, was driven for less than a mile to another house, where he was taken inside and told to lie on some blankets in the corner. Outside he heard the sounds of chickens, cows, and hogs.

After his two captors left the room, Urschel detected the voices of a woman and two men in an adjoining room, but the male voices didn't resemble those of the pair who had abducted him.

Early the next morning, Urschel was asked by the kidnappers if he had a friend who could be trusted, and he suggested John Catlett. Ordering the captive to look straight ahead, the men removed his blindfold briefly and instructed him to write a letter to Catlett and to E. E. Kirkpatrick.

Urschel was guarded by an older man and a younger man. Both of them were quite talkative. The older one boasted that he had been "a goddamned thief for

25 years," and sneeringly called the notorious killers Bonnie Parker and Clyde Barrow "just a couple of cheap filling station robbers and car thieves."[6]

When Urschel asked for a drink, he heard the eerie squeaking sound of a rope and pulley when the water was being drawn from a well outside the house. The drink was handed to him in an old tin cup without a handle.

Although the captive could not see his watch, he casually asked his guards the time when airplanes flew overhead at 9:45 each morning and 5:45 every afternoon—except Sunday, when a heavy storm apparently prevented the 5:45 from passing that way.

Although Charles Urschel had provided a fantastic amount of details on his nine-day ordeal, the FBI had few sound clues on which to push their investigation. Working painstakingly for countless hours, Hoover's men checked every airplane activity within 600 miles of Oklahoma City, and determined that an aircraft leaving Fort Worth at 9:15 o'clock each morning for Amarillo, Texas, would be in the vicinity of Paradise, Texas, by 9:45 A.M. Likewise, an airplane taking off from Amarillo for Fort Worth at 3:30 P.M. would be over the vicinity of Paradise around 5:45 P.M. These times coincided with the ones recalled by Charles Urschel.

Other G-Men checked meteorological records and found that the countryside around Paradise had been suffering from a drought, but that a heavy rain had fallen on the Sunday that Urschel reported. This had caused airplanes of the American Airways run between Fort Worth and Amarillo to skirt the region.

Further probing disclosed that the mother of the suspect Kathryn Kelly, Ora Shannon, and her husband had a ranch near Paradise. A closer look at the Shannon premises was needed. So an FBI agent, disguised as a government surveyor, was sent to the ranch.

There he asked Ora Shannon for a drink of water and heard the telltale squeaking pulley on the well near the house, just as Urschel had described. Mrs. Shannon handed the water to the agent in a tin cup without a handle, like the one in which Urschel had been given drinks. The water tasted bitter with minerals, again just as Urschel recalled.

Then the FBI man used a ruse to get inside the house, and he noted the layout and counted the number of steps leading upstairs—the same number that the blindfolded captive had counted.

A few days later, at dawn on August 12, a raiding party of heavily armed lawmen, led by FBI Agent Gus Jones, swooped down on the Shannon ranch and charged inside the house. They took into custody Boss Shannon, his wife Ora, and Shannon's 21-year-old son Armon, who lived a short distance away.

Asleep on a cot in the backyard was another man, whom Jones awakened by poking him in the mouth with the muzzle of a Tommy gun. When the figure raised up onto one elbow, blinking like a raccoon suddenly caught in the beam of a flashlight, the G-Man recognized him as professional bank robber and gunman Harvey Bailey, who had escaped from the Kansas State Penitentiary in the mass breakout on Memorial Day and was wanted as a suspect in the Kansas City Massacre.

"What in the hell is going on?" the sullen, gray-haired Bailey snarled.

"You are what's going on, Harvey," Gus Jones replied. "Going on back to the joint!"

"Well, it looks like it's just too bad," said Bailey, who had to endure the added indignity of being arrested while in his underwear.[7]

Near Bailey's cot was a Tommy gun and two pistols—all fully loaded. His 16-cylinder Cadillac was parked beside the house, ready for a quick getaway.

Gus Jones warned Bailey that he would be killed if the raiding party was fired on from the large barn or the two garages, where other outlaws might be hiding.

Bailey shrugged and muttered, "Go ahead and shoot me!"

On the back porch of the house was a second machine gun and a large quantity of ammunition. Inside, the G-Men found a large number of rifles and pistols.

Harvey Bailey had been a paying guest at the Shannon "fugitive farm" for two weeks. His apprehension came as a bonus, for the raiders had no idea that he would be present. Their main target had been Machine Gun Kelly.

Now the FBI brought Charles Urschel down from Oklahoma to inspect the Shannon premises. All the myriad of details his photographic mind had cataloged dovetailed. He identified the Shannon house as the place where he had first been taken and the nearby Armon Shannon home as the one where he had been kept until his release.

From their voices while his back was turned, Urschel also identified Boss Shannon and Armon as the talkative men who had guarded him while the two kidnappers (Kelly and Bates) were absent.

Questioned by the FBI, the three Shannons "sang like canaries," in the jargon of the underworld. They fingered George Kelly and Albert Bates as the actual kidnappers and Kathryn Kelly as a participant.

Meanwhile, the Kellys and Al Bates divided the Urschel loot and split company. While Kathryn drove into Fort Worth to try to gain information from the honest detective she thought to be a crook, Machine Gun sped south to Coleman, Texas, where he visited Will Casey and Cassey E. Coleman, who helped Kelly bury $73,250 of the ransom money in a remote cotton patch on Coleman's farm. Coleman was Kathryn Kelly's uncle.

Kelly hurried back to Fort Worth and picked up Kathryn, and the couple headed north. They disguised themselves as a poverty-stricken couple, like so many others in the Great Depression years. Machine Gun wore a faded shirt and trousers and a torn straw hat. She was garbed in feed-sack dresses, wore no makeup, and allowed her stylish coiffeur to deteriorate into tangled strands.

At Omaha, George dyed his hair blond, began growing a mustache, and donned octagon-shaped spectacles. Then it was on to Chicago for a few days and finally to Minneapolis.

In the meantime, the FBI circulated the serial numbers of the ransom bills to banks throughout the United States. A few days later, on August 5, an alert teller in the Hennepin State Bank in Minneapolis spotted several of the hot 20-dollar bills that had been exchanged there for a cashier's check.

Following that lead, FBI agents learned that a heavyset man who called himself "Collins" had cut a deal with a Minneapolis bootlegger named Edward Barney Berman. Collins paid Berman $5,500 for 125 cases of booze. Collins, the G-Men were convinced, was Machine Gun Kelly, for the $5,500 was part of the Urschel ransom money.

Kelly, the FBI learned, had then sold the 125 cases of booze for "clean" money, after which he and Kathryn drove to Cleveland. There Mrs. Kelly doffed the Oklahoma Okie disguise and went on a buying spree: a $1,000 dinner ring for the third finger of her dainty left hand, a platinum wristwatch imbedded with diamonds for her left wrist, and a replenished wardrobe of Chanel models.

Kathryn wanted a new automobile, even though the one the Kellys were driving was only two months old. George disagreed. Kathryn threw a profanity-punctuated tirade and her husband meekly caved in. She made one concession, however. Instead of a 16-cylinder vehicle, Kathryn settled for a 12-cylinder model.

They went back to their room at the Cleveland Hotel where George guzzled booze and read the afternoon newspaper. Moments later, he leaped to his feet.

"They've arrested the guys in Minneapolis who changed the money for me!" George exclaimed. "We've got to beat it—right now!"

Kathryn was reclining on the bed, painting her fingernails. Sparks flashed from her dark eyes.

"We've got to do *what*?"

"We've got to go on the lam! We've got to get to Chicago! We've got to start right now!"

Kathryn glared at her husband. "Don't be such a yellow-belly," she exclaimed. "I'm tired. We'll go in the morning."

Machine Gun continued to plead with her. Finally she yelled at him, "George shut up!"[8]

The next day, the Kellys drove to Chicago and from there to Des Moines, Iowa. In their hotel, they opened a newspaper and were thunderstruck: the blaring headlines told of the Shannon ranch being raided and that among those taken into custody by the FBI were her mother Ora and stepfather.

This shocking news caused Machine Gun to develop a serious case of the willies. For her part, Kathryn pitched a cursing diatribe against the FBI, storming wildly about the room, flailing her arms and hurling pillows. She vowed revenge against those who were "persecuting" her mother.

14

Rounding Up a Kidnapping Gang

Early on the morning of August 3, 1933, Albert Bates, the penny-ante con man and swindler, knocked on the door of an apartment in a shabby neighborhood of Denver. Clutched in his hand was a battered suitcase that held his $75,000 share of the ransom from the Charles Urschel kidnapping. Bates's wife, who went by the name of Clara Feldman, and her son Edward George Feldman lived at this address, where the kidnapper planned to hole up until the heat was off.

Nine days after his arrival in the Mile High City, Bates got into a brawl in a saloon and was arrested by Denver police on a drunk and disorderly charge, a misdemeanor.

Ironically, he was put in jail on the same day (August 12) that the FBI was raiding the Shannon ranch in Texas.

In the county jail in Denver, police found $660 in Bates's pockets, a tidy sum for such a disheveled man to be carrying. It would later be discovered that this money was part of the Urschel loot.

Clara and Edward Feldman were unaware of Al Bates's arrest until a man who had just been released from the Denver jail sneaked a note from Bates under the door of the Feldmans' apartment. It said that Bates was in custody and that Clara should "look in the suitcase." She removed the bag from its hiding place, opened it, and gasped: the suitcase was crammed with 20-dollar bills.

As instructed in the note, Clara Feldman and her son drove to the outskirts of Cheyenne, Wyoming, where they buried most of Bates's share of the ransom money at a point he had specified.

A few days after the woman and her son returned to Denver, they were contacted by Ben B. Laska, a local lawyer, who claimed he was representing Bates.

"Al told me to get in touch with you when I need some money for his defense," Laska said. Then he hit up Clara Feldman for $8,000 of the ransom money (she had kept some of it in the apartment) and the woman gave it to him.

Next, Laska took all identifying papers from Edward Feldman, told him to use the alias Axel C. Johnson, and urged the Feldmans to go East and live in large cities where they would be less likely to be found by the FBI. Then Laska insisted that Edward Feldman furnish him with a diagram of the spot where the bulk of Bates's ransom money was buried in Wyoming.

Deeply suspicious of the lawyer by now, the son provided him with a fictitious drawing. When Laska returned a few days later and demanded $2,000 more "for Al's defense expenses," Feldman gave it to him from the cache in the apartment.

Meanwhile, Harvey Bailey, who had boasted that no prison could hold him, pulled off a daring escape from the Dallas County Jail on September 4. He freed himself by cutting through three bars on his cell with a hacksaw. Bailey's freedom was short-lived, as he was collared by law enforcement officers at Ardmore, Oklahoma, on the afternoon of the same day.

Investigation disclosed that a man named Groover C. Bevill of Dallas had purchased the hacksaws and that the hacksaws and a pistol had been smuggled to Bailey by Thomas L. Manion, a deputy sheriff in the jail. Bevill and Manion were arrested and charged with aiding a jailbreak.[1]

In Des Moines, Kathryn Kelly tried to coax her husband George into driving to Texas with her to see her lawyers about cutting a deal with prosecutors to free her mother Ora. George refused.

"All right, you yellow son-of-a-bitch, I'll go myself," she screamed. Machine Gun finally agreed to accompany her.

What George didn't know was that he himself was to be the prized pawn. In return for the release of her mother and stepfather, Kathryn planned to squeal to the FBI about where her husband was holed up.

Kathryn telephoned her lawyers in Fort Worth to meet her at a certain Texas town. When the Kellys arrived there after a drive of 1,000 miles her attorneys were no-shows.

Now the Kellys began driving aimlessly while Kathryn tried to hatch a new scheme to free her mother. One morning they came upon three hitchhikers—Luther Arnold, his wife Hilda, and 12-year-old daughter Geraldine. They were typical of the legions of displaced American families hit hard by the Great Depression with no work and no place to go.

"Can we give you a lift?" Kathryn asked, flashing her pearly smile. Eager to get off their feet, the Arnolds climbed into the car.

That night the Kellys took the family to a tourist court in Cleburne, Texas, fed them and, the next morning, Kathryn bought new dresses for the mother and daughter.

Kathryn had hit upon a plan. She told the Arnolds her real name and said,

"You've seen me in the newspapers." Then, dabbing nonexistent tears from her eyes, Kathryn added: "They've taken my poor, dear, innocent mother into custody. I want you"—she nodded toward Arnold—"to get in contact with a lawyer and have him make a deal with the government."

Arnold was reluctant, saying he didn't want to get in trouble with the law. But when Kathryn handed him a $50 bill, he agreed to go on the mission.

Taking a car provided by the Kellys, Arnold drove to Enid, Oklahoma, and retained attorney John Roberts, who went to see U.S. Attorney Herbert H. Hyde at Oklahoma City in an effort to aid Mrs. Kelly's parents. Hyde refused to negotiate.

Knowing that Arnold was in touch with the Kellys, Hyde contacted the FBI and agents tailed the emissary to San Antonio. There Arnold went to the general delivery window at the post office and picked up a letter that gave directions to a particular address in the city. While Arnold was driving through heavy traffic to the meeting place, the FBI tails lost track of him.

At the house, Arnold found the Kellys, his wife, and his daughter. "Bad news," he told Kathryn. "The government will make no deal, and the district attorney said that all involved in the (Urschel) kidnapping would be prosecuted."

Kathryn was furious and pitched a wild, shouting tantrum. Eventually calming down, she came up with a new scheme, not to free her parents but to protect herself. Knowing that she and George would be less subject to suspicion if their "daughter" was with them, Kathryn asked the Arnolds if Geraldine could go on a trip with the Kellys.

"It'll only be a couple of hundred miles," she lied.

The Arnolds made no reply. Kathryn reached into her purse and handed the father $350. A few hours later, the Kellys and Geraldine drove off, heading for Des Moines on the first leg of what would be a desperate, 1,600-mile flight throughout the Midwest.

In line with Kathryn's prior instructions, Mrs. Arnold remained in San Antonio and Arnold drove back to Oklahoma City in the old car purchased for him by the Kellys. Arnold, it developed, was something of a swinger. Along the route, he picked up two teenaged girls in Texas and took them to Oklahoma City. There he was arrested by the FBI for violation of the Mann Act (transporting females across a state line for immoral purposes), a federal offense.

Arnold had in his possession a letter written by Mrs. Kelly to her father, J. E. Brooks of Oklahoma City, requesting that Brooks give him a pistol and any available money for lawyers.

Prosecutors explained that Arnold could beat the Mann Act rap. All he had to do was cooperate with the government. Arnold eagerly agreed.

"Where are the Kellys and your daughter now?" an FBI agent asked Arnold. Shrugging, he replied, "I don't have any idea."

At that time, the Kellys and little Geraldine were ensconced in a Des Moines hotel. Machine Gun was fearful and silent, sitting glumly in a chair and taking heavy belts of booze.

"Cheer up, George," the tough-minded Kathryn said. "Who'd ever suspect that a red-headed woman, a blond man wearing octagon glasses with their little girl would be kidnappers?"

One night, what remained of Machine Gun's nerve cracked. "We've got to get the hell out of here!" he declared. "The feds are closing in!"

Kathryn fixed him with an icy stare. "So you're the great Machine Gun Kelly, the fearless gangster," she snapped, biting off each word. "Why, you're nothing but a cheap, sniveling, gutless bastard. Come here and let mommy hold your hand."

Two days later, the Kellys and the child headed for Chicago. On the way, Kathryn read in the newspapers that the Shannons would soon be put on trial in Oklahoma City. Screaming and cursing, she forced George to write threatening letters to those involved, including the judge and Joseph Keenan, an assistant attorney general of the United States who would assist in the prosecution.

Mrs. Kelly was especially bitter at Charles Urschel. By dint of twisted logic, she blamed the kidnap victim for the Shannons' predicament. With Kathryn dictating, Machine Gun penned a series of letters to Urschel, one of which read:

Ignorant Charles—

If the Shannons are convicted look out, and God help you for He is the only one that will be able to do you any good. In the event of my arrest I've already formed an outfit to take care of and destroy you and yours the same as if I was there. I am spending your money to have you and your family killed—nice, eh? You are bucking people who have cash—planes, bombs and unlimited connections both here and abroad. . . .

Now, sap—it is up to you, if the Shannons are convicted you can get you another rich wife in Hell because that will be the only place you can use one. Adios, smart one.

Your worst enemy,
George R. Kelly

I will put my prints below so you can't say some crank wrote this.

On September 25, Mr. and Mrs. Luther Arnold in Oklahoma City received a telegram from their daughter, saying that she was arriving on the train from Fort Worth at 10 o'clock that night. When the bewildered girl stepped off the train, G-Men were at the station with her mother and father.

Questioned gently, Geraldine said she had left the Kellys at a Memphis, Tennessee, rooming house, which was owned by a man they called "Tich." She said she had ridden as far as Coleman, Texas, in an automobile driven by a friend of George Kelly, Langford Ramsey, who, it would be learned, was a Memphis lawyer and the brother of Machine Gun's first wife.

Ramsey was quite talkative, Geraldine said, and told her that he was on the way to a Texas ranch owned by Kathryn Kelly's uncle, Cassey Coleman, to get some "furs" (ransom money). At Fort Worth, the Arnold child told Ramsey that she was tired of riding in an automobile and begged to be allowed to go home on a train.

Awakened in the middle of the night at his home in Washington, D.C., and told of the red-hot lead, J. Edgar Hoover ordered agents from New Orleans, Cincinnati, St. Louis, and Birmingham to rush to Memphis. Working with Memphis police, the feds learned that a man named J. C. Tichenor owned a rooming house.[2]

At dawn on September 26, 1933, FBI agents led by William A. Roper and Memphis police officers surrounded the hideout at 1408 Raynor Street. Police Sergeant William Raney banged loudly on the front door. Moments later, the door swung open and Raney found himself face to face with Machine Gun Kelly, who was pointing a .45-caliber pistol at the officer. Raney stuck his shotgun in the fugitive's stomach.

"Drop that gun!" Raney ordered.

"Don't shoot, G-Men!" Kelly cried out, "don't shoot!"

Kelly meekly lowered his weapon.[3]

Taken into custody with Machine Gun was Kathryn Kelly, who glared icily at hapless George as though her predicament were all his fault.

Taken to the Memphis jail and grilled, Kathryn Kelly told the FBI that she had planned to go to Oklahoma City and voluntarily surrender, but that George had threatened to kill her if she left him.

"I'm glad we're both under arrest because I am not guilty and can prove it," she added. "I'll be rid of my husband and that bunch. I don't want to say anything about that guy Kelly, but he got me into this terrible mess and I don't want to have anything more to do with him."[4]

In his jail cell, Machine Gun Kelly seemed almost giddy, apparently delighted to be free of his shrewish, domineering wife. When asked for his occupation, he said he was "in the liquor business." Joking with the armed guards, Kelly called to one:

"Hey, buster, better watch out with that popgun—it might go off!"

There were more solemn moments when Memphis Police Commissioner Cliff Davis appeared at his cell. "Do you remember me?" Davis asked of Kelly, a native of Memphis.

"Sure I do," Machine Gun replied. "We were in high school together. You were on the debating team, and what a swell orator you were."[5]

Twenty-four hours later, at first light on September 27, FBI agents swooped down on the Cassey Coleman ranch in Texas and arrested Coleman and his sidekick Will Casey, charging them with harboring the Kellys. The $73,250 in Urschel ransom money was dug up from the cotton patch.

Three days after the Kellys were captured, an American Airways nine-passenger plane carrying the two prisoners and a group of heavily armed FBI men touched down at the Oklahoma City airport. When the aircraft rolled to a halt, a door flew open and out hopped two agents with Tommy guns trained on the crowd of several hundred persons who had come to gape at the notorious Machine Gun Kelly.

"Hello, gang!" Kelly chirped breezily as he stepped down from the plane. "Nice trip!" He was shackled hand and foot.

Watching Kelly alight were the kidnap victim, Charles Urschel, and U.S. Attorney Herbert Hyde. "That's the man," Urschel declared.

Mrs. Urschel also was looking on from her parked limousine. "That face will haunt me as long as I live," she said.

Behind Kelly came two more G-Men with Tommy guns. Then Kathryn Kelly, exquisitely garbed in a black silk coat and a black hat, made her entrance, smiling broadly and waving to the onlookers as she debarked from the plane.

Kathryn and George were rushed in a motorcade of ten cars from the airport to the little brick Oklahoma City jail. Surveying the decrepit structure, Machine Gun reverted to his Hollywood-inspired tough-guy role.

"I'll break out of this dump in no time," he declared.

Elsewhere in the jail, Kathryn wept copiously and protested her innocence in the Urschel kidnapping. She begged and pleaded with her interrogators. In her mule-skinner's vocabulary, she cursed her husband George for "bringing this disgrace on me and my family."

A jailer reported that Kathryn had offered him $15,000 to "put me on the street."

Meanwhile, in early October 1933, Albert Bates (who had been brought back from Denver), Harvey Bailey, Boss and Ora Shannon, and Armon Shannon were tried for their roles in the Urschel abduction. The Shannons claimed that the Kellys had coerced them into participating. All were sentenced to life in prison except for Armon Shannon, who was given ten years probation.[6]

Forty-eight hours after the verdict, a trimotored cabin plane carrying Harvey Bailey and Albert Bates, along with ten guards, landed at a military flying field outside Leavenworth, Kansas. Rushed by armored car the few miles to the federal penitentiary, Bailey surveyed the mass of concrete and steel and remarked with a grin: "Well, those walls look pretty high for me to get over any more."

It was almost a homecoming for the gray-haired desperado. Eight miles away stood the Kansas State Penitentiary, from which Bailey had joined with 11 convicts in a spectacular breakout on the previous Memorial Day.

A week later, Machine Gun and Kathryn Kelly were tried on kidnapping charges in a heavily guarded courtroom in Oklahoma City. Each took the witness stand and ripped the other one apart. Perhaps as a ploy to gain sympathy, Kathryn had her own daughter, now 14 years of age, brought into the courtroom. The jury was unimpressed. On October 12, the Kellys were found guilty and sentenced to life imprisonment. Less than four months after Charles Urschel was kidnapped, both were behind bars—Machine Gun in Alcatraz, a prison designed to hold America's most vicious criminals.

If ever there was a model prisoner, it was George Kelly, the Alcatraz warden would later report. Machine Gun often expressed his relief over being out of the clutches of his highly ambitious wife—even if it meant being locked up for life.[7]

In the meantime, FBI agents were trying to track down Albert Bates's wife Clara Feldman and her son Edward, who had fled Denver. On November 2, 1934, the feds got a break. Alvin H. Scott, Clara's brother-in-law, was seriously injured in an automobile accident at Roseburg, Oregon. Police found $1,360 in his pocket, money that turned out to be part of the Urschel ransom. A search of Scott's home turned up $6,140 of the kidnap loot hidden in a closet.

Five days later, Clara and Edward Feldman were arrested at Dunsmuir, California, with $1,100 of the ransom currency in their suitcase. When questioned, she designated a spot near Woodland, Washington, where she and her son had buried $1,520.

Clara Feldman swore that she had disclosed all the ransom money caches. Then, on December 4, she had a change of heart and told the FBI where $38,460 was buried near Cheyenne, Wyoming. At the same time, Alvin Scott, from his hospital bed in Oregon, disclosed where he had buried $5,000.

Altogether, 21 persons involved in the Charles Urschel case—kidnappers, harborers, lawyers, and money changers—were convicted. Six of them received life sentences.[8]

A few days after the final conviction, United States Attorney General Homer Cummings took to national radio to praise the work of the FBI in solving the Urschel kidnapping case.

"It was the greatest piece of deductive detective work in modern times," Cummings declared.[9]

While the Urschel trials were underway in Oklahoma City, two FBI agents, a U.S. marshal and a captain in the St. Petersburg, Florida, police department halted their vehicle at a poultry farm a short distance outside St. Petersburg. County real estate records showed that the farm was owned by an Edward Foley.

Dismounting from the car, the officers saw a tall handsome man wearing a pullover sweater repairing a chicken coup.

"Mr. Foley," the police captain said, "These are FBI agents."

"And you aren't Edward Foley, but Burlington Eddie Doll, the kidnapper and bank robber," a G-Man added.

"I'm afraid you've made a mistake," he replied in a pleasant tone. "My name is Foley."

The law officers knew that there was no mistake. Two weeks earlier, a female penitentiary inmate, being questioned by an FBI agent on an unrelated case, let slip information that indicated Burlington Eddie was living at the Florida place known as the "Sunshine Poultry Farm." Bureau men had quickly checked St. Petersburg real estate records and obtained handwriting specimens of the man who had purchased the Sunshine Poultry Farm.

"Have you any tattoo marks on your arms?" a G-Man asked the chicken farmer.

Indeed he did have tattoos on his arms—identical to those on the wanted posters.

"It's just a case of mistaken identity," Eddie told his bewildered wife Mary, as the officers bundled him into their car. "I'll be back in no time."

Mary, the farm girl from Vermont who had been picked up on a Chicago street corner by the dashing "cattleman" and "oil baron" Eddie Foley, had still not realized that her husband was a hardened, big-time criminal.

Grilled at the St. Petersburg police station, the prisoner was grim and cold, deflecting FBI questions with the deftness of a confirmed crook. He denied that he was Burlington Eddie, who had linked up with Machine Gun Kelly in the botched kidnapping of the South Bend manufacturer.

Suddenly his flinty attitude changed. Before him stood his wife Mary, her eyes red from weeping, her face pale with the jolt that her beloved Eddie was actually a vicious criminal.

"For God's sake, Eddie," Mary begged hysterically between sobs, "If you've done anything wrong, tell them!"

Eddie stared at the floor for long moments and said nothing. After she left the room, he slowly began to speak, then his words grew into a torrent. Out poured the story of his double life—heavenly bliss with Mary, the only woman he had ever loved, and his long career of bank robberies and kidnappings.

Burlington Eddie Doll was returned to Illinois, where he pleaded guilty to the interstate transportation of a stolen automobile, the only one of his crimes over which the FBI had jurisdiction at the time they occurred.

Sentenced to ten years in Leavenworth, Doll was escorted there by 11 armed officers. The FBI was grimly determined that there would be no repeat of the Kansas City Massacre.

15

Manhunt Orders: "Shoot to Kill!"

Michigan City, Indiana, lay dark and quiet just after midnight as a furtive figure, clutching a shopping bag, crept stealthily toward the thick walls of the Indiana State Penitentiary. Twenty-nine-year-old John Dillinger was on a lonely mission: smuggling weapons for ten of his cronies to break out of the prison. It was September 3, 1933.

Dillinger knew these bleak walls well. Only the previous May, Governor Paul V. McNutt had paroled him after he had served eight and a half years for armed robbery, the last four in prison in Michigan City.

Pausing briefly to scan the guard towers to either side of him, Dillinger reached into his bag, took out three loaded automatic pistols wrapped in cotton, and hurled them over the 30-foot barrier onto the athletic field. A crony, bank robber "Handsome Harry" Pierpont, was expected to retrieve the weapons. However, an inmate stumbled onto the pistols and notified Warden Louis H. Kunkel, and guards picked up the guns.

Former Indiana farm boy John Herbert Dillinger stood five feet nine inches, weighed 168 pounds, and had wavy brownish-red hair and a dimpled chin. He had met Harry Pierpont when the two men were cellmates in the Indiana State Reformatory at Pendleton in the mid-1920s. Pierpont had been arrested for the first time in March 1922, when he tried to kill a man in Terre Haute, Indiana. Soft-spoken and considered to be quite a ladies' man, Pierpont knocked over a Kokomo, Indiana, bank single-handedly and, upon his capture, was sent to Pendleton.

When in his teens, John Dillinger and an ex-convict, gaunt, jug-eared Edgar Singleton, the town pool shark, had cooked up a scheme to rob Frank Morgan, a 65-year-old grocer in Mooresville, Indiana, of his week's receipts, which he carried home each Saturday night.

Just before 11:00 P.M. on September 6, 1924, Dillinger and Singleton lay in wait in the shadows near grocer Morgan's Mooresville home. When the victim approached on foot, one man (it was never determined which one) leaped out and hit Morgan on the head with a large bolt wrapped in a rag, splitting open his skull. Woozy, the grocer struggled to his feet and was knocked down again by a heavy blow.

One robber brandished a small-caliber pistol. From a kneeling position, Morgan tried to knock it away with one hand and the weapon discharged. Dillinger and Singleton fled. Morgan was rushed to a hospital where 11 stitches were required to close his head wounds.

Mooresville youths tipped off police that John Dillinger may have been one of the culprits. So Deputy Sheriff John Hayworth and the grocer drove out to the family farm and Frank Morgan confronted the suspect.

Recalling how Dillinger had bought candy from him as a boy, Morgan said, "Why, Johnny, you wouldn't hurt me, would you?"

"No, Mr. Morgan," the youth replied.

Despite Dillinger's protests of innocence, he was charged with the crime and sent to Pendleton with concurrent sentences of two to 14 years and 10 to 20 years on two charges of conspiracy to commit a felony and assault intent to rob. Edgar Singleton was granted a change of venue and received a much lighter sentence (he would be paroled in two years).[1]

At Pendleton, Dillinger told the warden, "I won't cause any trouble except to escape." Within two weeks, the new inmate tried just that and was caught. A short time later, when a Pendleton guard was returning Dillinger after he had been escorted to Singleton's trial as a witness, the prisoner suddenly sent the officer sprawling in a train station and fled. The deputy gave chase, and trapped Dillinger when he ran down a dead-end alley.

Dillinger continued his efforts to escape. One night he was discovered missing from his cell and guards located him under a pile of excelsior in the foundry. A month later, working with a makeshift saw, Dillinger broke out of his cell and into a corridor where he was caught. A year later, in 1925, the inmate tried again, and once more was recaptured.

Meanwhile at Pendleton, Dillinger had developed a deep admiration for Handsome Harry Pierpont and Homer Van Meter, both crafty criminals. Pierpont and Van Meter were regarded by the inmates as the toughest, most incorrigible convicts at Pendleton. The two men spent more time in solitary confinement than in their cells. When reformatory officials decided that trying to control Pierpont and Van Meter was a hopeless task, the two inmates were shipped off to the state penitentiary at Michigan City to serve out their long sentences.

John Dillinger missed his two pals, who hated one another intensely. So he appeared before the Indiana parole board and talked the panel into transferring him to the Indiana penitentiary where he could play on the baseball team and "learn an occupation." In his precrime days, Dillinger was a crack second baseman on the town team in Martinsville, Indiana, where a teammate was Edgar

Singleton, who later joined with Dillinger in the brutal beating and robbery of the Mooresville grocery store owner.[2]

John Dillinger arrived at the Michigan City penitentiary on July 15, 1929, and was reunited with Harry Pierpont and Homer Van Meter. His old classmates from Pendleton introduced him to John "Three-Fingered Jack" Hamilton, a professional bank robber who was doing a 25-year stretch.

Hamilton began conducting "classes" in bank-robbing techniques, with Pierpont, Van Meter, and Dillinger as his attentive students. Three-Fingered Jack had been a disciple of Herman K. "The Baron" Lamm, once regarded by many in the underworld as America's most brilliant bank-robbing technician.

Lamm had been a young officer in the Kaiser's Germany army prior to World War I, but had been kicked out after being caught cheating at cards. Emigrating to the United States, The Baron worked as a holdup man in Utah, but was caught and sent to prison for a short stretch in 1917.

On his release, Lamm organized a gang and planned bank robberies as he would a military campaign, with a full range of options to allow for unforeseen development. He drilled members with precision and discipline, shouting at them in a manner that would have gladdened the heart of a Prussian drill sergeant.

Before hitting a bank, The Baron personally reconnoitered its interior, then drew up detailed floor plans and the location of safes and vaults, noting which employee's job it was to open them. Sometimes, Lamm would create a full mock-up of the bank's interior, as though it were an enemy fortress to be assaulted in a hit-and-run raid.

From the conclusion of World War I in 1918, Lamm and his gang knocked over scores of banks. After robbing the Citizens Bank of Clinton, Indiana, on December 6, 1930, The Baron and a few of his boys were trapped by an armed posse in a cornfield on the outskirts of town. Lamm, riddled with bullets, was killed. Two of his men, Walter Dietrich and James "Oklahoma Jack" Clark were captured and sent to the Indiana State Penitentiary.

There, Clark and Dietrich quickly became members of Harry Pierpont's clique, which also included Charles "Fat Charley" Makley, who had been in and out of prisons for a decade and was pulling 20 years for robbing a bank in Hammond, Indiana, and Russell Lee "Boobie" Clark (no relation to Oklahoma Jack), a hulking man with an introverted personality who was doing 20 years of hard time for bank robbery.

Boobie Clark was an incorrigible troublemaker behind bars. Sent up in 1927, he had led several thwarted breakouts, fomented riots, and tried to kill guards on three occasions.

This hard-bitten group, knowing that John Dillinger would be up for parole in the spring of 1933, began cultivating him. Dillinger would be their outside contact to help launch a mass breakout. Pierpont and Three-Fingered Jack Hamilton coached him on robbing a string of small-town banks to get funds for financing the prison escape and even provided Dillinger with a list of banks to be hit.

A man who served time with Dillinger at Michigan City would say of him:

> You get to recognize a killer in prison. First we thought (Dillinger) was just a hardheaded hick who got a lousy break. Then you'd see him in a fight, and it was like he didn't care whether he got killed or the other guy. We learned to keep out of his way.
>
> Some guys (behind bars) try to look tough. Then they forget it and it's gone. But Dillinger had that look all the time. I tell you, as soon as they let this guy out, we knew that someone was going to walk away from his hat.[3]

On his way back to his father's farm outside Mooresville after his release, John Dillinger could have passed for a farmer returning from the big city of Indianapolis or an unsuccessful traveling salesman in a cheap suit, denim shirt, and ankle-high black shoes.

Two weeks later, John Dillinger recruited a hoodlum named William Shaw to help rob the banks from the list given to him in prison. Shaw had a flare about him. He wanted everyone in the gang to wear white caps when pulling jobs as an identifying trademark to strike fear in the hearts of their victims—and to inspire newspaper headlines. Dillinger rejected the idea, claiming that the white caps would attract unwanted attention when the gang was approaching a targeted bank.

Harry Pierpont and Jack Hamilton had gotten out of touch with the banking business while in the Indiana slammer and the list of targets to be hit by Dillinger proved to be obsolete. Scores of banks had failed during the Great Depression, and when Dillinger and his gunmen went to a "ripe" target, they were often greeted by empty buildings.

Despite the outdated list, Dillinger carried out his mission by hitting substitutes for banks with locked doors. In just over three months, he and his companion William Shaw had accumulated some $75,000 for the Indiana Penitentiary Mass Escape Fund.

Now Dillinger began hatching a new scheme to help his pals at the Michigan City prison. He drove to Chicago and bribed a factory foreman to doctor one of the thread barrels being shipped to the shirt shop at the penitentiary. Harry Pierpont and a few others scheming to flee worked in the shop, Dillinger knew.

Seven loaded pistols were packed into the barrel. It was resealed and marked with a large red "X" on top. Word was smuggled into the prison for Pierpont and his cohorts at the shirt shop to be on the lookout for the coded barrel.

While the barrel was en route to Michigan City, Dillinger drove to Dayton, Ohio, to see his girlfriend of the moment, Mary Longnaker. She was the sister of Joseph Jenkins, who was serving a life term for murder at the Indiana prison and was slated to take part in the mass breakout.

Dayton Detectives Russell K. Pfauhl and Charles E. Gross were tipped off by Mary Longnaker's landlady that Dillinger was at his girlfriend's apartment. Armed with shotguns, the two officers burst into the apartment at 1:30 A.M.

"Stick 'em up, Johnny!" Pfauhl called out, aiming his weapon at Dillinger's head. Dillinger was ensconced in the jail at Lima, Ohio, for the robbery of the Citizens National Bank at Bluffton, Ohio.

On September 26, 1933, four days after Dillinger was locked up at Lima, Harry Pierpont, in the Indiana prison, sent a trusty to tell Assistant Warden Albert Evans he was needed in the shirt shop. When he arrived, Pierpont and other inmates pulled weapons they had retrieved from the marked barrel and held up Evans and D. H. Stevens, superintendent of prison shops.

Threatening to kill their captives if they failed to follow orders, the convicts led the two men into a ventilating tunnel leading from the shirt shop to the cell houses. Seven of the ten convicts, all desperate men imprisoned for murder and bank robbery, were armed. In the group beside Harry Pierpont were Fat Charley Makley, Joseph Jenkins (Mary Longnaker's brother), Edward Shouse, Russell Clark, Martin O'Leary, Joseph Fox, Three-Fingered Jack Hamilton, and Baron Lamm's old bank-robbing pupils, Walter Dietrich, and James "Oklahoma Jack" Clark.

Each convict provided himself with a bundle of shirts, and the weapons that John Dillinger had shipped in were concealed in these bundles. Walking through the cell houses, the escapers told guards that Assistant Warden Evans had ordered them to take the shirts to the main gate. Evans and Stevens, menaced by the hidden pistols, did not dare to speak out.

At the guard room just inside the main gate, guards Guy Burklow and Fred Wellnitz found themselves staring at drawn pistols and were ordered to open the big door. Wellnitz was slow in responding and was knocked to the ground by a blow to the head with a pistol butt. Burklow promptly opened the gate.

Outside, in the prison office, the convicts found 72-year-old Finley C. Carson and six other civilian clerks at work. Together with Evans and Stevens, they were herded into a vault. The elderly Carson became confused and one of the escapers shot him twice, in the leg and abdomen. Carson fractured his skull when he collapsed against a table.[4]

Now the ten convicts poured out of prison. Sheriff Charles Neel, who had just delivered two prisoners to the penitentiary, was preparing to leave when six of the convicts piled into his car and ordered him to drive off. The other four inmates dashed across the road to a filling station and ordered Joe Pawlawski, the attendant, to hand over the keys to his parked car. Instead, Pawlawski took to his heels and the convicts fired three shots, one of which grazed his shoulder while another ripped the skin from his forehead.

At that moment, Herbert Von Volkenburg of Oswego, Illinois, his wife and mother-in-law, drove along the road. Brandishing their weapons, the four escapees halted the vehicle, ordered the two women to get out, then forced Von Volkenburg to drive them away. After going for several miles toward Chicago, one convict took the wheel and the hostage was hit on the head with a pistol butt and pitched from the vehicle at high speed, seriously injuring him.[5]

Riding in Von Volkenburg's car, the convicts appeared at the farm of Valley Warner near Wanatah, Indiana, and stayed there until nightfall, holding the farmer and a mail carrier at gunpoint. After dark, they stole the farmer's car and drove away.

Meanwhile, 220 National Guardsmen were mobilized in the northern Indiana "war zone" to assist hundreds of state and local police in hunting down the escaped convicts. Searchers were told: "Shoot to Kill!"

The search centered about a large wooded area five miles south of Chesterton, where Pierpont, Makley, Clark, Hamilton, Shouse, and Jenkins had fled with their hostage, Sheriff Charles Neel, after wrecking a car they had stolen from a farmer.

Neel was forced to hide by day and stumble through woods by night for three days as his captors sought to elude the swarms of police, deputies, and guardsmen. Near Hobart, Indiana, in the darkness of early morning, the sheriff and Oklahoma Jack Clark became ill and weak from lack of food, so the five convicts abandoned them.

Side by side, the haggard law officer and convict staggered through the black forest in the direction of the flickering lights of Hobart. There the hungry man climbed onto a streetcar and rode it for a few miles to the city limits of Gary, Indiana, just east of Chicago, where Neel got off.

"If you tell I'm on this car, I'll kill you!" were Clark's parting words to the sheriff.

Clark continued on the streetcar into Hammond, where he was intercepted by law officers armed with Tommy guns and shotguns.

"I'm glad to get it over with," Clark said resignedly.

Just after dark on September 30—three days after the mass escape—William Alltop was at his father-in-law's house near Bean Blossom, Indiana, 50 miles from Indianapolis. There was a knock on the door, and when Alltop answered he was confronted by a man in ill-fitting clothes and with a scruffy beard. The stranger asked how far it was to the general store in Bean Blossom, and when told it was a mile away, the man departed.

Alltop turned to his father-in-law and said, "I bet that's one of the convicts who escaped at Michigan City."

Alltop got his shotgun, loaded it, stuffed extra shells in his pockets, and drove toward Bean Blossom. Halfway there, his headlights shone on the stranger walking along the side of the road. Driving on, Alltop reached the town and picked up Herbert McDonald, a storekeeper, and the two men walked back to confront the stranger. By that time, the man had reached the edge of town, and as Alltop and McDonald walked toward him, the man moved one hand up and across his breast as though reaching for a gun.

Suddenly, the stranger (later identified as escapee Joseph Jenkins) dashed down an alley. Alltop and McDonald cut back in front of a store to head him off when he came through the end of the alley.

When Jenkins realized he was cornered, he fired a pistol and the bullet hit McDonald in the arm. Benjamin Kantor, a resident of Bean Blossom, now joined Alltop and both men flopped to the ground and fired their shotguns. Riddled with buckshot, Jenkins fell to the ground and died an hour later.

Throughout Indiana the manhunt intensified. Airplanes, linked by radio with police squad cars, were crisscrossing the prairies. Squads armed with machine guns were posted on bridges crossing the Ohio River into Kentucky. Suspicious automobiles were stopped and searched. Thousands of frightened Indiana families bolted doors long left unlocked night and day.

Pierpont, Makley, Clark, Hamilton, and Shouse, riding in a stolen car, managed to infiltrate the dragnet and reach the Indianapolis home of 22-year-old Mary Kinder, whose brother was serving time in a penitentiary. Before his latest capture, John Dillinger had left money from his string of bank holdups with Mary. With these funds, Harry Pierpont outfitted himself and his men with new clothes and a new car and reinforced the gang's arsenal of weapons. This spending splurge depleted Dillinger's funds, so more money was sorely needed.

Just after noon on October 3, Fat Charley Makley strolled nonchalantly into the First National Bank of St. Mary's, Ohio, his home town. Makley promptly ran onto an old friend, W. O. Smith, the bank president. Not having seen Fat Charley for a few years and apparently unaware that he had escaped from prison, Smith engaged Makley in casual conversation about the crops, the weather, and the Great Depression.

During the pleasant cracker-barrel conversation, Harry Pierpont and other gang members entered the bank, pulled their weapons, and left with a $14,000 haul.

16

Murder in Cold Blood

Shortly after supper had been served to prisoners in the Lima, Ohio, jail on October 12, 1933, John Dillinger and two other inmates were playing cards. At 6:20 P.M., three sharply dressed men wearing snap-brim hats entered the jail office where Sheriff Jess L. Sarber, his wife Lucy, and deputy Wilbur L. Sharpe were sitting. Sarber looked up and spoke pleasantly to the visitors: "What can I do for you?"

Handsome Harry Pierpont glanced at his companions, Charley Makley and Russell "Boobie" Clark, and replied, "We're Michigan officers, and we'd like to see John Dillinger."

Mary Sarber continued working on a crossword puzzle. The sheriff remained seated at his desk. "Let me see your credentials," Sarber said.

Pierpont whipped out a gun and snarled: "These are our credentials."

A pistol was lying on the desk before the sheriff. When he moved a hand, one of the gunmen yelled, "Let him have it!"

Pierpont fired two shots, hitting the sheriff in the stomach and the hip. Bleeding profusely, Sarber slumped to the floor in agony.

"Give us the keys to the cells," Pierpont ordered the shocked Mary Sarber and deputy Sharpe.

Sheriff Sarber tried to raise on his elbow. Makley leaped forward and swung his gun butt with terrific force onto Sarber's head, splitting it open to the bone. Then he struck him a second time.

Deputy Sharpe was ordered to open the door into the cell block. When it seemed to the gunmen that Sharpe was stalling for time, a shot was fired through the cell-block door, as Dillinger and nine other inmates inside ducked.

Sharpe finally unlocked the door, and he and Mrs. Sarber were locked in a cell. Pierpont, using Sharpe's keys, opened Dillinger's cell and handed him a pistol. Rushing from the jail, the three gunmen and Dillinger paused briefly in the door of the office where Sheriff Sarber was sprawled on the floor in a pool of blood.

"Why did you do this to me?" the law officer whispered hoarsely.

The gang ran down the jail steps and fled in a waiting car. Moments later, Sarber died.

Despite murdering a sheriff and breaking a prisoner out of jail, the gang had violated no federal laws. However, Ohio and Indiana law enforcement officers invited the FBI to join in the search for the Michigan City escapers, especially the ones who had gunned down and beat Sheriff Sarber.

John Dillinger and his companions, meanwhile, headed for Indianapolis, where they holed up with Mary Kinder and hatched plans to equip themselves for a string of bank jobs. Harry Pierpont and the shapely Mary quickly developed a romantic attachment.

Dillinger also had a new girlfriend, Evelyn "Billie" Frechette, a raven-haired, part Menominee Indian, whom the gangster had met earlier in Chicago and had been brought to Mary Kinder's home at his request. Billie's husband was pulling a long term for bank robbery at the Leavenworth penitentiary.[1]

Seven days after Dillinger was sprung from the Lima jail, he and Harry Pierpont, posing as tourists, entered the police station at Peru, Indiana, and engaged officer Ambrose Clark in casual conversation. What preparations had the local lawmen made in the event "that horrible Dillinger gang roared into town?" they asked.

Proudly, policeman Clark and a desk sergeant showed the "tourists" their arsenal—Tommy guns, shotguns, rifles, pistols, bags full of ammunition and bullet-proof vests.

"Just what we need," Pierpont remarked, as the two outlaws pulled pistols from their pockets.

While the Peru policemen stood with upraised arms, Dillinger and Pierpont strolled out to their car with armloads of weapons and equipment. Mary Kinder was waiting in the vehicle as a lookout.

A week later, two members of the Pierpont-Dillinger gang appeared at the Auburn, Indiana, police station and identified themselves as writers for the popular *True Detective* magazine. Eager to be written up, Auburn policemen were interviewed in depth and told the visitors everything they needed to know about the arsenal in the building. Then the "writers" whipped out their weapons and carried off rifles, Tommy guns, shotguns, cartons of ammunition—and two police badges.

On October 12, 1933, Boobie Clark sat behind the wheel of a Studebaker touring car while Pierpont, Dillinger, and Makley got out and walked into the Central National Bank of Greenville, Indiana. Jack Hamilton was the "tiger"— he stood outside the front door to keep an eye open for the police or other dangers.

The gang knew precisely where the vault and the tellers' cages were—a few days earlier two of them had visited the bank posing as newspaper reporters and obtained a detailed rundown on the operation of the facility. Seven minutes after they reached the bank, the gang members, without firing a shot, sped away with a haul of $75,346 in cash and negotiable bonds.

Ditching their hot Studebaker, the gang stole another car, put pilfered license plates on it, knocked off three more banks within a six-day period in Michigan, Ohio and Illinois, and headed for Racine, Wisconsin.[2]

On November 20, well-dressed Harry Pierpont strolled into the American Bank and Trust Company in Racine just before closing time. A bookkeeper, Mrs. Henry Patzke, watched in puzzlement as the stranger unrolled a huge Red Cross poster in the lobby and pasted it in the middle of the large picture window.

That was the all-clear signal for John Dillinger and Fat Charley Makley to enter with guns drawn. Makley went up to teller Harold Graham and snarled, "Stick 'em up, Buster!"

Thinking the heavyset man was joking, he replied, "Go to the next window, please."

Makley raised his voice a decibel: "I said, stick 'em up, goddamn it!"

Graham made a sudden move and Fat Charley fired; a bullet tore into the frightened teller's arm and he fell, triggering an alarm button. The alarm, silent in the bank, went off at the Racine police department. Two policemen drove routinely to the bank. They were in no hurry. Numerous accidental soundings by careless tellers had occurred in the past.

When the officers, Wilbur Hanson and Cyril Boyard, sauntered into the bank, Pierpont leaped forward and ordered them to drop their weapons. When Hanson didn't react soon enough, Pierpont's pistol barked and a bullet tore into him. Women in the bank loosed piercing screams. All the while, Dillinger and Hamilton had been looting the vault.

"Okay, I've got all of it," Dillinger calmly said. "Let's get the hell out of here!"

At that moment, an off-duty policeman walked into the bank, but before he could draw his pistol, Dillinger had him covered and disarmed.

A large crowd of gapers had assembled outside the bank after the first shot had been fired. The three robbers pushed a few women out the door as a shield, while policemen across the street fired at them, the shots sent high to avoid the hostages.

The gang piled into a black Buick in which Boobie Clark had been waiting at the wheel. Then, with the bank president and bookkeeper Mrs. Patzke as hostages, the car rushed out of town and along premarked back roads for several miles where the hostages were released.

Now Dillinger and Pierpont decided to make the gang's headquarters in Chicago. Members lived in several North Side apartments, changing addresses every month or so. Dillinger took up light housekeeping with 27-year-old Billie Frechette, who was a singer in a cheap nightclub on North Clark Street.

Not long after arriving in the Windy City, Edward Shouse, one of the Michigan City prison escapees, fell into disfavor with Pierpont, Dillinger, and the others. Shouse was drinking heavily, had tried to con Jack Hamilton into independently knocking off banks with him, and had been making passes at the gangsters' girlfriends. Shouse was booted out of the gang.

Two weeks later, on the night of November 15, John Dillinger was driving his Hudson Terraplane to a dentist's office for an appointment. Billie Frechette was seated beside him. Nearing the office on Irving Park Boulevard, Dillinger smelled a trap. Several automobiles were parked in front of the office, all of them facing in the wrong direction.

Dillinger changed gears, pressed hard on the accelerator, and raced away with tires squealing. Several police cars gave chase. Soon, only a vehicle driven by Sergeant John Artery remained in hot pursuit along crowded Irving Park Boulevard at speeds of up to 70 miles per hour. Both of the vehicles careened in and out of the traffic, dodging trucks, streetcars, and buses.

Artery finally managed to bring his car alongside the Hudson, and his partner, Officer Arthur Keller, leaned out the window and fired a shotgun. Glass was blown out of the Hudson's windows, but neither Dillinger nor his woman were hit by pellets.

Now Dillinger drove even faster and, after rounding a corner on two wheels, he spotted an alley and sped into it. The police car occupants did not see the maneuver and raced on past. By the time Artery and Keller turned around, Dillinger was long gone.[3]

Dillinger, Pierpont, and the others were furious, convinced that Ed Shouse had tipped off the police about the dentist appointment. They swore to kill Shouse, but their plans were thwarted when police captured him in Paris, Illinois. Shouse was returned to the Michigan City prison, along with two other escapees, Joseph Burns and James Fox, who had also been apprehended, one in Chicago and the other in Ohio.

Early in December 1933, John Dillinger and Fat Charley Makley were out for a stroll in Chicago and saw a notice posted at the Unity Trust and Savings Bank. It said that the bank was closed down, but the room containing the safe deposit boxes would remain open for business as usual.

A day later, Dillinger and Pierpont, posing as salesmen of burglar alarms, approached the bank's only attendant, a 73-year-old man. He advised them that the facility had no need for their product, explaining, ''We don't have enough wiring for burglar alarms.''

That night Dillinger and his gang laid plans to hit the Unity Trust Bank, using an innovative technique—a real, live Santa Claus. Fat Charley Makley was a natural for the role—red-cheeked and with no need for the customary padding of the stomach.

At two o'clock in the afternoon of December 13, Makley, with his fake white beard, red suit, and a pair of .45 automatics tucked in his belt under his shirt, took up his post outside the bank. He rang his hand-held bell, ho-ho-ho'd and thanked passersby who dropped coins in his iron pot. Santa was the gang's lookout.

Soon John Dillinger, Harry Pierpont, and Three-Fingered Jack Hamilton sauntered past the red-suited Makley and on into the bank. Ten minutes later, the three men, one carrying a suitcase crammed with $220,000 in cash and negotiable bonds from the safe deposit boxes, came out, bid Santa Claus a merry Christmas, dropped a few coins in his iron pot and disappeared into the crowd of holiday shoppers.

A day later, Chicago Police Sergeant William T. Shanley received an underworld tip that Three-Fingered Jack would be at a certain automobile repair shop on the North Side. Along with Detective Frank Hopkins, the 42-year-old Shanley hid near the place. An hour later, Hamilton and a woman friend entered the shop to pick up his car.

Sergeant Shanley confronted Hamilton, saying, "I'm a police officer."

Hamilton whipped out a pistol, shot Shanley dead, and headed for the door, dragging the woman with him. Detective Hopkins, who had been posted outside the door, seized the woman, but she scratched and clawed like a tigress while Hamilton scrambled into his car and fled.

Sergeant Shanley, who left a wife and two children, was the eleventh Chicago policeman to be killed by criminals that year.[4]

With the approach of New Year's Day 1934, John Dillinger's picture was on the front page of newspapers on a regular basis, on magazine covers, and flashed on movie screens in newsreels. Radio newscasts led off with the latest word on the desperado.

So Dillinger decided it was time to lay low—and to get away from the icy blasts of a Chicago winter. Pierpont and Mary Kinder, along with Makley and Boobie Clark, headed for the luxury hotels of Tucson, Arizona. Dillinger and Billie Frechette, accompanied by Jack Hamilton, Homer Van Meter, and two women, drove to balmy Daytona Beach, Florida, where they rented several plush cottages on the water's edge.

A Hot Tip from "Old Joe" the Alligator

Edward G. Bremer, the 37-year-old president of the Commercial State Bank, dropped off his daughter Betty, age eight, at the Summit Hill Girls School in St. Paul on the bleak and frigid morning of January 17, 1934, and was driving to work through the rush-hour traffic. His wealthy father was Adolph Bremer, a good friend of President Franklin D. Roosevelt and principal owner of the Jacob Schmidt Brewing Company in St. Paul.

In the wake of the William Hamm, Jr., kidnapping in St. Paul nine months earlier, police picked up underworld rumors that Edward Bremer was to be snatched and held for ransom by a Chicago gang. Bremer employed bodyguards for five months, but dropped them when the reports seemed to be groundless.

As Edward Bremer paused for a stop signal before crossing heavily traveled Lexington Avenue, he glanced at his watch: it was 8:25 A.M. Moments later, a large sedan braked to a halt in front of the bankier's sleek Lincoln sedan. Four masked men brandishing pistols leaped out. One gunman tried to enter Bremer's car on the driver's side and the banker sought to get out the opposite door. A second member of the gang stopped him.

Both gunmen scrambled into the car and struck Bremer on the head with a lead pipe, causing him to lose consciousness. So swift had been the maneuver that no one in the scores of automobiles going both ways on Lexington Avenue had noticed the brutal scenario.

James Quinehan, a milk wagon driver, had halted about a half-block away for a group of children crossing Goodrich Avenue, and he had seen the car whip in front of the Lincoln. Thinking that a minor accident had taken place, he watched idly as the big car drove away and the Lincoln followed.

When Edward Bremer regained consciousness, his eyes were bandaged and he was lying on a narrow bed. An hour later, two kidnappers entered the room and beat him on the head with a blunt object, possibly a pistol butt.

In the days ahead, he heard automobiles frequently passing, indicating that he was close to a heavily traveled road. However, he did not hear any streetcars, which led him to believe that his prison was not in a large city.

Although his blindfold was removed from time to time during his captivity, Bremer was forced to sit facing the bedroom wall, so he never saw the faces of two guards who worked in shifts and remained constantly behind him. Although the room was darkened, he etched in his mind the wallpaper design, which one day might permit him to identify the hideout. Only later would Bremer learn that he was being held in the Chicago suburb of Bensonville.

Meanwhile, back in St. Paul on January 18 (24 hours after the kidnapping), Walter Magee, a wealthy contractor and friend of the Bremer family, received an anonymous telephone call from someone representing the abductors.

''Well, we've got your friend Ed Bremer, and if you ain't careful we'll get you too,'' the menacing voice said.

After threatening to kill Magee if he told the police about the call, the voice told the contractor to look for a note on the back porch of his office; then the caller slammed down the telephone.

The note demanded $200,000 in ransom and instructed the Bremer family to insert a notice in the *Minneapolis Tribune* saying, ''We are ready, Alice,'' indicating that the Bremer family was willing to negotiate. This was done.

Two nights after Magee received the telephone call, a milk bottle crashed through the glass front door at the St. Paul home of Dr. H. T. Nippert, the Bremer family physician. There were three notes in the bottle: one was to Nippert and signed in a shaky scrawl by Edward Bremer, and the other two were for Adolph Bremer and Walter Magee.

The message to Dr. Nippert instructed him to meet two or more of the kidnappers at a specified street corner in St. Paul and to accompany them to the hideout to treat Edward Bremer's numerous head wounds.

In great secrecy, Nippert met the abductors. He was blindfolded and taken on a night automobile ride of about six hours before the hideout was reached. After administering to young Bremer, with gang members standing behind them out of their view, Nippert was again blindfolded and returned to St. Paul.[1]

The note for Adolph Bremer designated Walter Magee as the intermediary. A few days after the abduction, Magee received instructions from the gang. He was to take a bus from St. Paul at a specified hour, go to a certain hotel in Des Moines, Iowa, and register under an assumed name, having in his possessiosn the $200,000 ransom in five- and ten-dollar bills. There he was to await further word.

However, when Magee received the communication, the money was under a time-lock in a St. Paul bank and the plan had to be abandoned. Several days passed without further signs from the captors, prompting Adolph Bremer, father of the victim, to issue an appeal to the kidnappers to contact him or Walter Magee.

Final instructions followed almost immediately. Magee was to go to a specified corner in St. Paul where a 1933 Chevrolet with Shell Oil signs on each door would be parked. There would be a note on the front seat.

On the night of February 6, Magee reached the Chevrolet and read the note, which said:

Go to Farmington, Minnesota. The Rochester bus will arrive there at 9:15 P.M. and leave at 9:25 P.M. Follow one hundred yards in back of the bus, when it leaves Farmington until you come to four red lights on the left of the road; turn on the first road to the left and proceed at fifteen miles per hour until you see five flashes of lights; then stop and deposit packages of money on right hand side of road. Leave the money; get in car and go straight ahead.

As instructed, Walter Magee left the ransom at the designated point along the dark road, then drove away without looking back. Twenty-four hours later, Edward Bremer, weak from numerous head wounds and nervous exhaustion, was shoved out of a small sedan by three of the kidnappers on a desolate street in Rochester, Minnesota, 85 miles south of St. Paul.

As soon as his son arrived home, Adolph Bremer, who had been in failing health, issued a public statement:

I am so happy to tell you that my boy is back at last. The hideous hours of suspense have been almost unbearable for all of us.

I gratefully appreciate the personal interest of President Roosevelt and the Governor (Floyd B. Olson) and the splendid cooperation given by the press and radio. The Federal, State and City law-enforcing authorities have been most kind in their efforts.

When the hundreds of employees at the Jacob Schmidt Brewery were told that young Bremer was back home, they let out a rousing cheer. Governor Olson called for an all-out effort to "crush the menace of kidnapping."

Law enforcement agencies, headed by the Federal Bureau of Invesigation, plunged into the formidable task of identifying the kidnapping gang. In Washington, D.C., J. Edgar Hoover and Assistant Director Harold Nathan took personal charge of the probe and were working nearly around the clock. FBI Agent Frank J. Blake, who had directed the search for the kidnappers of Oklahoma oil millionaire Charles Urschel, flew from Dallas to St. Paul to coordinate the investigation.

Once Edward Bremer had rested for 48 hours (under his doctor's orders), he was questioned in depth about his ordeal by Blake and other G-Men. His story of his imprisonment in what seemed to be a farmhouse, his treatment by the kidnappers (which was brutal at times), the sounds of their voices (one man used a phony Mexican accent) and the distinguishing characteristics of the room where he had been confined (the wallpaper design), were all discussed in detail.

Then Bremer mentioned a seemingly insignificant incident that occurred when three of the abductors were driving him back to Rochester. About half-way into the trip, the car stopped and two of the men got out and filled the gasoline tank from a large can, then tossed the container to the side of the road. Bremer had been blindfolded, but could tell what was taking place by his captors' conversation and the sounds of the refilling operation.

Finding a gasoline can somewhere along an unknown road within a 300-mile radius of St. Paul appeared to be an impossible task. Possibly the container had been pitched into high weeds or into thick brush, which would make it invisible from the road. However, three days after Bremer's release, FBI agents located the discarded gasoline can near Portage, Wisconsin.

The container was rushed to Washington, D.C., where two latent fingerprints were lifted in the FBI laboratory. They were positively identified by technicians as being those of Arthur "Doc" Barker, one of Ma Barker's notorious sons.

J. Edgar Hoover now knew the identity of the kidnapping gang, and he sent out a teletype message to FBI field offices:

"Pick up the Barker-Karpis Gang . . . Wanted for kidnapping of Edward George Bremer . . . Urgent."

In the meantime, most of the $200,000 ransom was turned over to gang member Shotgun George Ziegler, the former Illinois University football star and graduate engineer, who stashed it in a garage belonging to his wife's uncle, where it was left to "cool." That action proved to be a serious mistake. Ziegler began drinking heavily, talking wildly in underworld circles, and boasting of his role in the Bremer kidnapping.

On March 22, 1934, just two months after the abduction, the nattily dressed Ziegler strolled out of his favorite restaurant in the gangster-controlled Chicago suburb of Cicero. A long black Buick roared up and two blasts were fired from shotguns. Handsome George Ziegler's head was nearly blown off.

FBI agents gained valuable information from Shotgun George's mutilated corpse. In his wallet were membership cards to the Chicago Yacht Club and the Mohawk Country Club of Bensonville, a northwestern suburb of Chicago. Investigators also found the names and addresses of numerous members of the Karpis-Barker mob.

With Ziegler gone, only his widow knew where the bulk of the ransom money was hidden. Ma Barker took care of that matter by consoling and cajoling the grieving Mrs. Ziegler into disclosing the hiding place of the loot. George, Ma convinced the trusting widow, had been rubbed out by enemies from his days with the Al Capone mob.

Suddenly, things had become hot for the Karpis-Barker gang, whose members were holed up in Chicago and St. Paul. Thousands of wanted posters of gang members had been sent by the FBI to hundreds of post offices and were hanging conspicuously in lobbies. Photographs of Doc and Freddie Barker, Alvin "Old Creepy" Karpis and other gang members were splashed across newspaper front pages and prominently displayed in such popular magazines as *Liberty* and *True Detective.*

Feeling the heat, Freddie Barker, Ma's favorite son, and Creepy Karpis decided to have plastic surgery performed to alter their appearances. They contacted a 39-year-old Chicago physician, Dr. Joseph P. Moran, an ex-convict who operated (literally) on the shady side of the law for hefty fees. A former honor student at Tufts Medical School, Boston, following an honorable tour of duty as a lieutenant in the army signal corps in France during World War I, young Moran came to LaSalle, Illinois, and hung out his shingle.

In LaSalle, he was highly regarded by the citizens and gained a reputation as a skilled surgeon. However, he had a serious failing—he was a heavy drinker. While reputedly drunk, he performed an illegal abortion on a young woman and served a year and four months in the Illinois penitentiary at Joliet.

After his release, Moran's license to practice was restored and he opened an office in a suburb of Chicago. From his contacts while in the Joliet prison, Dr. Moran soon found himself to be a gangland physician and surgeon for Chicago.

These were bloody days in the Windy City on Lake Michigan, and large numbers of citizens wondered why only dead gangsters were found sprawled in gutters—where were the wounded ones? When guns blazed in gangster warfare, the wounded were hauled off to a secluded hotel or apartment, then a telephone call went out to Doc Moran.

Moran, still a heavy drinker, specialized in plastic surgery and fingertip alterations at his office on Irving Park Road in Chicago. After injecting Freddie Barker and Creepy Karpis with heavy doses of morphine, the underworld quack worked on their noses, chins, and jowls. Freezing their fingers with cocaine, he scraped them with a scalpel in an effort to distort their tell-tale fingerprints.

Dr. Moran had botched the job. Ma Barker and 19-year-old Delores Delaney, Karpis's girlfriend, nursed Freddie and Alvin as best they could. Both men were in extreme pain, their faces were black and blue, and ghastly incisions would not heal. Worse, the two men could see no appreciable change in their facial makeup.[2]

One night, Freddie, in great pain yelled, "I'm going to kill that bastard (Moran) as soon as I get out of here!"

In August, Doc Moran disappeared, never to be seen again. Melvin Purvis, special agent in charge of the FBI office in Chicago, and his men picked up underworld rumors that Moran had been put in a concrete-weighted barrel and dropped into Lake Michigan.

Meanwhile, the FBI was painstakingly pursuing every clue in the Bremer kidnapping, ferreting out the figures involved one by one. John J. "Boss" McLaughlin, a Chicago political ward heeler was picked up by G-Men who had traced a hot Bremer 100-dollar bill to him. McLaughlin was charged with exchanging ransom money. Then FBI agents tracked down and arrested Oliver A.

Berg, an escapee from the Illinois State Penitentiary, who was charged with furnishing the ransom money to McLaughlin.[3]

The net was growing tighter. Ma Barker and Freddie fled to Florida; Creepy Karpis and his girlfriend Delores Delaney departed for Havana, Cuba, where they were traced by FBI agents and fled back to Miami. However, Doc Barker, Russell "Slim Gray" Gibson, Bryan Bolton, and other gang members remained holed up in Chicago.

On the night of January 8, 1935, a squad of FBI agents led by Melvin Purvis surrounded an apartment on Pine Grove Street in Chicago after being tipped off by an informant that Doc Barker and Slim Gray Gibson were living there. Then a G-Man went to the speaking tube in the hallway, called the fugitives, and ordered them to come out with their hands up.

There were several minutes of silence. Agents, gripping their weapons tensely, waited. Then out of the front door walked Bryan Bolton and two women with raised arms. Slim Gray, wanted for murder, scrambled down a shadowed, rear fire escape to the ground.

Wearing a bulletproof vest and brandishing a Browning automatic rifle, Gibson came out shooting at the FBI agent assigned to cover that point. With his powerful .351 rifle, the G-Man returned the fire, and a bullet penetrated the fugitive's steel vest. Slim Gray collapsed in the snow, shot through the heart.[4]

Despite the success of the raid, Melvin Purvis and his agents were disappointed. They had failed to root out Doc Barker. However, an apartment on Surf Street, about 15 blocks to the south, had been under observation and it was thought that Barker might be hiding there. Purvis and his men quickly drove to Surf Street and staked out the building.

Unaware of the developments on Pine Grove Street, Barker leisurely strolled from the apartment building and moments later found himself staring at the muzzles of several rifles and pistols. The fugitive was searched, but no gun was found.

"Where's your weapon, Doc?" one G-Man asked.

"Home," Barker replied with a wince, "And ain't that a hell of a place for it?"[5]

Doc Barker was taken to the downtown Chicago FBI office in the Bankers Building and grilled for hours. As the hardened criminal he was, Doc sat in a chair, jaws clenched, staring straight ahead. He refused to reply to the simplest question. However, Bryan Bolton, who said he had "taken care" of the gang's women while the Bremer kidnapping was in progress, had a loose lip and co-operated with the FBI.[6]

In Doc Barker's apartment agents found a map of Florida with a penciled circle drawn around the town of Ocala. Bolton said he knew Ma Barker and her boy Freddie were in Florida, but he didn't know where. Bolton himself had recently been in Florida, and he had accidentally met Doc Barker and Slim Gray Gibson in Georgia. They had all returned to Chicago together.

Along the way, Bolton told the G-Men, Barker and Russell jokingly talked about an alligator that lived in a Florida lake or bayou and had been nicknamed "Old Joe" by the local people.

Informed of this hot lead, J. Edgar Hoover ordered a team of agents from Chicago to fly to Florida and join with other agents from the Jacksonville office. It was leanred that Old Joe inhabited Lake Weir in Oklawaha, 16 miles south of Ocala in the central part of the state.[7]

Descending on Oklawaha, the team of FBI agents, headed by Earl J. Connelly of the Cincinnati office, rapidly focused on a rambling, nine-room frame house on the banks of Lake Weir. For two months it had been the mystery house of the town and its occupants the subject of widespread gossip and conjecture. The owner had leased the house to a couple who went by the names of Mr. and Mrs. J. E. Blackburn.

The locals considered the couple to be strange. They kept to themselves and never mixed with neighbors. About the only time Mrs. Blackburn was seen was on Sundays when she attended services at the Moss Bluff Baptist Church. She was a middle-aged, roly-poly, black-haired woman. Her husband was far younger, perhaps in his late twenties or early thirties, and diminutive.

What especially got local tongues wagging were the high-powered automobiles that beat a path to and from the old house, day and night. One neighbor liked to fish, and when he started his car engine at 5:00 A.M. on many mornings, he spotted men peering out from behind curtains.

Disguised as county road workers, two FBI agents reconnoitered the premises and caught several glimpses of the Blackburns. There was no doubt about it. They were Ma Barker and son Freddie and, judging by the vehicle traffic reported by townspeople, other members of the Barker-Karpis gang were probably keeping under cover inside the house.

Old Joe the alligator had led the FBI to its quarry.

Just before dawn on January 16, 1935, a caravan of black sedans rolled along a dirt road leading to Lake Weir and the big frame house. All was deathly still, except for the gentle murmuring sound of the rubber tires. Fourteen FBI agents, bearing high-powered rifles, machine guns, and tear gas, poured out of the cars when the caravan halted about a half-mile from the house. Each G-Man was wearing a steel vest.

Led by Earl Connelly, a tall, lean-faced veteran of the Bureau, the G-Men stole through the semi-darkness and surrounded the Barker-Karpis gang's hideout. When the trap had been set, Connelly shouted:

"This is the FBI! You're surrounded! Come on out!"

Silence.

A minute later, Connelly yelled: "Unless you come out, we're going to start shooting!"

More silence.

Finally, Ma Barker, her voice bitter and grating, shouted from the dark house: "All right, go ahead!"

Connelly and his men thought that Ma Barker was telling the other gang members to surrender. So Connelly walked out into the open, only some 90 feet from the house, and called out:

"All right, you won't be hurt! Come out one at a time with your hands up!"

Moments later a machine gun began chattering from an upstairs window, and Agent Connelly dived for cover as a string of bullets kicked up sand around him. An ear-splitting crescendo erupted as the G-Men loosed a withering fusillade of fire with their Tommy guns and rifles. Off and on, the blistering shootout raged four hours.

Along the highway about 300 feet from the house, some 400 curious rubberneckers were watching the gun battle from ditches, on store porches, from parked automobiles, and lying flat on the ground. Oklawaha had never known such excitement.

At midmorning, 25-year-old George Albright entered the general store in Weirdale to pick up a copy of the *Jacksonville Times-Union*, part of his daily routine.

"There's a regular war goin' on over at Oklawaha," the clerk declared. "Machine guns shootin' and all that stuff."

Albright's curiosity got the better of him. So he hopped into his Model A Ford and drove the five miles to where the gun battle was raging. Parking his car, Albright slipped through a patch of woods and suddenly found himself only 100 feet from the bullet-riddled house. Just then, bursts of fire erupted and slugs hissed past his head in both directions. Caught in the crossfire, Albright leaped behind a large oak tree.

"I suddenly remembered that there were some important things I had to do back at my orange groves," George Albright would say later. "So I left in a hurry."[8]

Just before 11:00 A.M., a stillness hovered over Lake Weir and its shoreline. Tear gas, propelled from short-barreled guns, was flung into the hideout. Cautiously, weapons at the ready, Agent Connelly and his men entered the house. In an upstairs bedroom, Freddie Barker was sprawled grotesquely in a pool of blood, his body punctured by 11 bullets. Clutched in one hand was a Tommy gun. Under him was a .45 automatic. Freddie had remained true to his mother's admonition over the years: "Barker's always die with their boots on!"

A short distance from Freddie lay the lifeless body of Ma Barker, clinging to a Tommy gun, its barrel still hot. She had been hit by three bullets, one of which had gone through her heart. In Ma's pocketbook, agents found $10,200 in bills of large denominations.

Poking their Tommy gun muzzles through the doors of rooms in the rambling house, the G-Men hunted for other members of the gang, particularly for Creepy Karpis, who had gained the newspaper nickname of "Magic" Karpis because of his seeming knack for escaping the clutches of the law.

Hundreds of empty shells littered the house. On a table sat a pan of newly risen biscuits ready for the oven. Freddie loved Ma's biscuits.

In Washington, D.C., J. Edgar Hoover and the man called his shadow, Clyde

Tolson, were hovering over a clicking teletype in FBI headquarters. A message read:

> Ma Barker and son Freddie killed in fight at Oklawaha, Florida. Karpis escaped from house hour before we arrived. Another man, believed to be (Harry) Campbell, and two girls left with him. Standing by for orders.
> —Connelly.

In the wake of the big Lake Weir shootout, morbidness prevailed in Ocala, 16 miles from the scene of the battle. Thousands of people from many states streamed into the little town, crowding around the mortuary where Ma and Freddie had been taken. Ropes failed to hold back the surging, jostling waves of humanity to get a glimpse of the dead outlaws. Hordes of souvenir hunters ransacked the big white house on Lake Weir. Finally, the owner charged admission, and the curious shelled out their money.[9]

In the meantime, within hours after the Oklawaha gun battle, a Jacksonville, Florida, florist reported that his car was stolen. Since it was the only vehicle stolen that night in the state, J. Edgar Hoover theorized that Creepy Karpis and his sidekick Harry Campbell had ditched their car in Jacksonville and were fleeing north in the florist's automobile.

A description of the stolen car and its license number was flashed from FBI headquarters to every police department and sheriff's office east of the Mississippi River. Three days passed with no sightings reported.

Then, on the afternoon of January 20, Patrolman Elias Saab of the Atlantic City, New Jersey, police department was on his Kentucky Avenue beat, about a half-block from the famed boardwalk. Saab was cold—it was sleeting—and the streets were nearly deserted. Then he spotted a car with the Florida florist's license number parked at the curb.

Officer Saab rushed to police headquarters and excitedly reported his find to Captain Harry Yates, chief of detectives. Yates and a few of his men drove swiftly to Kentucky Avenue, where they learned that two men and two women had arrived in the Florida car and registered at the Danmore Hotel, which was less than a block away.

Inquiry at the Danmore disclosed that the couples had registered under the names of Carson and Campbell, and that the two men had left the hotel earlier that afternoon. The wife of Carson, the desk clerk reported, was about to have a baby and arrangements had been made for having her taken to a hospital.

As the Atlantic City officers had surmised, Carson was actually Old Creepy Karpis, wanted for two murders and the Hamm and Bremer kidnappings. Karpis had his hair cropped short and wore glasses with owl-like lenses in an effort to disguise himself. The other man was Harry Campbell, also wanted for the two abductions.

There was added urgency to capturing the pair of outlaws: Karpis had just been designated Public Enemy Number 1.

Delores Delaney, the younger sister of a member of the John Dillinger gang, was Karpis's pregnant girlfriend, and the other woman was Winona Burdette, whose ambition had been to become a singer of radio commercials before she had taken up with Harry Campbell.

Detective Captain Yates and a few officers staked out the Danmore Hotel, and when they saw Karpis and Campbell return at about 5:00 A.M., Detectives Edward Mulhern and Arch Whiteman, with drawn automatic pistols, stole upstairs to the rooms singled out by the desk clerk. In unison, the two officers kicked open the door to Room 23 and confronted Creepy Karpis.

In a split second, Harry Campbell charged out of the bathroom with Tommy gun in hand. Karpis leaped for his weapon and the two men opened fire. Mulhern and Whiteman ducked out of the door to escape the torrent of bullets and began shooting. Whiteman was struck in the face by a pellet and slumped to the floor, while the two fugitives dashed down the corridor toward the rear steps.

A door to another room was flung open and Delores Delaney and Winona Burdette rushed into the hall. There was a loud scream as a bullet grazed the pregnant Delaney's leg; the other woman pulled her back into the room and slammed the door.

By this time, Detective Mulhern had emptied his pistol, and he crouched beside the wounded Whiteman, whose face was covered with blood. Officers posted in the lobby heard the shooting and were charging up the steps two at a time, but Karpis and Campbell were racing down the rear stairs.

Bolting out a back door, the two gangsters were greeted by a burst of fire from a pair of detectives. But when the officers ran out of bullets at the same time and had to reload, Karpis and Campbell ran into a garage next to the Danmore. There they scrambled into a pea green Pontiac owned by an Atlantic City woman. With Campbell at the wheel and Karpis firing out the open window, the vehicle rushed from the garage amidst a hail of police bullets and roared out of town.

Detective Whiteman was taken to a hospital where it was found that the bullet had grazed his cheek. The two women were arrested. Captain Yates notified the FBI in Philadelphia, and agents were sent to Atlantic City. The G-Men questioned the women, who had played the game before and remained silent.[10]

At 9:30 on the night of January 21, less than 24 hours after Karpis and Campbell had made their daring escape from Atlantic City, Dr. Horace H. Hunsicker, a staff member at the Pennsylvania State Hospital at Allentown, was lying bound and gagged on the floor of a deserted Grange hall, 15 miles southwest of Akron, Ohio. He was struggling frantically to get to a telephone hanging on the wall.

Earlier, Hunsicker had been driving his brand new Chevrolet coach along the Allentown-Philadelphia Pike at Sellersville, Pennsylvania, when two men in a pea green Pontiac forced him to the curb and took over his automobile at gunpoint. The young doctor was bound, gagged, and pitched into the back seat. Then the two men drove off with their captive after abandoning the Pontiac.

Hours later, the car stopped, Dr. Hunsicker was thrown into the Grange hall, and his abductors disappeared.

Hunsicker finally reached the telephone, managed to rip off the gag, and called for help. Sheriff Roy Kruggle and a deputy responded, and the FBI in Washington was notified about the two men in the pea green Pontiac, the one previously stolen from the Atlantic City garage. In less than an hour, FBI agents and law enforcement officers in five states were on the alert for Dr. Hunsicker's 1935 Chevrolet.

Dell Clarke, a rural mail carrier working out of Monroe, a resort town on the Lake Erie shore, found Hunsicker's car, riddled with bullet holes, abandoned along a deserted country road. There the trail of Karpis ended as abruptly as if the earth had swallowed him.

In Washington, D.C. a few days later, a crude note scribbled in longhand arrived at FBI headquarters. It read:

Mr. Hoover:
    You ain't going to take me alive, and before you get me, I'm going to get you. If I die, I'll kill you first.
                                                                    —Alvin Karpis

While the intense search for Karpis continued in the East, the FBI's focus now turned to the Southwest.

18

Winter Guests in Tucson

Most guests were asleep early in the morning of Tuesday, January 22, 1934, when the cry "Fire! Fire!" resounded in the posh Congress Hotel in Tucson, one of the oldest towns in the United States, with a population of around 25,000. Tucson's dry desert air and winter sunshine made it a popular health and play resort.

While the hotel was burning, a group of six men and four women guests collared a few firefighters and paid them large tips to lug their baggage outside. Several of the suitcases were exceptionally heavy, the luggers noticed.

When the blaze was extinguished two hours later, the Congress had been so heavily damaged that many of the guests, including the group of ten, had to locate lodgings elsewhere in Tucson.

Twenty-four hours later, one of the firefighters was whiling away the time in a Tucson station by reading *True Detective* magazine. Suddenly, he leaped to his feet, waved the publication, and called to his comrades. He pointed to a spread of mug shots of the John Dillinger gang that had been terrorizing the Midwest. The firefighters had recognized two of the men in the pictures as those whose baggage he had helped carry out of the burning Congress Hotel.

Two days before the fire, John Dillinger and his girlfriend, Billie Frechette, Three-Fingered Jack Hamilton, and Homer Van Meter checked into the Congress, where Handsome Harry Pierpont, Fat Charley Makley, Boobie Clark, and their women had been ensconced for two weeks. Dillinger and his entourage had quickly tired of Florida's beaches, so they climbed into a Buick touring car at Daytona Beach and drove westward to Tucson to join the rest of the gang.

Police were quickly notified of the firefighter's discovery. This was their first inkling that the Dillinger gang was in Tucson, presumably to spend the winter. Congress desk clerks and bellhops were shown pictures of the gang and identified them as the guests who had arrived at different times in flashy, powerful automobiles.

Bellhops recalled these particular guests because of their stylish clothing, lavish tips, and the heavy weight of pieces of their baggage. Only later would they learn why these suitcases had been so heavy—they held Tommy guns and hundreds of rounds of ammunition.

Investigators found that gang members and their women had created a stir around Tucson when they went on spending binges at expensive clothing stores and in nightclubs. Most locals pegged the strangers flashing the big rolls of currency as wealthy tourists from the East.

Acting on tips from townspeople, lawmen began rooting out the gangsters. Harry Pierpont and his sweetheart Mary Kinder were nabbed as they were leaving a tourist camp. Perhaps impressed by the meek manner in which Pierpont surrendered and his friendly banter, the police did not search him.

While being processed at the Tucson police station, Pierpont suddenly whipped out two concealed pistols and began backing toward the door. Patrolman Frank Eymans leaped at the prisoner, knocked his guns aside, and thrust the muzzle of his own pistol against Pierpont's stomach. Then Handsome Harry was finally searched, and a third small pistol was found in his sock.

In the meantime, other policemen rushed to a radio store in a shopping center where they arrested Fat Charley Makley and his girlfriend of the moment. Makley was buying a short-wave radio capable of getting the police alarms.

Makley's companion turned out to be a local cabaret entertainer who had known nothing of her big-spending man's true identity, and she was released from custody.

Boobie Clark was traced to an apartment in the northern part of Tucson. Posing as a door-to-door salesman, a detective knocked on the door of Clark's unit. Boobie, who was with a woman, opened the door, cursed the "salesman," and was about to slam the door in his face when he spotted policemen coming up the hall.

Clark spun around and made a dive for a pistol that was lying on a table. The detective leaped on the husky hoodlum and the two men were thrashing about on the floor when the other officers rushed into the room. Clark refused to quit, and had to be beaten into submission with blows to his head from pistol butts.

Now Tucson officers cast their dragnet for the biggest fish of them all—John Dillinger. Several hours elapsed and it was feared that he had skipped town. In the meantime, police staked out the apartment from which Boobie Clark had been taken on the off chance that Dillinger might come there.

By now, virtually the entire countryside had heard on the radio about the manhunt—but Dillinger apparently had not tuned in. Police at Clark's apartment tensely gripped their weapons as they saw Dillinger and his woman friend drive up. The outlaw, carrying a Tommy gun only partly concealed by his coat, stepped out to reconnoiter.

Then Dillinger walked up to the front door and inserted a key. At that moment, six policemen closed in on the porch and ordered the fugitive to put up his hands. Dillinger wheeled and started to lift his machine gun.

"Drop it, or you're dead!" an officer called out.

The wanted man raised his arms.

While being put in a cell at the Tucson police station, Dillinger said to the men who had captured him: "My God, how did you know I was in town? I'll be the laughing stock of the country! How did I know that a hick town police force would ever suspicion me?"[1]

Posted around the jail were 15 heavily armed officers, a hedge against the Dillinger gang's outside cohorts trying to free him from captivity.

Far into the night, Tucson law enforcement officers counted the currency found in Dillinger's possession: more than $30,000. Most of the money had been hidden in a flour sack in Dillinger's quarters, and the outlaw carried $9,175 in his pockets.

John Dillinger was furious to find himself behind bars. "You can't keep me in any two-by-four jail like this!" he snarled while shaking a fist at guards. "I'll get out and kill you all!"[2]

Governor B. B. Moeur visited the jail to inspect the precautions being taken to prevent the prisoners from being helped by friends on the outside. Charley Makley chatted freely with the governor and was almost cockey. "I'll be out of here soon, Gov," Makley told Moeur. "I've broken out of a hell of a lot better Bastilles than this one!"

John Van Buskirk, a Los Angeles lawyer retained by the gang to fight extradition to other states, flew to Tucson and filed a writ of habeas corpus on behalf of the prisoners. If granted, Dillinger and his henchmen would be released from jail.

Perhaps encouraged by the arrival of Van Buskirk, Dillinger grew boastful while in his cell. "I'm an expert in my business," he told guards with considerable accuracy. "I can play tag with police any time. They just dodge around on old trails like fox hounds that don't know what's going on.

"And the dumbest ones in the world are the Chicago kind. Right now none of these smart-alec coppers have got a bit of evidence that I killed anybody or robbed a bank.

"And they can't keep me penned up anywhere," Dillinger continued. "Not here, Atlanta, Leavenworth or Alcatraz,"[3]

Chained together, Dillinger and his henchmen were brought into court the day after their capture for a hearing. Four states had put in claims for gang members, mainly on charges of bank robbery and murder. Mary Kinder and the other two women were also led into the courtroom.

The four male prisoners were in a defiant mood and tried repeatedly to disrupt proceedings. When his name was called, Dillinger refused to stand up. "I ain't John Dillinger," he growled in a surly tone. At the order of Magistrate C. V.

Budlong, Dillinger was yanked, still protesting, to his feet by husky guards. "I'm being framed," Dillinger exclaimed.

Harry Pierpont kept up a running fire of jesting comment on the proceedings, so that at times he had to be forcibly silenced. When his own name was called he stood up, looked around and said, "Hell, that must be me!"[4]

Boobie Clark, still pale from loss of blood and dressed in the blood-stained suit he had worn in his struggle with police a day earlier, remained silent, other than to deny that he was Russell Clark.

Pierpont, Makley, and Clark were extradited to Lima, Ohio, to stand trial for the murder of Sheriff Jess Sarber at the time three gunmen broke Dillinger out of jail on the night of October 22, 1933. Dillinger was picked up in Tucson by a contingent of Indiana law enforcement officers and flown to Chicago, then taken in a 13-car caravan escorted by armed lawmen to a jail at Crown Point, Indiana. There he was charged with the murder of Policeman Patrick O'Malley in the holdup of the First National Bank of East Chicago, Indiana, on January 15, 1934.[5]

Two bank officials identified Dillinger and pictures of Three-Fingered Jack Hamilton (who was still at large), as the bandits who had gunned down Officer O'Malley, but Dillinger denied any involvement, claiming that he was in Florida at the time. If convicted of O'Malley's murder, Dillinger would receive a mandatory death sentence.[6]

John Dillinger's jailer at Crown Point was Lake County Sheriff Lillian Holley, widow of a former sheriff who had been killed while trying to arrest a drunken farmer. The Crown Point jail was reputed to be escape-proof: there were six steel doors between any ambitious escaper and freedom. "It will take a Harry Houdini to break out of this jail," a deputy told the horde of newspaper people who descended on Crown Point.

Something of a carnival atmosphere prevailed in and around the jail. Dillinger was often taken from his cell to the office of Sheriff Holley, where the notorious outlaw and Lake Country Prosecutor Robert Estill posed, with arms around each other and beaming, for newspaper and magazine photographers.

In Chicago, FBI Special Agent in Charge Melvin Purvis and his men were outraged by such conduct on the part of law enforcement officials. "I wonder at the impulse which creates the desire on the part of any responsible person to shake hands and pose with a criminal or otherwise indicate an unmistakable friendliness for him," Purvis declared.[7]

On the afternoon of March 4, Deputy Sheriff Ernest Blunk and jailer Sam Calhoun walked into the cellblock and were greeted by a pistol in the hands of John Dillinger.

"I don't want to kill anybody," the inmate said, "Just do as I tell you."

Dillinger disarmed the two men and forced them to open the cellblock door. Then he dashed for the sheriff's office, grabbed a pair of Tommy guns, and rounded up the other guards, locking them in the cellblock.

"Anyone want to go?" Dillinger yelled at the 15 or 20 prisoners. Only Herbert Youngblood, who was awaiting trial for murder, accepted his offer.

Dillinger and Youngblood ran out the front door and leaped into Sheriff Holley's Ford V–8. Taking along Deputy Blunk and a mechanic, Dillinger and Youngblood sped out of town, apparently heading for Chicago to the northwest. Fifty miles west of Crown Point, near Peotone, Illinois, Dillinger released the two hostages along a deserted stretch of road.

Both men were shaken over the ordeal of being at the mercy of one of the nation's most wanted desperadoes. They had been especially nervous during the drive, when Dillinger would occasionally sing the lyrics of a popular ditty of the time, *I'm Heading for the Last Roundup*.

Then, as the escapees drove onward from Peotone, Dillinger told Youngblood, a black man, to lie flat on the rear floorboard, since the two of them together, one white and one black, would be easily detected by searching law officers.

Before reaching Chicago, Dillinger and Youngblood separated. Nine days later, on March 13, Youngblood was cornered by three policemen in a tobacco store in Port Huron, Michigan. A shootout erupted. Youngblood killed one officer, wounded the other, and took six bullets himself. The escapee's dying words were that Dillinger had been with him the previous day. That untrue disclosure triggered an extensive manhunt in the area, and there were numerous reports that Dillinger had been seen crossing the border into Canada.

Actually, Dillinger was hiding out with Billie Frechette, the former Chicago saloon singer, in unit 303 of the Lincoln Court apartments in the exclusive Hill section of St. Paul. After a short stretch in the Tucson jail as a material witness, Frechette had been released.

The spectacular breakout from the "escape-proof" Crown Point jail triggered a rash of blaring headlines. Radio newscasts led off with the latest details on the hunt for John Dillinger. When the outlaw made it a point to advise the press about his wooden-gun ploy, the media coverage exploded in an orgy of stories— some of them true—about the cold-blooded thug.

Dillinger claimed that he had pulled off the breakout by using a razor blade to carve a crude-looking wooden pistol from the top of a washboard and darkening it with bootblack provided to him earlier by accommodating guards impressed with the prisoner's friendliness and national renown.

John Dillinger emerged as a kind of Robin Hood folk hero among many Americans, many of whom were impoverished and embittered by the ravages of the Great Depression. "I am for Johnnie," an admirer in Indianapolis wrote to the local newspaper. "Dillinger never robbed poor people—he robbed those who became rich from robbing the poor.[8] Such sentiment was widespread, neatly skirting the fact that some of the money stolen from banks belonged to poor people.

Dillinger projected an image of swashbuckling glamour, which resulted in large numbers of people overlooking the widows and young children of law officers gunned down by him and his gang. When holding up a bank, the agile outlaw would leap the barrier to the tellers' cage to grab the loot. This caused one major newspaper to dub him, "The Leaping Bandit." He had been known to tip his straw hat to frightened elderly women caught in the center of his bank heists.

Movie newsreel shots of Dillinger were greeted with applause, cheers and whistles. "This nation," an indignant editorial declared, "seems to have taken leave of its senses."

President Franklin Roosevelt, in one of his famous radio "Fireside Chats," said that he was "shocked by the public adulation of a vicious criminal. . . . it permits police to be corrupted and intimidated, and romanticizes men who are nothing but insane murderers."[9]

In Washington, J. Edgar Hoover was also outraged by the mood of much of the public, and he went out of his way to call John Dillinger and other desperadoes "scum from the boiling pot of the underworld," "craven beasts," "public rats," "vermin," and "vultures."

In the wake of the Crown Point jail breakout, a London newspaper editorial asked: "What on earth is happening in America?" In Germany, where a Nazi dictator with a Charlie Chaplin mustache named Adolf Hitler was solidifying his grip on the nation, a newspaper shrieked, "No voice in America should be raised against the Fuehrer (Hitler) as long as John Dillinger is on the loose." The piece went on to offer advice on how the United States could curb the outbreak of lawlessness: "Round up the gangsters and sterilize them."[10]

Shortly after the outlaw had released his two hostages near Peotone, Illinois, Sheriff Holley's Ford got stuck in a roadside ditch and had to be abandoned. Discovery of the getaway car officially brought the FBI into the search for Dillinger. (Actually, G-Men, invited by local and state law enforcement agencies, had been on his trail for months.)

Until now, Dillinger had broken only local and state laws. But the moment he crossed the Indiana-Illinois state line, he violated the National Motor Theft Act (commonly known as the Dyer Act), which prohibits transportation of a stolen automobile or truck into another state.

J. Edgar Hoover turned his bloodhounds loose, teletyping orders to FBI field offices: "Urgent. Bring in John Dillinger."

Throughout the Midwest and South, every spot where Dillinger had ever been known to have spent time was "planted" (FBI agents observing a place from another point, usually a rented room or apartment across the street). Dillinger's relatives at Mooresville, Indiana, were put under surveillance, and G-Men checked out the fugitive's underworld acquaintances.

Tips flooded FBI offices and police and sheriff departments. Many were spite tips, seeking to embarrass a neighbor or relative against whom the anonymous callers held grudges. G-Men put in thousands of manhours and wore out shoe leather and automobile tires running down leads, most of which were fruitless.

Dillinger became a popular phantom of everyone's imagination. In less than a week after his Crown Point escape, he was reported by citizens to be in New

York, Chicago, Phoenix, Savannah, New Orleans, and Detroit. A New York newspaper editorial declared: "John Dillinger—wherever he is—seems to have kept out of London, Paris, Berlin, Rome, Moscow, Vienna and Paducah, Kentucky."

Police departments in scores of Midwest cities formed Dillinger Squads, whose single purpose was to capture or kill the outlaw. The American Legion offered to arm 50,000 of its World War I veterans to join in the search, a proposal that was diplomatically rejected. The Indiana National Guard suggested it use its airplanes and tanks in the manhunt.

Dillinger, meanwhile, was apparently basking in his widespread publicity. In a letter to his sister in Indiana, he boasted about his escape from the Crown Point jail:

> Dear Sis:
>   I thought I would write a few lines and let you know I am still perculating. Don't worry about me honey, for that won't help any, and besides I am having a lot of fun. I am sending Emmett (Audrey's husband, Emmett Hancock) my wooden gun and I want him to always keep it. I see that Deputy Blunk says I had a real forty five thats just a lot of hooey to cover up because they don't like to admit that I locked eight deputys and a dozen trustys up with my wooden gun before I got my hands on the two machineguns and you should have seen their faces. Ha! Ha! Ha! Don't part with my wooden gun for any price. For when you feel blue all you have to do is look at the gun and laugh your blues away. Ha! Ha! I will be around to see all of you when the roads are better, it is so hot around Indiana now that I would have trouble getting through.
>
>   Lots of love,
>   Johnny

Within 48 hours of Dillinger's flight from the Crown Point jail, he formed a new gang. His right hand man was tall, blue-eyed Homer Van Meter, a crony from his Michigan City prison days, where the two men plotted their war on society. Van Meter left the penitentiary on May 18, 1933, when Governor Paul McNutt, on the recommendation of the State Clemency Commission of Indiana, paroled him. The commission declared that it felt Van Meter would "make good in the future."

Van Meter, 35 years of age, brought into the gang Eddie Green, who was renowned in the underworld as a jugmarker (one who singled out bank plums to be hit), and Tommy Carroll, a virtuoso with a "Chicago piano" (Tommy gun), who had once been a promising professional boxer. Three-Fingered Jack Hamilton, an old standby, rejoined the gang, and a newcomer, 25-year-old Lester J. Gillis, was recruited.

Lester Gillis, a name he had discarded long ago because it "sounded sissy," preferred to be known as Big George Nelson, even though he was five feet, four inches tall and weighed about 133 pounds. However, he was known in the underworld as ''Baby Face''—but no one dared to call him that to his face, for even hardened criminals were awed by Nelson's brutality. He loved to kill for the sake of killing. ''Baby Face would shoot his own mother and not blink an eye,'' one outlaw told lawmen. Nelson had an especial hatred for ''G-Men and coppers.''

Baby Face Nelson, the son of a tanner, was born in Chicago on December 6, 1908. As a boy, his friends would recall, he was active, daring, and intelligent, a leader in his neighborhood. He was often in fights, and was skillful with his fists.

Nelson launched his crime career at age 13, when he engaged in petty thievery and reportedly held up the patrons of a Chicago whorehouse at gunpoint. Sent to the St. Charles Home for Boys after being arrested for stealing car accessories, he was paroled a year later. After getting into more trouble and breaking parole, Nelson was returned to the reformatory, and he was again paroled a few months later.

When only 19 years old, Nelson hooked up with the Al Capone mob as a goon to enforce kickbacks from reluctant union bosses. In 1931, Baby Face decided to go into business for himself. He was caught while robbing the Hillside State Bank in suburban Hillside and sentenced to a term of one year to life. However, he didn't go to prison, but was held for trial on charges of an earlier robbery of the Itasca State Bank in Itasca. Again Nelson was convicted, and received a second term of one year to life in the Illinois State Penitentiary at Joliet.

After the second trial, Baby Face was escorted by a prison guard, who was to take him to Joliet. The two men rode a train to that city, some 35 miles from Chicago, and then got into a cab. On the ride, Nelson, who was handcuffed to the guard, suddenly drew a concealed revolver (which had been slipped to him by pals on the train, police would theorize).

Nelson forced the guard to open the handcuffs and drove both the taxi chauffeur and the guard to a lonely cemetery, where he ordered them out and fled. For the next two years, Baby Face and John Paul Chase, a hoodlum he had met in California, knocked off a string of banks in the West and Midwest.

Two days after John Dillinger escaped at Crown Point, he assembled his new, five-man gang in a St. Paul hotel room. Baby Face Nelson, no shrinking violet, displayed no awe over being in the presence of Dillinger, the most famous bank robber of them all. While Dillinger listened, newcomer Nelson delivered a lengthy monologue on how to rob banks. Baby Face's theory was to barge into a bank, begin shooting, grab the loot, and roar out of town with Tommy guns blazing.

Homer Van Meter, an old pro in the bank heisting business, broke out laughing. Baby Face was infuriated, and both men went for their guns. Only Dillinger's quick intervention kept Nelson and Van Meter from killing one another.

Later that day, Dillinger was in a car being driven by Baby Face, who was inept at the wheel. Nelson's car collided with a vehicle at a St. Paul street intersection. Theodore Kidder, the other driver, leaped from his damaged automobile and ran back to Nelson.

"Are you blind?" Kidder screamed. "You ran a stop sign."

Baby Face had already drawn his pistol, and he sent a slug right between Kidder's eyes, killing him instantly.[11]

In the meantime, jugmarker Eddie Green had targeted two banks, one in Sioux Falls, South Dakota, and the other in Mason City, Iowa. Dillinger, Baby Face Nelson, Hamilton, Van Meter, Green, and Carroll drove all night and hit the Sioux Falls bank that afternoon.

Less than a minute after three gang members entered the bank, a teller punched a security button, triggering a raucous burglar alarm. Dillinger, Van Meter, and Green, veterans of many such situations, routinely emptied the cages as the bantam Baby Face, brandishing his Tommy gun wildly, leaped onto a desk and kept shouting "I'll kill the bastard who set off that alarm!"

While the robbery was in progress, Nelson spotted off-duty policeman Hale Keith getting out of a car in front of the bank. Baby Face fired several shots through a large picture window, winging Keith, who had not known that a holdup was taking place.

"I got one of them! I got one of them!" Baby Face yelled excitedly.

Scrambling into a large Packard sedan, the gang raced out of town with their $49,000 loot in a white sack. Five miles from Sioux Falls, the driver braked hard. John Dillinger and Three-Fingered Jack Hamilton sprang from the car and sprinkled hundreds of roofing nails along the road to halt or slow any pursuing police vehicles.

Hardly pausing to catch their breath, the gunmen drove to Mason City, Iowa, and entered a bank.

"Stick 'em up!" one bandit yelled.

Willis Bagley, the bank president, came out to see what the shouting was about and met Homer Van Meter approaching with a Tommy gun. Bagley ran back into his office, and slammed and locked the door. Van Meter loosed a burst of fire that splintered the wooden door, but missed Bagley.

A guard in a steel cage hovering over the main lobby fired a tear-gas shell that struck Eddie Green in the back, nearly knocking him off his feet. Green spun around and sprayed the cage with Tommy gun bullets, one of which went through a crack and hit the guard in the shoulder.

A terrified customer ran from the bank down an alley where she bumped into a short, muscular man wearing a cap and holding a Tommy gun.

"Quick! Quick!" the nearly hysterical woman called out. "They're robbing the bank!"

"You're damned right they are," Baby Face Nelson replied. His job was to stand guard by the parked Buick getaway car.

Racing over back roads, the gang headed for St. Paul with some $52,000 from the Mason City bank to sweeten their $49,000 kitty from the Sioux Falls job.

Meanwhile, In Lima, Ohio, the wheels of justice were grinding swiftly. Town folk were still seething over the cold-blooded murder of Sheriff Jess Sarber. Handsome Harry Pierpont was put on trial first. Deputy Sharpe and a jail attendant testified that they had seen him shoot the sheriff. Pierpont's tearful mother took the stand to swear her son was with her at the time, eating a dinner she had cooked for him.

After the verdict was rendered and Pierpont returned to the lockup, Fat Charley Makley called to Pierpont from his cell.

"What was it, Harry?"

"Well, what would it be?" Pierpont replied dejectedly.

"It" was death in the electric chair.

Makley was put on trial next. When the verdict came in, he shuffled past his pal Pierpont's cell.

"What'd you get, Charley?" Handsome Harry asked.

"Well, what the hell," Makley responded. "We've all got to die sometime."

Russell "Boobie" Clark was sentenced to life imprisonment for his part in the slaying of Sheriff Sarber.

On the windy night of March 31, 1934, FBI agents R. C. Coulter and R. L. Nalls and a St. Paul policeman slipped quietly up the stairs of the Lincoln Park Apartments in St. Paul. Earlier, the building manager had reported two suspicious tenants, Mr. and Mrs. Carl Hellman. The couple "acted nervous" and refused to admit the building's caretaker.

Billie Frechette answered the agents' knock and explained that her husband was asleep and she was not dressed properly to admit them. Coulter and Nalls insisted that they speak with Carl Hellman. Telling them to wait, Billie relocked the door and ran to the bedroom, awakened John Dillinger, and told him the FBI was outside the door.

While waiting, the G-Men turned to see a man coming up the stairs. Flashing their badges, the agents asked, "Who are you?"

Homer Van Meter, one of the most brutal members of Dillinger's gang, responded pleasantly, "I'm a soap salesman."

"How do we know that?"

"Come downstairs to my car and I'll show you my identity."

Coulter followed Van Meter down the stairs, and on reaching the first floor, the outlaw spun around and aimed a pistol at the FBI man.

"You asked for it, you bastard!" Van Meter snarled.

Before he could fire, Coulter dashed into a nearby room, and Van Meter fled out the front door. Leaping onto a horse-drawn delivery wagon, Van Meter donned the driver's cap and whipped the horses down the street—a bizarre getaway for a modern outlaw.

Suddenly, the door of the "Hellman" apartment opened and the muzzle of a Tommy gun began spraying the hallway with bullets. Then, holding tightly to

Billie Frechette's wrist, Dillinger ran down the corridor to the back stairs with the G-Men in hot pursuit. Just as the fugitive went through the doorway leading to the alley, a bullet struck him in the leg. However, he managed to get into his Hudson Terraplane, back it out of a garage, and race away at high speed.

Gang member Eddie Green was contacted and took Dillinger to an apartment hideout reserved for just such an emergency, and an underworld quack was summoned to treat his wound.

At the Lincoln Park Apartments, the FBI found a Tommy gun, two automatic rifles, a Colt automatic pistol, and two bulletproof vests. They also discovered jottings on a piece of paper that indicated Eddie Green and a girlfriend were living in an apartment across town under the names "Mr. and Mrs. Stephens."

On April 3, four days after the Lincoln Park Apartments shootout, FBI agents and St. Paul policemen surrounded Eddie Green's apartment building. When Green answered a knock on his door, saw three G-Men standing there, and tried to go for his pistol, he was shot. Eight days later, Green died in a hospital.

Dillinger and Billie Frechette, meanwhile, drove to Mooresville, where they stayed with Dillinger's father until the outlaw's leg wound had nearly healed. Then the couple went back to Chicago where Billie wanted to visit a woman friend. FBI agents had "planted" the home, and Billie was arrested. Unseen by the G-Men, John Dillinger, a Tommy gun beside him, was seated across the street in his Hudson.[12]

A few days later, Dillinger and Homer Van Meter barged into a police station at Warsaw, Indiana, held up two officers on duty there, and made off with several rifles, pistols, and three bulletproof vests.

On the afternoon of Sunday, April 22, 1934, Melvin Purvis, special agent in charge of the Chicago FBI office, received a call from the United States marshal in the city. He said that a man named Voss had telephoned and had important information about a wanted criminal. Purvis immediately called Voss in Rhinelander, in the far north woods of Wisconsin.

"The man you want most is up here," Voss said in a low voice.

As the guarded conversation continued, Voss seemed to be hesitant to mention the outlaw's name over the telephone.

"Do you mean John Dillinger?" Purvis asked.

"Yeah. Him and five of his gang are at a resort called Little Bohemia."

Purvis felt a surge of excitement, for the man sounded sincere. He told Voss to meet him at the closest airport, near Rhinelander, which is 50 miles from Little Bohemia.

"Wear a white handkerchief around your neck so I can identify you," the FBI man instructed.

Purvis promptly telephoned J. Edgar Hoover in Washington, D.C. and was given permission to go after the Dillinger gang with as many G-Men as he could muster in a hurry.

Late in the afternoon, three airplanes, two from Chicago and one from St. Paul, were converging on Rhinelander. On board were 16 FBI agents, together with small arsenals: rifles, pistols, Tommy guns, tear-gas equipment, and bulletproof vests. It was as though they were headed for war—and indeed they were. Each knew there was a good chance that he might not return from this mission.

19

Siege in Wisconsin's North Woods

America's crime kingpins loved to vacation in the pristine tranquility of the Wisconsin north woods. Back in 1925, Al Capone, at age 27, had set the trend when he bought a charming rock and wooden house known as the Hideaway, near Couderay. Until he was ensconced in Alcatraz for income tax evasion in 1930, the undisputed boss of the Chicago underworld often came to the house overlooking Cranberry Lake on his rolling 400-acre estate.

In his spacious and bright second-floor bedroom, Capone enjoyed listening to his favorite singer, Enrico Caruso, on his Victrola. Capone's favorites were operas including *Aida* and *Il Travatore*.

A unique feature of the Hideaway was a machine-gun turret, which seemed out of place in the quiet setting. Planes carrying illegal booze from Canada during Prohibition days landed on Lake Cranberry, and Capone's henchmen then shipped the liquor to Chicago by road in large, tarpaulin-covered trucks marked "Lumber."

A short distance north of Little Bohemia was the refuge of Ralph "Bottles" Capone, Al's brother, who was the director of liquor sales for the Chicago-based crime empire. Ralph was especially fond of the nearby town of Mercer, known as "The Loon Capital of the World." Many persons in that resort community had warm feelings for Bottles. A Mercer realtor called him "a fine human being."[1]

At that time, the Capone brothers were raking in perhaps $300 million per year from bootlegging, prostitution, extortion rackets and slot machines, while protecting their kingdom against infringement by ordering countless murders of rival gangsters and others.

In north Wisconsin, however, there were stories of Bottles Capone helping out with Mercer family mortgage problems during the Great Depression, donating to the needy, and even being active in the local Lions Club. What Ralph Capone may have been doing in Chicago was given little, if any thought by many of the locals.[2]

Knowing of the region's reputation as a hospitable place for hard-working outlaws to relax and plot new jobs, John Dillinger checked in at Little Bohemia on April 19, 1934. With him was most of his pack: Baby Face Nelson, Homer Van Meter, Tommy Carroll, Three-Fingered Jack Hamilton, and Pat Reilly, along with Nelson's wife Helen and two other women.

After Melvin Purvis and the other G-Men landed at the Rhinelander airport on April 22, he spotted his tipster Robert Voss, who was wearing a white handkerchief as instructed. Voss told Purvis that his brother-in-law, Emil Wanatka, owned the Little Bohemia Lodge and that Wanatka, his wife, their eight-year-old son, and two employees feared for their lives. A day earlier, Voss said, Wanatka had scrawled a note telling of the Dillinger gang's presence, placed it in a pack of cigarettes, and slipped the pack to Voss when he happened to visit the lodge.

An agent was sent with Voss to his home, about two miles from Little Bohemia, with instructions to wait there. A few minutes later, while Purvis and his men were unloading weapons and gear from the three airplanes, Voss ran up and called out excitedly, "I just met my wife on the road. She's learned that the gang has changed their plans and that they're leaving tonight after supper!"

It was then about 6:30 P.M. and dusk was settling over the north woods of Wisconsin, painting the thick clumps of trees with shades of purple. Dillinger and his henchmen no doubt were eating supper at the moment and then would be gone, Purvis reflected. The 16 G-Men and their weapons and equipment sill had 50 miles to go over back roads—and there were no automobiles available to get them to Little Bohemia.

Purvis had hoped to reach the lodge in time to reconnoiter the terrain before surrounding the gang's hideout in a systematic manner to assure maximum success in bagging Dillinger and his cronies. However, time was in short supply.

Purvis caught a ride from the airport into nearby Rhinelander, commandeered five automobiles (much to the howls of the owners), raced back to the airport, told the 16 agents to climb into the vehicles, and drove off for Little Bohemia. Two of the cars were so dilapidated that they soon began to chug and cough.

It was a ride that none of the FBI agents would ever forget. Packed into the automobiles around them were rifles, Tommy guns, tear-gas canisters, large amounts of ammunition, and other accoutrements of battle. Each man was wearing a bullet-proof vest, an ordeal in itself since the garment weighed 24 pounds and restricted normal breathing. The roads were horrible, narrow and twisting. The night was black, and a light April snowfall was smearing the windshields, making it difficult for the drivers to see the road.

Before the tiny convoy was halfway to Little Bohemia, two of the motorized relics broke down, and their seven occupants had to climb onto the running boards of the three remaining cars. Holding on for dear life with bone-cold hands, the outside riders were pelted in the face with freezing snow as the three cars sped through the night.

A half-mile from Little Bohemia, the caravan halted and headlights were extinguished. The G-Men got out of and off of the cars, stamped their numb feet to restore circulation, blew hot breaths onto their hands, and checked the mechanisms of their weapons.

Then everyone got back into and onto the automobiles and, in total blackout, the convoy proceeded at a snail's pace to the driveway leading from the road for 400 yards to the lodge. Again the feds dismounted. Peering through the timber they could detect the glowing lights of the lodge, a structure built of rustic logs. Inside was a bar, a popular place for guests and residents in the region. On either side of the lodge were several small cabins for guests.

Whispered orders were given, and the G-Men began to steal through the inky-black woods to take up assigned positions to the front and to either side of Little Bohemia. Spider Lake to the rear would probably prevent flight in that direction. Melvin Purvis's plan was to ring the lodge before calling on the Dillinger pack to surrender.[3]

None of the grim agents really expected the band of desperadoes to emerge with their arms in the air. Each agent recalled the warning of hard-bitten Ed Shouse, who had escaped from the Michigan City prison the previous year and belonged to the Dillinger gang until defecting earlier in 1934. Shouse, captured in Peoria, Illinois, after Eugene Teague of the state police was killed in a shoot-out, had told officers that the Dillinger gang intended to "spread death rather than be captured."

Shouse added, "If you policemen are married with families, I warn you to be careful about trying to take those boys. They'll shoot it out to the last bullet, and they have plenty of guns and bullets!"[4]

Before the FBI agents reached their assigned positions, dogs outside the lodge let loose with an incessant and prolonged crescendo of barking and howling, an enormous racket which, in the words of one G-Man, "could wake up the dead in a cemetery five miles away."

Through the woods, a few agents at the driveway entrance saw that the barking of the canine sentinels had touched off a commotion. Five men inside the lodge hurried out the front door. Two of them promptly dashed back inside, and the other three scrambled into a Ford V–8 coupe.

The men at the driveway entrance shouted at the top of their lungs that they were federal officers. Either not hearing or choosing to ignore the warning, the three men in the Ford, with headlights blazing, charged down the long driveway. Three G-Men yelled, "Halt!" several times, and when the car continued to bear down on them, they opened fire. Riddled with bullets, the vehicle lurched to a halt.

One figure in the Ford jumped out and ran into the woods, another was hit by four bullets and the third, killed instantly, slumped over the steering wheel.

It had been a tragic mistake: the three men were not members of the Dillinger pack, but rather they were locals who had come to Little Bohemia to drink beer.

Meantime, FBI men picking their way through the thick woods to take up positions on the right were slowed when they became entangled in two barbed-wire fences. On the left, other G-Men were delayed when they stumbled into a drainage ditch.

Suddenly, a withering fusillade of gunfire erupted from the upper floors of the lodge, and the FBI men returned the fire. The noise was ear-splitting. Bullets hissed like angry bees through the woods, cutting off branches that dropped on the heads of the agents who were using the larger trees for cover. Two agents were wounded.

After the deafening racket continued for several minutes, shooting abruptly ceased. An eerie stillness hovered over Little Bohemia. At the time, the G-Men were unaware of the reason for the calm: Dillinger and his men were climbing out of rear windows on the second floor and they escaped before all the agents were in place.

As silence continued to reign, the FBI men shouted repeatedly for those inside to come out with hands raised. Finally, three men filed through the front door-way. They were Emil Wanatka (the owner) and two waiters, all of whom had taken refuge in the basement when the gun battle broke out.

Wanatka, badly frightened and shivering from the cold, told Melvin Purvis that the Dillinger gang was still inside the lodge. (Actually, they had already fled.)

Earlier, Purvis had sent two agents, J. C. "Jay" Newman and W. Carter Baum, to the nearby home of Alvin Koerner to telephone the Rhinelander airport with instructions for other FBI men who had flown in to reinforce the group at Little Bohemia.

Carter Baum was 29 years old, popular with his fellow agents, and known for his devotion to duty and high ideals. Always cheerful, Baum loved to engage in sports, with handball being his favorite. He was a loving family man and the father of two small children.

On reaching the Koerner home, Carter Baum, Jay Newman and a local con-stable, Carl Christensen, saw a car with three occupants parked in front.

"Do you know whose Chevrolet that is?" Baum asked the constable.

"It's okay," Christensen replied. "It belongs to Mr. Koerner."

Braking their automobile, the three lawmen stepped out and walked toward the Koerner vehicle, unaware that the Dillinger gang had escaped the trap at Little Bohemia. Suddenly, Baby Face Nelson, a pistol in each hand, leaped from behind the Koerner car and opened fire on the unsuspecting officers. Baum was hit in the head by a bullet and crumpled like a rag-doll to the snow-covered ground, dying instantly. Jay Newman was also hit in the head and fell, and Constable Christensen was singed by a slug.

Nelson ran to the FBI men's car, jumped in, and roared off into the blackness. Agent Newman, bleeding profusely and eyes blurred, struggled to his knees and emptied his automatic pistol at the fleeing vehicle, but his bullets missed the target. Then Newman collapsed into unconsciousness.

Jay Newman and Carl Christensen were rushed to the nearest hospital, which was a considerable distance away in Ironwood, Michigan. There they joined other FBI men who had been wounded in the shootout at the lodge.

Later, the shaken Alvin Koerner told agents that Baby Face Nelson had bolted into his house, demanded his car keys, bundled three locals into the vehicle as hostages, and was about to drive away when Baum, Newman, and Christensen drove up.

In the meantime, J. Edgar Hoover had been pacing the floor at FBI headquarters in Washington, D.C. From an agent who had been posted at a telephone known to locals as the Central, a short distance from Little Bohemia, Hoover had been receiving an ongoing play-by-play report of the siege.

Shortly before dawn, while the bone-chilled, hungry, and weary G-Men remained at their posts around Little Bohemia, not knowing that their prey had escaped, Pat Reilly, a minor member of the Dillinger gang, was driving toward the lodge. Beside him in the Buick sedan was Pat Cherington, a nightclub dancer and entertainer. Two days earlier, Reilly, a former batboy for the Minneapolis Millers professional baseball team, had been sent to St. Paul to fetch more ammunition.

Reilly turned into the lodge driveway and halted abruptly, apparently sensing a trap. Three G-men sprinted toward the car and shouted for the occupants to get out with their hands in the air. Swiftly, Reilly backed the car, spun it around, and raced off with FBI bullets riddling the vehicle. Pat Cherington was cut on the forehead by flying glass splinters, but Reilly was not hit. A few miles down the road, the automobile broke down, and the couple spent the remainder of the night and after daylight tramping through the frigid woods.[5]

Meanwhile, two miles from Little Bohemia, John Dillinger, Three-Fingered Jack Hamilton, and Homer Van Meter burst into Ed Mitchell's Rest Lake Resort. Tearing the telephone from the wall, the outlaws threatened to kill Mitchell and grabbed Robert Johnson, a guest at the resort, forcing him to drive them in his Ford for 35 miles to Park Falls. There they released Johnson and continued their flight in his automobile.

At dawn, the G-Men fired tear-gas shells through the windows of the Little Bohemia lodge, then started to storm the building. Moments later, the trembling voice of a woman cried out, "We'll come out if you'll stop firing!"

Three women emerged, one of them being the wife of Baby Face Nelson.[6]

Then the agents barged into the lodge, now pock-marked with bullet holes, and conducted a room-by-room search. Melvin Purvis and his men were chagrined. Not a single gang member was flushed out.[7]

When word of the ill-fated raid spread, the FBI—Melvin Purvis in particular—was the target of heavy criticism. Liberal members of Congress and a few newspapers were leading the charge. One blaring headline screamed: "DEMAND PURVIS QUIT IN DILLINGER FIASCO."

Purvis, a slightly built South Carolinian, offered to submit his resignation, but J. Edgar Hoover rejected the proposal. Had the Director thrown the beleaguered Purvis to the wolves, FBI morale would have plunged to the depths.

While John Dillinger and his desperadoes had been featured in newspaper headlines for many weeks, Clyde Barrow, the misfit, and his partner, Bonnie Parker, were continuing their murderous escapades in the South.

On April 1, 1934, two young Texas highway patrolmen pulled over the couple's car for a routine inspection. As the officers approached on foot, a hail of bullets came from the car. Neither patrolman had a chance to draw his weapon before both went down, seriously wounded.

Five days later, at Miami, Oklahoma, Barrow and Parker were halted by suspicious Constable Cal Campbell. Again a burst of gunfire, and the constable's head was nearly blown off.

All the while, a dragnet had been closing in on Clyde and Bonnie. An FBI agent learned that the couple, along with a few members of the Henry Methvin clan, had flung a wild party at Black Lake, near Ruston, Louisiana, on the night of May 21. Methvin had escaped earlier in 1934 from the Waldo, Texas, prison, when he gunned down two guards with a pistol smuggled to him by Bonnie and Clyde.

The G-Man also learned that Barrow and Parker planned to return to the Black Lake locale in two days. So a posse of lawmen, led by former Texas Ranger Frank Hamer, quickly made plans to intercept the couple.

Frank Hamer was the most legendary Texas Ranger of the twentieth century, one who would have fit the mold 60 years earlier when shootouts with the bad guys were an almost daily occurrence. Born in 1884, Hamer's career began when portions of the West were still wild, complete with cattle rustlers, horse thieves, bank robbers on horseback, and "walkdowns" in dusty cowtown streets.

Although only 21 years of age when he joined the famed Texas Rangers in 1906, Frank Hamer was promptly assigned to clean up a few of the rough, dirty, boisterous, crime- and vice-laden Texas towns that had sprouted during the turn of the century oil booms. Those jerry-built communities were loaded with gunmen, card sharks, con men, loose women, and an array of other disreputable characters.

Over the years, Hamer gained a reputation for tracking down bank robbers. Once he surprised three men while they were pulling a heist at a bank, and killed two robbers when they tried to shoot their way out. Although wounded in the leg, the tall, lean, young Ranger marched the surviving robber down the middle of the main street and locked him in a jail cell.

Frank Hamer's scintillating career spanned both the horse-borne, six-shooter era of the early 1900s and the speeding, high-powered automobiles and chattering Tommy guns of the 1930s. Now, on the trail of Clyde and Bonnie at age 49, Hamer was determined to bring them to justice, for the couple had murdered several police officers, a few of whom had been his friends.

On the morning of May 23, 1934, Hamer and six other lawmen crouched behind bushes and trees by the side of a road eight miles from Gibsland, Louisiana. From information obtained by the G-Man, they knew precisely the description of the car that Clyde and Bonnie would be driving—a gray Ford sedan. Shortly after 9:00 A.M., the waiting officers heard the faint purr of an approaching engine, and moments later, a gray Ford rounded a curve and headed toward the trap.

When the car was less than 50 yards away, deafening bursts of gunfire erupted from the roadside foliage. Bonnie and Clyde, each struck by some 20 bullets, died instantly.

Inspecting the bullet-riddled Ford and the mutilated bodies, one law officer remarked grimly, "Well, those who live by the sword, die by the sword."

Ranger Frank Hamer drove to Gibsville and telephoned a terse report to his headquarters: "There wasn't much to it. They just drove into the wrong place at the right time. They had plenty of guns in the car, but didn't have a chance to use them."[8]

The bodies of Clyde Barrow and Bonnie Parker were taken to Dallas for separate burials. Many of the flowers at their funerals came from admiring strangers. Onlookers pilfered the gladioli, roses, and peonies from the coffins. At the cemetery, the crush of morbid humanity was such that Clyde's sister could get no closer than 50 feet to his grave.[9]

On May 18, 1934, President Roosevelt sat at his desk in the Oval Office in the White House, flanked by Attorney General Homer Cummings and FBI Director J. Edgar Hoover. While Movietone News and Pathé newsreel cameras were rolling and press photographers' flashbulbs were popping, Roosevelt signed into law six dramatic anticrime bills enacted two days earlier by the Senate, whose members had been getting heavy heat from constituents demanding that the FBI be granted increased authority to fight the nation's criminal army.

"Federal (Bureau of Investigation) agents are constantly facing machine-gun fire in the pursuit of gangsters," the President told the American people. "I ask citizens, individually and in organized groups, to recognize the facts and meet them with courage and determination."[10]

The tough new laws made it a federal offense to transport a kidnapped person from one state to another; to extort by means of telephone, telegraph, radio or oral message; to kill or assault an FBI agent; to transport stolen goods from one state to another; to rob federal banks; or to facilitate the escape of inmates from a federal penitentiary. Heavy penalties, including fines and imprisonment, were provided for violation of the new laws.

Most major newspapers hailed the new powers given to the Department of Justice. Editorialized the *St. Louis Post-Dispatch*:

The nation has waited with the patience of Job for this hour. In a determined Department of Justice backed by the resources of the national government, gangsters face an invincible foe.

Armed with a much heavier club, J. Edgar Hoover wasted no time in accelerating the war against the kidnappers and desperadoes. On June 1, two weeks after Roosevelt signed the anticrime bills, the Director sent for Agent Samuel P. Cowley, who was serving in the Washington headquarters as an aide to Harold Nathan, assistant director in charge of investigations.

Cowley was a husky, 34-year-old attorney from Utah who had served as a missionary in the Mormon Church before being accepted into the FBI. Hoover had a special assignment for Cowley: taking charge of the search for John Dillinger.

"Stay on Dillinger," the Director stressed, his iron jaw thrust out defiantly. "Go anywhere the trail takes you. Take (arrest) anyone whoever is remotely associated with his gang. Get Dillinger alive if you can, but protect yourself."[11]

In Washington, D.C., on June 7, President Roosevelt gave another boost to the war on America's criminals by signing a bill authorizing the Department of Justice to offer up to a $25,000 reward for the capture of criminals, such as John Dillinger and other "public enemies." The measure authorized smaller rewards for information leading to an arrest. In the midst of the Great Depression, Attorney General Cummings and J. Edgar Hoover hoped that money would talk.

That same day, more than 1,000 miles to the west, the Waterloo, Iowa, police department received a tip that John Dillinger's lieutenant, Tommy Carroll, was in town. Carroll had been one of the outlaws who escaped the FBI trap at Little Bohemia six weeks earlier.

A pair of Waterloo detectives spotted a man they thought was Carroll and a pretty young woman walking along a street. The lawmen tailed the couple to a point in front of the Waterloo police station, then called on the man to halt. Tommy Carroll spun around, tried to go for his weapon, and was shot five times by the detectives.

Carroll was taken to the hospital, but refused to admit his identity. "I've got 700 bucks on me," he said in a weak voice to officers. "Be sure the little girl gets it. She doesn't know what it's all about." An hour later, Tommy Carroll was dead at 33 years of age.[12]

At first, the gangster's woman refused to talk, but she finally gave her name. She said she was 21 years of age and originally from Aberdeen, South Dakota, and was Tommy Carroll's wife. She had been captured by the FBI at Little Bohemia, but had been turned loose by judicial authorities on her promise that she would have nothing more to do with known gangsters.

Meanwhile, FBI agent Sam Cowley, whom Hoover had designated to coordinate efforts to snare John Dillinger, set up his headquarters in Chicago, where he and Melvin Purvis planned their strategy. A squad of agents under Cowley worked with two East Chicago, Indiana, policemen, Sergeant Martin Zarkovich and Captain Timothy O'Neil, in tracking down the torrent of tips and rumors that poured in from jittery citizens.

Cowley's search convinced him that John Dillinger—now proclaimed to be Public Enemy Number 1 in newspaper headlines—was hiding out in Chicago. Reliable information indicated that he was recovering from a surgeon's efforts to disguise his facial features through plastic surgery.

Only later would the FBI learn of the circumstances surrounding Dillinger's medical operation, which had taken place on May 28, a month after he had escaped from Little Bohemia. Dr. Wilhelm Loeser (who was out on parole from a federal prison on a narcotics charge), Dr. Harold B. Cassidy, and James Probasco had been involved in the face-lifting job.

Loeser, who performed the operation, received a hefty $5,000 fee. He was assisted by Cassidy, who administered the anesthetic. Probasco, for a reputed $1,000 had permitted his house to be used for the surgery and Dillinger's convalescing period.

A mole was removed from the patient's forehead; a dimple deleted from his chin; two slices were taken from his cheeks near his ears, and an attempt was made to alter his nose.

In the middle of the operation, Dr. Loeser nearly lost his patient. Dillinger swallowed his tongue and his heart stopped beating. Through artificial respiration and powerful heart stimulants, he was resuscitated.

America's arch desperado was delighted with his new look. So he sold his sidekick, Homer Van Meter, on coming to Chicago from his St. Paul hideout to go under Dr. Loeser's knife. Van Meter's face job was performed on June 3.[13]

On the afternoon of July 21, 1934, Agent Melvin Purvis received a telephone call from Captain O'Neil and Sergeant Zarkovich, the East Chicago officers. In a guarded tone, they said they had some "hot information." A few hours later, Purvis and Sam Cowley huddled with the two policemen in a hotel room in downtown Chicago.

There the East Chicago officers unfolded a tale of intrigue. Anna Sage, the madam of a popular whorehouse in Gary, Indiana, an eastern suburb of Chicago, had gotten in touch with the two lawmen in an effort to cut a deal with the U.S. government. A middle-aged, dark-haired woman of fading beauty, Anna had come to the United States in 1914 from a small Romanian town. Now she was in big trouble. The U.S. Immigration and Naturalization Service wanted to deport her as an undesirable alien because of her profession.

Earlier in the month, a man calling himself Jack Lawrence had been in a Chicago diner and picked up Anna Sage's apartment roommate, blond Polly Hamilton. Polly, who had been one of Anna's working girls at the Gary brothel, brought her new friend to the apartment. Anna thought she recognized the man and soon realized that he was the notorious John Dillinger, whose picture she had seen countless times in newspapers and movie newsreels.

In the Chicago hotel powwow, the East Chicago officers said that Anna wanted to meet with the FBI, and a rendezvous was set for the same night. Purvis and Zarkovich drove to a prearranged point in west Chicago, parked along the curb, and extinguished the headlights. Tree limbs shadowed the car from the dim glow of a nearby street light. Cowley and O'Neil, trailing in a second car, parked a discreet distance to the rear.

At about 9:00 P.M., Purvis and Zarkovich heard the faint tap-tap-tap of a walking woman's high heels and moments later the dim figure came into view. Anna Sage strolled past the car and down the desolate street, seemingly to make certain that no trap had been set for her. Then she retraced her steps and scrambled into the back seat of the FBI automobile.

Purvis and Zarkovich drove to a secluded spot on Lake Michigan and stopped. Anna quickly told of her proposition: she would lead the FBI to John Dillinger in return for a substantial reward and for something being done to permit her to remain in the United States. Purvis promised her the reward, but pointed out that the FBI had no control over deportation proceedings. However, he pledged that her cooperation would be called to the attention of the Immigration and Naturalization Service.

Then Anna related her plan. She said that Polly, Dillinger, and she had gone to the Marbro Theater on Chicago's west side to see movies a few times, and that the threesome planned to go again soon. Dillinger had told her that he loved movies, especially gangster films, and that his favorite Hollywood actor was Douglas Fairbanks, Sr. Anna said she would notify the FBI when they were going to the theater. In order to be easily recognized by the lawmen, she would wear a bright red dress.

Early the next morning, Melvin Purvis and Samuel Cowley collected most of the Chicago agents in their nineteenth floor office and laid plans for capturing Public Enemy Number 1 at the Marbro Theater. Just before 5:00 P.M., while the confab was still in progress, the telephone jangled impatiently and Purvis picked up the instrument.

A whispered voice came over the wire: "He's here! We're going either to the Marbro or the Biograph!" Then a click and Anna Sage was gone.

Purvis and Cowley rushed agents to both the Marbro and the Biograph theaters to discreetly reconnoiter the entrances, exits, seating arrangements, adjoining alleys and streets, and other pertinent features. On their return, five G-Men were dispatched to each theater with instructions to stake out the premises and telephone back to the FBI office every five minutes.

Samuel Cowley would remain to take their calls and to coordinate overall operations. Purvis would lead one squad to the Biograph. Should Dillinger be spotted at one movie house, the agents at the other theater were to speed there.

20

High Drama Outside a Movie Theater

A stifling, humid night gripped Chicago. Patrons were streaming into the Biograph Theater for the first show, not only to see the movie *Manhattan Melodrama* starring a handsome Hollywood newcomer named Clark Gable, but also to take refuge in the air-cooled comfort.

G-Men Melvin Purvis and Ralph Brown were sitting in the front seat of their parked automobile about 50 feet south of the theater entrance. They faced forward, away from the ticket window. Neck-craning, as if to observe in all directions, could tip off John Dillinger.

At five-minute intervals, Brown left the car to telephone the FBI office from a nearby drugstore, advising Inspector Sam Cowley that he had nothing to report. Other FBI men took up positions at designated points. It was Sunday, July 22, 1934.

Twenty minutes passed. Thirty minutes. Forty. Forty-five. Where was Public Enemy Number 1? Had he gone to the Marbro?

Suddenly, the agents on the stake-out tensed. Three figures—a man with a woman at either side—were approaching along the sidewalk. All eyes were on the medium-sized man wearing dark glasses, a straw sailor hat, gray trousers, and a white shirt. The G-Men were relieved to see that he was not wearing a suit coat; that meant he could carry only one or two weapons.

Although Dillinger appeared to have undergone plastic surgery, he was promptly recognized by the lawmen. Anna Sage, chicly garbed in a bright red dress, and buxom Polly Hamilton casually studied the stills of Clark Gable (who played the role of a gangster who went to the electric chair at the end of *Manhattan Melodrama*) while Dillinger bought tickets.

Agent Ralph Brown telephoned Sam Cowley back at the FBI office, and the G-Men at the Marbro Theater were contacted and told to rush to the Biograph.

Cowley then called J. Edgar Hoover, who had been pacing the library of his modest Washington home, waiting for word of developments.

Hoover cautioned Cowley to have the agents wait outside and take Dillinger after he emerged, rather than to risk a gun battle inside the dark theater, which could result in a large number of movie-goers being killed or wounded.

The Director emphasized that the G-Men were not to unnecessarily endanger themselves, and if Dillinger tried to resist, each agent was "on his own." Then Cowley departed for the Biograph.

In the meantime, Melvin Purvis, nattily dressed in a straw sailor hat, single-breasted blue coat, white trousers, and white shoes, bought a ticket and entered the theater. Two pistols were tucked in his belt and concealed by his coat. Purvis hoped that there would be three empty seats behind America's arch desperado, so that G-Men could occupy them and, in unison, pounce on and overpower him.

It was so dark inside and the seats were so crowded that Purvis never spotted Dillinger, who munched on sunflower seeds as he watched Clark Gable perform.

Purvis returned outside to wait. He visited the agents on the stakeout, and informed them that the second show would let out at 10:30 P.M. Two East Chicago officers were stationed on the north side of the theater; two G-Men with Purvis on the south side. These were the five men selected to close in on Dillinger when he emerged.

Slowly, the seconds and minutes ticked past. A thin veil of tension hovered over the men on the stakeout. Melvin Purvis idled away the time by chatting with the ticket seller. Each lawman had his eyes on Purvis; when he lit a cigar, that would be the signal that a positive identification of Dillinger had been made. A wave of Purvis's hand was the sign to close in and capture the outlaw.

Minutes before the movie was to conclude, a Chicago Police Department squad car manned by two officers drove up and halted before the Biograph. The theater's employees, noticing the FBI agents loitering about the entrance for two hours, had grown suspicious that the box office was about to be robbed and had sent for the police. An agent quickly dashed to the police car and identified himself, and the Chicago officers rapidly departed.

Then the house lights went up and patrons began pouring out of the Biograph into the sultry night. Purvis scanned the faces. Suddenly, he felt a strange inner surge: walking directly toward him was John Dillinger, flanked by the two women. It seemed to Purvis that half the women and children in Chicago were around the outlaw. For a split-second, Dillinger's and Purvis' eyes locked, but America's most wanted fugitive walked on.

Purvis struck a match and lit the same cigar that he had been chewing on nervously for more than two hours. It was the preliminary signal. Moments later, when the crowd had thinned, the G-Man gave the signal to close in.

Glancing up the street, Purvis's heart skipped a beat. The two East Chicago policemen were talking with a passerby and did not see his hand wave. Purvis took a few steps and repeated the sign. Still the pair of policemen did not see it. Then, from out of the shadows, two G-Men, who had not been designated as part of the five-man arrest force, came to the rescue by cutting off any escape in that direction.

Purvis got in step with Dillinger, behind him and a few feet to the left. In his customary squeaky voice, the G-Man called out, "Stick 'em up, Johnny! We've got you covered!"

Dillinger's reply was to pull a Colt automatic from his trouser pocket and bolt toward an alley. Agents Herman E. Hollis, Clarence O. Hurt, and Charles B. Winstead, all expert marksmen, fired a total of five shots. Three of them struck the desperado; he went down with his head in the alley and his feet on the sidewalk.[1]

Melvin Purvis and the other agents gathered around the wounded man, and one took the pistol from his outstretched hand. Purvis leaned over the blood-stained figure.

"Johnny, can you hear me?"

There was no reply.

An ambulance was called and rushed Dillinger to the Alexian Brothers Hospital, where he was pronounced dead at 10:51 P.M. The greatest manhunt in American history to that time was over.

Once more the FBI got its man. But the agents had hoped to take Dillinger alive, for even the most hardened criminals talk eventually, and when they talk, they often aid lawmen in solving many crimes. By drawing his weapon, Dillinger had forced the issue.

"Protect yourselves at all times!" had been J. Edgar Hoover's instructions.

Word spread with lightning speed that John Dillinger had been killed, and a surging, jostling pack of humanity filled the street in front and to each side of the Biograph. Traffic was blocked. Horns honked. People were shouting to one another. G-Men looked on in amazement when several women, some of them crying, kneeled and dipped their handkerchiefs in the arch-desperado's blood.[2]

A newspaper account the next day mentioned that a bit of Dillinger's blood had come onto the cuff of Melvin Purvis's white trousers as he was kneeling over the outlaw. A few days later, a Chicago man came to the local FBI office and said he would pay $50 for the trousers Purvis had worn, wanting them as a souvenir. The morbid individual received neither the pants nor a courteous response.[3]

Shortly after Dillinger had been brought down, Inspector Sam Cowley received a letter from J. Edgar Hoover. It read, in part:

> I want to write and to repeat to you my expression of commendation and pleasure upon the excellent results you attained. . . . Your persistence, dedication and energy have made it possible to attain this success, and I am proud and grateful to you.

Blaring headlines across the nation told of the drama outside the Biograph Theater. Hundreds of editorials praised the FBI and the G-Men directly involved.

Sackfuls of mail and telegrams poured in from citizens in the United States and from foreign countries. Most of the communications were highly laudatory.

A few of the letters and telegrams condemned the FBI for "ambushing" and killing John Dillinger. Some threatened revenge against Purvis and his G-Men. The latter communications were dismissed as the bleatings of crackpots.

A handful of editorial writers, safely ensconced in their ivory towers, heaped abuse on the FBI. A Virginia newspaper declared: "Any brave man would have walked down the aisle and arrested Dillinger. . . . Why were so many cowards afraid of one man? The answer is that the (FBI) agents are mostly cowards."

When two other desperadoes resisted arrest and were gunned down by FBI agents, a woman wrote a letter that was published in a Baltimore newspaper:

> Those poor dear boys should have been detained and preached to. If the G-Men had told them to go and sin no more, that would be true Christian example.

Such critical letters and editorials, although few in number, irritated J. Edgar Hoover, who knew his agents had put their lives on the line in shooting it out with hardened criminals. "Dillinger was just a yellow rat!" the Director told the press. "And the country may consider itself fortunate to be rid of him!"[4]

After a routine inquest by the Cook County coroner, John Dillinger's body was put on display at the Chicago morgue, and thousands of persons—mainly women—filed past in a line a mile long. Inching ahead at a snail's pace, most of the people were gripped by morbid curiosity. However, some women were weeping. Barkers passed back and forth along the line, hawking innovative souvenirs—swatches of white cloth with Dillinger's "original, fully guaranteed" blood on them.[5]

John Dillinger was buried in the same Indianapolis cemetery that had been the final resting place for such notable Hoosiers as President Benjamin Harrison, a vice president, two governors, three U.S. senators and poet James Whitcomb Riley. Unlike the others, Dillinger's grave was reinforced with iron and cement to thwart ghouls.[6]

A week after the desperado was buried, his father, John Dillinger, Sr., left his Indiana farm to go on a vaudeville tour of the nation, taking along his daughter and son-in-law. Handbills drawing attention to their show stated:

> Hear from their own lips incidents in the life of the late John Dillinger, Jr., and of his last visits to the home of his kindly father, when the entire nation was searching for him.

When Dillinger's girlfriend, Billie Frechette, was released from the Federal Detention Center at Milan, Michigan after serving a year for harboring a criminal, she joined a touring carnival sideshow. Throngs shoe-horned into her tent to hear Billie tell first-hand of her life with Public Enemy Number 1. Among the revelations that caused her audiences to react with awe: "I think John liked bread and gravy better than any other food."[7]

In late 1934, a *Literary Digest* poll to pick the outstanding figures in the world resulted in 31-year-old G-Man Melvin Purvis coming in eighth, ahead of such renowned persons as Secretary of Labor Francis Perkins (America's first woman cabinet member) and Rear Admiral Richard E. Byrd (the first man to fly over both North and South Poles). Franklin D. Roosevelt finished first in the poll.

Ironically, in view of the enormous favorable publicity that engulfed the FBI, the Dillinger episode seemed to intensify the friction that had been simmering for months between Purvis and his boss, J. Edgar Hoover. Many Bureau veterans felt that SAC (special agent in charge) was the best job in the FBI. Agents for 15 or 20 years doggedly pursued that goal, for a SAC is a ruler of his own kingdom, far removed from daily scrutiny by the Washington headquarters. Even though he is guided by countless rules and regulations prevailing at any given time, the SAC can mold a field office according to his own style, personality, and views on how the workload can best be handled.

The SAC can choose to be a tyrant, frightening his agents into compliance, or take on the role of teacher, advisor, and mentor to gain maximum efficiency and production from his men—or perhaps a little of both. Through the use of his discretionary fund he is free to decide which informants will be cultivated. In short, the SAC is the one who directly controls people and priorities.

There were many in the Bureau who privately expressed the view that Melvin Purvis's collision course with the Director had resulted from a certain amount of free-wheeling on the Chicago SAC's part. Of all the regional offices of the FBI, the Chicago office was the only one that did not begin its press release with "J. Edgar Hoover announced . . . " Melvin Purvis's name was substituted for Hoover's in the releases.

As much as Purvis admired Inspector Samuel Cowley and respected his courage and dedication, he allegedly had been slightly miffed that the Director singled out Cowley for a letter of praise for bringing John Dillinger's career to an end. Purvis had been on the desperado's trail for months, and had personally led the squad that got the job done, while Cowley had been assigned to the search only seven weeks before the Biograph affair.[8]

What's more, Purvis was said to believe that J. Edgar Hoover had been behind the decision by Attorney General Homer Cummings to refuse Bureau help in filming a Hollywood movie about Purvis's seven-year career with the FBI. For his part, the Director vigorously denied that there was or ever had been a rift between the two strong-willed men.

Purvis, close associates would indicate, was also annoyed about the fate of Anna Sage, the whorehouse madam who had led the FBI to John Dillinger. Although she was paid $5,000 out of funds Congress had allotted for such purposes, she was deported by the U.S. government to her native Romania, from which she had left 20 years earlier.[9]

In their clandestine rendezvous with Anna Sage on the Lake Michigan waterfront, Purvis had been scrupulously careful to point out that the Bureau had no direct control over deportation proceedings, but that they would contact the right people and tell of her cooperation. After Anna had been put on a boat heading eastward, Purvis was said to have felt that Director Hoover had not done all that he could to avoid her deportation.[10]

A few months after the episode at Chicago's Biograph Theater, visitors waiting in the reception room to see J. Edgar Hoover were greeted by a startling white plaster facsimile of John Dillinger's death mask. From under the glass of an exhibit case, it stared, empty-eyed—a compelling symbol of the invincibility of the FBI. There were numerous other exhibits in the anteroom, but this one, resembling a prized scalp, was the closest to the Director's door.

Grouped around Dillinger's mask were the straw hat the most-wanted outlaw had been wearing when killed, a soiled snapshot of a woman found in his pocket, a cigar he had been carrying in his shirt pocket, still in its cellophane, and the silver-rimmed glasses he was wearing to enhance his disguise, one of the lens rims cracked by a bullet. The Dillinger death mask exhibit would remain in place for 40 years.

Elsewhere in the nation during the second week of August 1934, the relatives of a young St. Paul woman became suspicious of a man with whom she had started to keep company. Although he said he was a waiter, Henry Adams (as he called himself) was constantly flashing large rolls of currency. St. Paul police were informed.

Chief of Police Frank Cullen took a personal interest in the report when he learned that the physical description of Henry Adams—five feet, 11 inches tall, blue eyes, thin, and about 27 years of age—matched that of John Dillinger's longtime partner in crime, Homer Van Meter.

Chief Cullen put detectives on Henry Adams's tail and their investigations convinced the chief that Adams was actually Van Meter, who had escaped with Dillinger from the FBI trap at Little Bohemia. On August 23, Cullen and three detectives, armed with automatic rifles and Tommy guns, concealed themselves near the front of Van Meter's rented house at Marion and University Avenues, only three blocks from the imposing Minnesota capitol.

When the fugitive appeared and walked toward the front door, the officers leaped out and ordered him to surrender. In reply, Van Meter pulled out a pistol and fired twice. Cullen and his men started shooting as Van Meter ran across the street and dashed down an alley. Hard on the fugitive's heels was Detective Thomas Brown, who loosed a burst of fire with an automatic rifle. Struck by seven bullets, Van Meter staggered for a few steps, then sprawled face downward and died a few minutes later.[11]

Officers inspecting Van Meter's body found that, like Dillinger, he had had his face lifted and his hair, naturally chestnut, dyed black. A tattoo on his forearm depicting an anchor with the word ''Hope'' had been blanked out by the surgeon to leave merely a dark blotch on the skin. In Van Meter's pockets was $938 in currency.[12]

A month after Homer Van Meter was killed, two other members of Dillinger's gang, Handsome Harry Pierpont and Fat Charley Makley, were confined to Death Row at the Ohio State Penitentiary. Time was drawing near for their executions for the murder of Lima, Ohio, Sheriff Jess Sarber the previous October.

Thirty-two-year-old Pierpont was an unusual character. He could, and did, kill cold-bloodedly, yet he gave way to tears under stress or emotion. When the death sentence had been passed on him he heard the pronouncement with no show of emotion. Then he kissed his mother while being taken back to prison and tears coursed down his face.

Handsome Harry, ensconced on Death Row, often taunted guards. ''I'll never fry in that (electric) chair!'' he boasted. No doubt he was convinced that John Dillinger would spring him in a daring breakout. Then, on the night that Dillinger was killed, a mysterious car circled the prison three times and honked sharply four times at intervals. This was a prearranged code, and told Pierpont and Makley that Dillinger was dead.

''They got John,'' Pierpont said. ''I'd be willing to trade places with him tonight.'' Harry Pierpont had been depressed for several weeks—and not just because of his pending electrocution. Amanda Thomas, daughter of the warden and postmistress at the prison, noted that Pierpont, who usually penned a letter to his sweetheart Mary Kinder nearly every day, suddenly stopped writing. Mary, her intercepted letters indicated, was no longer interested in a man who would soon be dead—she had a new boyfriend on the outside.

Pierpont's most recent letter to Mary declared: ''I wish it was over.''

On the morning of September 22—two months after John Dillinger had been gunned down while fleeing—Ohio penitentiary guard O. E. Slagle was putting a meal into Harry Pierpont's cell. As Slagle turned away to leave, the convict hit him a staggering blow with his fist, knocking the guard to the floor.

''Give me the goddamned key!'' Pierpont snarled.

Sprawled on the floor in a daze, Slagle refused to obey. Pierpont pulled the guard to his feet, smashed him again in the face, and took the key.

Outside his cell, Pierpont produced a pistol, rushed to Makley's cage, and unlocked his door. Makley, too, had a pistol. Actually, both weapons were carved of soap. The two convicts hoped to gain freedom by a ploy similar to the wooden-gun escapade in which John Dillinger had fled from the ''escape-proof'' jail at Crown Point, Indiana.

From a distance of five or six feet, the soap guns looked realistic. They were modeled after automatic pistols, and the makers had even put holes at the ends of the muzzles to resemble the bores of real automatics. Wooden pieces of a jigsaw puzzle and small bits of tin were used to reinforce the stocks. Tin foil from cigarette packages gave the soap weapons their steel gray appearance.

Pierpont and Makley opened all the cells and turned loose the other eight men on Death Row, then backed Slagle and another guard toward a steel door, behind which a third guard was watching events through a peephole. Desperate, the convicts broke a big table into pieces and tried to smash their way through the door.

Suddenly, at 10:32 A.M., alarm bells clanged throughout the large prison—the signal that a breakout was in progress. Eight members of the riot squad, always held ready in the main guard room, rushed to the L block where they found Pierpont and Makley leading an assault on the steel door. Armed with rifles, the riot squad lined up, the door was flung open and, as Pierpont and Makley poked their realistic looking soap weapons toward them, the riot squad opened fire.

Pierpont and Makley crumpled to the floor. One bullet entered Fat Charley's side, took a downward course, and came out on the left side. Another slug remained in his body. Pierpont was hit by a pellet, which came out his back, partially paralyzing one leg.

The two wounded convicts were taken to the prison hospital, where Fat Charley died less than an hour later. Pierpont was found to be not seriously wounded, and five hours after the confrontation he was returned to his cell on Death Row.

That night, Handsome Harry broke down and cried, prison physician Dr. George Keil told the press. "He said he wants to die," Keil added.

Shortly before midnight on October 16, Pierpont, dressed in a blue serge prison suit and wearing a light blue dress shirt, was flanked by two guards as he walked toward the electric chair at the Ohio penitentiary. He kissed a crucifix and handed it to a Catholic priest just before he sat down. His eyes were bloodshot, showing the effects of numerous crying spells. At 12:09 A.M., Pierpont was strapped to the chair and pronounced dead at 12:14 A.M.

Meanwhile, far to the east, two years, six months and 14 days after two-year-old, golden-haired Charles Lindbergh, Jr., had been kidnapped from the family's Sourland Mountain mansion in New Jersey and brutally murdered, investigators finally got their first big break in the baffling case. The hunt for the kidnapper of the son of famed aviator Charles A. Lindbergh and his wife Anne had been one of the most intense in U.S. history, and was a cooperative effort between the FBI, the New Jersey State Police, and the New York City Police Department.

On September 15, 1934, a motorist purchased five gallons of gasoline at a filling station in the fringes of the Bronx, one of New York City's five boroughs, and paid with a ten-dollar gold certificate. After giving the driver his change, the attendant scribbled on the bill the license number of the car—4U–13–41. He had been suspicious because these notes had been called in by the federal government in April 1933, when the United States went off the gold standard.

Three days later, a teller at the Corn Exchange Bank noticed the license number written on the bill and checked the note against the list of Lindbergh ransom serial numbers that the FBI had sent to thousands of banks and other business firms. The serial number on this particular bill was on the list. The FBI was notified of the find, and a check with the State Motor Vehicle License Bureau disclosed that New York plate 4U–13–41 had been issued to Bruno Richard Hauptmann, of 1279 East 22nd Street in the Bronx.

Hauptmann, a carpenter, was promptly arrested and a 20-dollar ransom gold certificate was found in his pocket. Incriminating evidence against Hauptmann began to pile up. Investigators discovered another $13,000 of the Lindbergh ransom money stashed in his garage. Dr. John Condon, the Lindbergh family's go-between with the kidnapper, identified Hauptmann as the "Cemetery John" to whom he had paid the $50,000 ransom.

Mrs. Cecilia Barr, a ticket agent at Loew's Sheridan Square Theater, who had sold a ticket to a movie patron in November 1933, identified Hauptmann as the man who had paid for it with one of the Lindbergh bills. John Perone, a taxi driver, picked the suspect out of a lineup as the Cemetery John he had taken to a meeting with Dr. Condon. An elderly man fighting advanced stages of rheumatism, Amandus Hochmuth, identified Hauptmann as the man he had seen driving close to Sourland Mountain at the time of the kidnapping. The suspect's car had a long ladder strapped to its side, Hochmuth said.

FBI investigators, working with New Jersey and New York City officers, matched the wood of the ladder the kidnapper had left at the Lindbergh mansion to a missing board in Hauptmann's attic. Also they discovered the telephone number of go-between Dr. Condon written on a closet wall in the suspect's home in the Bronx.

Bruno Hauptmann, a 36-year-old native of Germany, vehemently claimed that he was being framed. He was merely keeping the ransom money for a fellow German, Isidore Fisch, who had returned to the Old Country for a visit in 1933, and died there.

As damning evidence against the suspect was made public, Americans were incensed. When Mrs. Anna Hauptmann, the accused's wife, left a New York City police station after being questioned, a screaming mob of people closed in on her. Later she told reporters:

> I thought they were going to kill me. The detective who was with me sheltered me and rushed me to a nearby restaurant. The maddened mob, continuing to shout, "There she is!" followed me to the door of the restaurant and tried to batter their way to lay their hands on me. . . . The entire world seems to have gone crazy.[13]

Bruno Hauptmann's kidnapping trial was held in January 1935 in Flemington, New Jersey. A carnival atmosphere prevailed. Large crowds stayed up all night in the near-freezing weather to try to get one of the few seats available in the courtroom. Hollywood movie stars and Manhattan society matrons joined the throngs in shoving and pushing matches. Vendors passed up and down the long lines of hopeful spectators to what the press had billed ''the trial of the century,'' and hawked their morbid ''souvenirs.'' These included dolls with golden hair dressed to look like the murdered Lindbergh child and miniature replicas of the makeshift ladder used in the kidnapping.

Hordes of press and newsreel cameramen were frantically snapping pictures and grinding out film footage of the waiting crowds. Men and women, beaming broadly, held up their miniature Lindbergh dolls for the photographers.

After a sensational trial that grabbed the world spotlight, Bruno Hauptmann was found guilty and sentenced to die in the electric chair. New Jersey Governor Harold Hoffman granted a stay of execution to permit authorities to hear new evidence that the convicted man claimed would prove his innocence. When none was produced, the kidnapper/murderer was scheduled to be executed on April 3, 1936.

A bizarre aspect of the windup of the four-year Lindbergh abduction case was when Gabriel Heatter, a widely known radio newscaster and commentator, conducted an electronic death watch at the New Jersey State Prison. During the final four hours, Heatter gave millions of radio listeners a minute-to-minute play-by-play of events, including Hauptmann's electrocution in the little green room.[14]

Long before Hauptmann's execution, Charles and Anne Lindbergh had sailed from the United States to make their home in England. With them was their three-year-old son, John, who had been born three months after Charles A. Lindbergh, Jr., was murdered. The Lindbergh's decision to leave their homeland came after they received several letters threatening to kidnap their new son.

21

Violent Confrontations

Residents in a middle-class neighborhood of Buffalo, New York, were relieved to awaken on the morning of October 20, 1934, and discover that the two strange-acting couples cooped up in a single apartment unit for the past 15 months had left town. Neighbors knew them as Mr. and Mrs. Eddie Brennan and Mr. and Mrs. George Sanders, but the FBI and other enforcement officers across America knew them as Pretty Boy Floyd, Adam Richetti, and their girl-friends, Rose and Beulah Baird.

Floyd and Richetti were high on the FBI's most wanted list. Among numerous other crimes of violence they were sought as the gunmen in the Kansas City Massacre and for murdering two state policemen in Columbia, Missouri.

Twelve hours after slipping out of Buffalo at 3:00 A.M. under cover of a thick fog, Floyd was at the wheel of a new Ford V–8 sedan that had been bought for a trip back to the Cookson Hills, the outlaw haven in northeastern Oklahoma. Near Wellsville, Ohio, Pretty Boy lost control of the car. It skidded into a ditch and was damaged when it struck a telephone pole.

Floyd and Richetti removed their small arsenal from the Ford, sent Beulah and Rose into Wellsville to get the car repaired, and walked into the edge of the woods to await the women's return. A short time later, Alonzo Israel, a local, drove past and grew suspicious of the two strangers he glimpsed loitering in the woods.

Israel informed Wellsville Chief of Police John W. Fultz, who, with two of his officers, went to the scene to investigate. Nearing the woods on foot, Fultz shouted at Floyd and Richetti to come out with their hands raised. Moments later, a fusillade of bullets raked the officers, who returned the fire. Richetti barricaded himself in a farmhouse and Floyd got into an advantageous position on a knoll.

Between bursts in the gun battle, Chief Fultz and his men heard Pretty Boy shout to his partner: "Kill the bastards!"[1]

As the shootout raged, Fultz's ankle was grazed by a bullet, and one of his officers was hit in the shoulder. Floyd's Tommy gun jammed, and he pitched it aside and continued blazing away with a pistol.

After expending his ammunition, Richetti came out of the farmhouse with his hands in the air and was collared by the Wellsville policemen. Floyd fled back through the woods, and a short time later he reached a road and waved down a Model T Ford driven by George McMullen. Unaware of the gun battle or Pretty Boy's identity, McMullen accepted ten dollars to drive Floyd to a town about 15 miles away.

Soon the driver became suspicious of his jittery passenger, and when about halfway to their destination, McMullen pulled the choke on his Tin Lizzy (as the Model T's were known) and the engine flooded. He told Pretty Boy that the car was out of gas.

Floyd left the stalled vehicle, went into a nearby greenhouse, drew his gun on the proprietor, 65-year-old James H. Baum, and told him in a menacing tone, "You're going to drive me to Youngstown!"

For two hours, Baum drove his captor along back roads, dodging posses that were looking for the desperado. Near East Liverpool, Ohio, a car filled with armed officers gave chase and a few miles down the road, Floyd ordered the greenhouse owner to halt the car, and the two men got out. Moments later, the car filled with lawmen roared up, and Floyd fled into the woods. Mistaking James Baum for one of the outlaws, an officer shot him in the shoulder.[2]

Notified by Wellsville Police Chief Fultz that Adam Richetti was in custody and Pretty Boy Floyd cornered, Melvin Purvis, special agent in charge of the Chicago FBI office who had led the squad that killed John Dillinger, chartered an airplane. Along with a few of his agents, Purvis flew to Wellsville, where he took charge of 21 G-Men who were pouring into the small town from around the Midwest.

Grilled by Purvis and Fultz in the Wellsville jail, Richetti gave a phony name and denied being involved in the Kansas City Massacre or the killing of the Missouri policemen. His companion was named James Warren, a gambler he had met in Toledo a few days earlier, Richetti said. The two men had hitchhiked from Toledo and had stopped in the woods to rest when suddenly several men (Chief Fultz and his officers) began shooting at them, Richetti explained.

Purvis and Fultz didn't buy the "James Warren" story.

"I got a good look at the guy," the police chief said, "and I've seen his face hundreds of times on wanted posters. It's Pretty Boy, no doubt about it."

Purvis held up an FBI wanted bulletin with Richetti's photograph on it and asked the question, "Recognize this guy?"

Richetti shrugged and said nothing. When the G-Man reminded him that his real identity would be established as soon as his fingerprints reached the FBI laboratory in Washington, D.C., Richetti admitted his true name. However, he clung to his yarn about "James Warren" being a gambler from Toledo.

"I ain't seen Charlie Floyd (Pretty Boy) since I left him in Texarkana, Arkansas, a couple of years ago," the prisoner declared.

Purvis set up an FBI command post in a small hotel in East Liverpool, near the place where Floyd had last been sighted, and sent his heavily armed agents to join with local sheriff's deputies and policemen in patrolling roads in the region.

Pretty Boy Floyd, who had often led the high life off the loot from his criminal endeavors, had now turned into a hunted animal. On his first night in the woods, he slept in a corn shock, covering himself with a stolen tarpaulin. Hungry, thirsty, shivering from the cold, he could hear the sounds and glimpse the headlights of lawmen's automobiles rolling up and down the roads. Floyd had put only 20 miles between him and the point where he and Adam Richetti had engaged in the shootout with Wellsville policemen.

After daylight, a disheveled and bearded Floyd knocked on the door of a farmhouse owned by Mrs. Ellen Conkle, a widow, and asked politely for a meal and a place to wash. Mrs. Conkle had not heard of the big manhunt for America's Public Enemy Number 1, but she was frightened by the stranger's slovenly appearance and the fact that he kept glancing back toward the road.

The stranger explained that he had been hunting squirrels with his brother and had gotten lost in the woods. When Mrs. Conkle appeared dubious of that story, Floyd grinned and admitted that he had been drunk and had passed out in the woods.

After eating a meal the widow prepared for him, Floyd asked if she could arrange to get an automobile and driver to take him to Youngstown, adding that he would pay $20 for the trip. Mrs. Conkle replied that she could not, that all the men were working in the fields. Pretty stalked off through tall rows of corn.

In the meantime, Arthur Conkle, brother-in-law of the woman, who lived on an adjoining farm, had spotted Floyd talking with Ellen Conkle and quickly telephoned the FBI command post in East Liverpool. Two squad cars carrying Melvin Purvis, four other G-Men, East Liverpool Chief of Police Hugh J. McDermott, and three of his officers, raced toward the locale.

Pretty Boy Floyd had gone to another farm owned by Stewart Dyke and, by offering $50, persuaded the farmer to drive him to Youngstown. With Dyke behind the wheel and Floyd beside him, the car reached the main road just as Purvis, Chief McDermott, and the other lawmen drove up.

"Those men want me!" Floyd declared to the startled Dyke.

The fugitive leaped from the still-moving automobile and sprinted into a field, where he took refuge behind a corn crib. Since the crib was on stilts, Floyd's blue trouser legs could be seen.

Braking hard and scrambling from their two vehicles, Purvis, McDermott and their men, weapons at the ready, fanned out and edged in a skirmish line toward the corn crib.

"Come out, Floyd!" Purvis shouted.

Pretty Boy fired five shots, then ran hell-bent for a nearby patch of woods. A terrific racket erupted as the lawmen opened fire with Tommy guns and rifles. Shooting periodically, the G-Men and officers chased the fugitive, and they saw him go down and then disappear behind a grassy knoll. Although hit by several bullets during his dash, Floyd got to his feet and began running again, seeking the cover of the woods. This time bursts of fire brought the desperado down and he lay motionless.[3]

Melvin Purvis was the first to reach Pretty Boy, who was conscious and bleeding profusely from several wounds. Face down, Floyd was still clutching a .45 caliber pistol in his right hand. The G-Man took the weapon and a second pistol carried in Floyd's belt.

"Who tipped you?" Floyd muttered through clenched teeth.

Purvis ignored the question and asked if he was involved in the Kansas City Massacre.

"You'll never know!" the outlaw gasped.

An ambulance was summoned, but 15 minutes after he had been shot, Floyd died.

That night in East Liverpool, Melvin Purvis issued a statement:

> The killing of Charles Arthur "Pretty Boy" Floyd brings to a close the relentless search and effort on the part of the (FBI).
>
> The search was directed by J. Edgar Hoover, Director, from Washington, and I have been in constant contact with him by telephone and telegraph. Mr. Hoover has been particularly anxious, as have we all, to bring about apprehension of this and other similar hoodlums.[4]

For his part, J. Edgar Hoover was unhappy with Wellsville Police Chief John Fultz. "Now all we have to do is obtain the custody of Richetti," the Director told the press. Hoover wanted to return the prisoner to Missouri to stand trial for the Kansas City Massacre and for the slaying of the two Missouri state policemen.

Hoover flatly charged that Ohio authorities were obstructing the work of his agents by refusing to permit them to question Richetti. Chief Fultz steadfastly refused to give up his prisoner to the feds.

"Richetti tried to kill me," Fultz declared. "He shot one of my citizens. Therefore I have a right to take care of our case. I want to keep him here where we can keep an eye on him until his trial. We'll make certain that he doesn't get away."[5]

When FBI Inspector Sam Cowley and Sheriff Thomas Bash of Columbia, Missouri, arrived in Wellsville with two federal warrants for Adam Richetti, Ohio authorities had a change of heart and the prisoner, shackled at hands and feet, was taken back to Kansas City to stand trial for first degree murder, which called for the death penalty on conviction.

Meantime, Rose and Beulah Baird, who had been sent into Wellsville to get the damaged Ford repaired, were also in Kansas City. While waiting in the Wellsville garage, they had heard about Richetti being captured and Floyd fleeing, so they drove to Missouri.

In Washington, J. Edgar Hoover released information that Pretty Boy Floyd had tried to cut a deal with the U.S. government to avoid being hanged or sent to the electric chair. On four separate occasions, Hoover said, Floyd had sent messages to the FBI, the most recent one two weeks before he died in an Ohio cornfield. "Floyd offered to give himself up if promised immunity from a death sentence," the Director said.

But the word that went back to the fugitive was that no promises would be made and that Floyd would have to take the consequences for the brutal crimes he had committed.

In Salisaw, Oklahoma, the slain outlaw's mother, Mrs. W. F. Floyd, took the news stoically and sighed, "My boy was not bad at heart."

Mrs. Floyd also revealed that her son Charles had picked his own grave site at a cemetery near the village of Akins, Oklahoma.

"Right there is where you can bury me," her son told his 55-year-old mother in May 1933.

For more than a year, Mrs. Floyd had tended the cemetery plot, seemingly assured that she would live to bury her wayward son. When Charles Floyd was laid to rest, grieving along with his mother were Pretty Boy's girlfriend Rose and her sister Beulah.

A short time after Pretty Boy Floyd was gunned down, on the morning of November 26, 1934, a pair of small-time hoodlums who hit the Chandler National Bank of Lyons, Kansas, and fled with $2,090, failed to realize that they were making history—they would receive the first life sentence imposed under the Federal Bank Robbery Act.

Taking two officials of the bank as hostages in a stolen Ford V–8, the bandits immediately switched on a radio that was located on the floorboard of their getaway car in order to listen to police broadcasts. It was an innovative technique for bank robberies. Ten miles from Lyons, the hostages were released, badly frightened, but unharmed.

The Ford used in the getaway was found abandoned in Hutchinson, Kansas, and contained $143 in silver from the Lyons Bank, four pistols, and assorted paraphernalia used in the robbery. FBI agents investigating the bank heist determined that the serial numbers on the stolen currency matched the $351 in bills that had been placed in circulation in Hutchinson.

On December 4, six days after the Lyons bank robbery, Hutchinson police arrested Burton Phillips. G-Men looking into his background found that he had previously been in the Kansas State Reformatory for bank robbery. While there, he had been a good friend of Homer Binkley, who was also doing time for bank robbery.

Binkley was then taken into custody in Hutchinson, and eyewitnesses identified Phillips and Binkley as the men who had hit the Lyons bank. Both men were put on trial in Wichita, Kansas, and a guilty verdict was returned. Binkley and Phillips escaped the death penalty they could have received, but they were given life in prison.

Prior to the enactment of the Federal Bank Robbery Act on May 18, 1934, the American Bankers Association reported that there had been an average of 16 robberies of national banks per month for the preceding five years. However, since the FBI had been given jurisdiction, the yearly average of bank robberies fell to 11.8 month, and during 1935 the figure would plummet to 6.4 per month.[6]

One of the earliest cases investigated by the FBI under the new federal law was the robbery of the Caledonia National Bank at Danville, Vermont, on June 4, 1934. After prolonged sleuthing, agents tracked down and arrested in Brooklyn an old pro in the bank robbing trade, Edward Wilhelm Bentz.

Eddie Bentz had gained his greatest acclaim in the underworld when he masterminded the heist of the Lincoln National Bank in Lincoln, Nebraska, on September 17, 1930. At that time, he and four henchmen made off with some $3 million in cash and negotiable securities—history's largest bank loot at that time.

However, the U.S. Justice Department decided to charge Bentz with the Vermont bank job, having a much stronger case against him for that heist.

Bentz seemed to enjoy being the center of attention when questioned by G-Men, and he told them that he had knocked off so many banks he had lost count of them. Now, in his cell, Eddie bemoaned the changing conditions since the FBI had been given authority to investigate bank holdups.

"Many yeggs (old bank robbers) have gotten out of the racket because they aren't likely to get away with it any more," Bentz declared.[7]

With the death of Pretty Boy Floyd, the "honor" of being designated Public Enemy Number 1 went to Baby Face Nelson, the surly bantam who had gunned down FBI Agent W. Carter Baum at Little Bohemia in Wisconsin. Since fleeing from that shootout, Nelson and his pal John Paul Chase had been holed up in Chicago, where they were joined by Helen Gillis, Baby Face's wife. She had been taken into custody by the FBI in the Little Bohemia affair, but a judge released her.

After John Dillinger was killed by G-Men only a short distance from his Chicago hideout, Nelson felt the heat and headed for California by motor car with Chase and Helen. In Kansas, the constable in a small town arrested Baby Face for speeding and hauled him into an improvised courtroom in a drug store, where a judge fined him five dollars and released him. Nelson's car, which was loaded with Tommy guns, rifles, and ammunition, had never been searched.

In mid-November 1934, Nelson, his wife, and Chase returned to Chicago and rented an apartment. Baby Face, now 25 years of age, and the 32-year-old Chase had been close friends since they had first teamed up in a booze-smuggling operation in California back in 1930. Chase frequently introduced Nelson as his half-brother.

On November 27, FBI Inspector Samuel Cowley, who had been designated by J. Edgar Hoover to lead the search for Baby Face Nelson, and Agent Herman Hollis were driving along a lonely road near Fox River, Illinois, a short distance west of Chicago. Although they were on another assignment that morning, by an amazing coincidence a car driven by Nelson, with his wife and John Paul Chase as passengers, happened to pass them from the opposite direction.

Apparently the keen-eyed G-Men, trained to be observant at all times, had spotted Nelson as his car zipped past. Cowley and Hollis executed a sharp U-turn and, with tires squealing, gave chase at high speeds. Just outside the northwest suburb of Barrington, Nelson braked hard.

Nearby, a group of road construction workers looked up curiously. They saw Nelson leap out of his car clutching a Tommy gun and Chase scramble out the other side with a Browning automatic rifle.

Hollis and Cowley also brought their car to a sudden halt and jumped out of the vehicle. Hollis, armed with a shotgun, crouched behind the car, while Cowley, cradling a Tommy gun, jumped into the roadside ditch. Moments later, a tremendous racket erupted as the two sides began blasting away at one another. The construction workers belly-flopped to the ground as swarms of bullets hissed past their heads.

Later, Baby Face Nelson's wife told the FBI about the episode:

Les (Nelson) hollered at me to duck, and I jumped into a ditch and kept my head down. I could see Les firing back at the federal men who were trying to kill him.

A few seconds after the firing started, I saw Les jump up and grab his side. I knew that it was all over. I was in that ditch until the firing stopped.

Our car had been damaged by bullets, so we climbed into the federal car. Les tried to drive, but he was too weak (from gunshot wounds). John (Chase) took the wheel and we drove to a house somewhere near Chicago.[8]

When the smoke of battle had cleared, G-Man Herman Hollis, his shotgun and pistol empty, lay dead. Inspector Cowley, critically wounded, was rushed to a hospital where he was visited briefly that night by Melvin Purvis.

"Who did this, Sam?" Purvis asked softly.

"Baby Face Nelson," Cowley gasped.[9]

An hour later, the inspector died.

At 7:35 that night, Baby Face Nelson drew his final breath at the home of a suburban Chicago politician where he had been taken after the gun battle.

Early the next morning, Phillip Sadowski, a Chicago undertaker, received a mysterious telephone call. A man's voice said, "Hello, is that you, Phil?" Sadowski replied in the affirmative.

"Phil, I want you to go out to Long and Niles (avenues). You'll find a body there. He's a friend of mine named Gillis."

Sadowski promptly notified the Niles Center Village police, who in turn contacted the FBI. A short time later, FBI Inspector Hugh H. Clegg, whom J. Edgar Hoover had rushed to Chicago on hearing of the Barrington shootout, and local police came upon the naked, bullet-riddled corpse of Baby Face Nelson lying along a road near St. Paul's Cemetery. Nelson was wrapped in a dirty blanket, and a strip of white cloth was bound around his abdomen to cover a gaping wound from a shotgun blast.

That night, Nelson's 133-pound body, rigid and white, lay on a cold slab in the Raben Mortuary in Niles Center. It was the same slab on which John Dillinger's corpse had lain 128 days earlier.

In Washington, D.C., a grim J. Edgar Hoover told reporters: "Yes, we got the guy—but he killed two of my fellows. It was two lives for one."[10]

An examination of the weapons, the Director said, had shown that Inspector Cowley had discharged 51 bullets from his Tommy gun and Agent Hollis had fired all of the ten shells for the type of shotgun he carried.

"Make sure you say our fellows got Nelson—and they quit firing only after all of their ammunition was gone," Hoover stressed.[11]

In Chicago, Mrs. Herman Hollis and Mrs. Samuel Cowley had become nearly hysterical on learning of the deaths of their husbands. Friends, including wives of several FBI agents, tried to comfort them. Word that Baby Face Nelson had been killed seemed to have a calming effect on the distraught widows.

Later in the day, with her arms around her four-year-old son, Mrs. Hollis told reporters: "They got him (Nelson) too late. I'm glad my husband and Mr. Cowley had something to do with getting him. But it's terrible that two good lives had to be sacrificed for one bad one."[12]

Meanwhile, an intense search was launched for Helen Gillis, widow of Nelson, who was thought to be hiding in Chicago. She unofficially became the nation's first female public enemy. Hundreds of FBI men, police, sheriffs, and their deputies scoured highways and gangster haunts to ferret out the 22-year-old woman.

22

Lashing Out at "Sentimental Moo-Cows"

In the aftermath of the killings of G-Men Samuel Cowley, Herman Hollis, and H. Carter Baum, Director J. Edgar Hoover and other top men in the Federal Bureau of Investigation were taking a hard new look at the role of female accomplices of the desperadoes. The Bureau leadership held that outlaw gangs could not operate on such a widespread and deadly scale without their customary array of "contact" women.

In Washington, rumors spread through the press corps that Hoover had issued "shoot to kill" orders in the search for Helen Gillis, Baby Face Nelson's wife. Hoover vigorously denied the report.

"We're not a Cossack outfit!" he barked.[1]

However, the Director noted that if a federal judge had not suspended Helen Gillis's sentence after she was captured at Little Bohemia and confessed to aiding the John Dillinger gang, she would not have been free to assist Baby Face Nelson in his bloody rampages.

When Nelson's widow heard a public appeal from her father, a law-abiding Chicago citizen of Polish ancestry, to give herself up and "answer for what you have done," she came out of hiding and surrendered. She was questioned intensely about the identity of the man involved with her husband in the shooting deaths of G-Men Hollis and Cowley, and she said he was John Paul Chase, a crony of her late husband.

Chase had been the one who telephoned the Chicago undertaker and had helped her put Nelson's body alongside the road in Niles Center. Then Chase departed, the widow added, and she said she didn't know where he had gone.

Sob-sister journalism had a field day after the arrest of Helen Gillis. One maudlin newspaper story said:

Baby Face Nelson died in the arms of his young wife with a smile on his lips, but with tears in his eyes for his two small children. This was among the highlights of a thrilling story told by Nelson's pretty widow, in which she gave a heartbroken account of his death at the hands of FBI agents.

In that same story, Nelson's sister was quoted as describing the outlaw's widow as "one of the most devoted mothers I have ever known." Actually, Helen Gillis and Baby Face had abandoned their two children, who knew their mother only as an infrequent visitor they called "Aunt Helen."

No mention was made in these stories of the widows and children of the FBI agents Nelson had killed.

Although the overwhelming weight of public opinion remained solidly with the FBI, J. Edgar Hoover was outraged by the sympathy heaped on dead outlaws and their female accomplices. Noting that Baby Face Nelson, whom he described as "one of the most vicious public rats," had murdered three G-Men within a span of a few weeks and had been paroled three times, the Director lashed out at the U.S. parole system. He declared that "sentimental moo-cows, yammerheads, venal politicians, sob-sisters, and those afflicted with itching palms" had made the parole system a "horrible, filthy mess." Stressing that he was not opposed in principle to parole for first offenders, he spoke out against "giving easy freedom which indiscriminately turns loose on society the human mad dog side by side with the reformable character."

In a speech before a civic group, Hoover declared:

"The biggest job of law enforcement is not the capture of new criminals. It is the chasing down of hardened, shrewd, canny repeaters who know all the tricks and therefore are ten times as costly in their recapture as the inexperienced offender.

"It is a disgrace that, of our more than twelve thousand desperate bank robbers, kidnappers, thugs, confidence men, holdup men, hijackers, arsonists, rapists and professional murderers, that fully twenty-nine percent of them have been cloaked by the mantle of parole or other clemency."

On the day after Baby Face Nelson's bullet-riddled body was found, John Paul Chase slipped out of his place of hiding to buy Chicago newspapers. He breathed a sign of relief; Nelson's companion in the Barrington gun battle was not mentioned by name. In fact, press accounts indicated that lawmen were conjecturing that the unidentified gunman with Nelson had been Old Creepy Karpis, a kingpin in the Barker-Karpis gang who was still at large.

Chase thumbed through the classified advertisements and responded to one that sought men to convoy cars to Seattle. Applying for the job under the name of Elmer Rockwood, he was photographed for a chauffeur's license at a Chicago police station. This was only three days after he had helped gun down G-Men Cowley and Hollis, but since Chase's only known arrest had been for drunkenness in 1931, no wanted circulars with his picture and fingerprints had ever been issued.

As uneasy as Chase may have felt to be surrounded by blue-uniformed policemen in the station, he was encouraged by the fact that none of them recognized him.

By the time Helen Gillis was in custody and had identified Chase as the second gunman, "Elmer Rockwood" was driving across the United States toward Seattle, unaware that the FBI was on his trail. G-Men in the San Francisco office contacted Chase's former employers and fellow workers at the California State Fish Hatchery at Mount Shasta with instructions to notify the Bureau if the fugitive was seen.

On December 27, Chase appeared at the hatchery and tried to borrow money from employees. The FBI was contacted, and agents rushed to the scene and apprehended the fugitive.

Chase was flown back to Chicago, where his trial for murdering FBI Inspector Samuel Cowley began on March 18, 1935. He was the first person to be tried under the recently enacted federal law that made it a violation to kill an FBI agent while in the performance of his duties. One week later, John Paul Chase was found guilty and was sentenced to life imprisonment at Alcatraz.[2]

While J. Edgar Hoover's bloodhounds had been tracking down Baby Face Nelson and John Paul Chase, G-Men in Kansas City discovered the rooming house where desperado Volney Davis was holed up. Back in 1932, Davis had been serving a life sentence for murder in the Oklahoma State Penitentiary when Governor Alfalfa Bill Murray granted him what was called a "two-year leave of absence." Presumably, the hardened criminal, facing a lifetime behind bars, would voluntarily return to prison after the two years had expired.

On his release from the Oklahoma penitentiary, Davis had gone to St. Paul, where he joined the Barker-Karpis gang and was involved in the 1934 kidnapping of wealthy banker Edward Bremer.

Now, on February 5, 1935, a few G-Men broke into Volney Davis's Kansas City hideout and overpowered him before he had time to draw a loaded automatic pistol from his pocket. A day later, Davis, shackled at wrists and ankles, was put on a chartered airplane to be flown to Chicago. Two FBI agents were assigned to escort him.

Just before 7:00 P.M., the private pilot had to make a forced landing on a farm near Yorkville, Illinois, 58 miles southwest of Chicago. As soon as Volney Davis stepped out of the plane, the agents removed his handcuffs and leg irons.[3]

In a car owned and driven by a neighbor, William Ford, the two agents and their prisoner went to the Hotel Nading in Yorkville. One G-Man put in a telephone call to the Chicago office of the FBI, while the other took his unbound prisoner into the hotel bar.

"What'll you have?" asked the agent.

"I'll take beer," replied Davis.

With a swift motion, the prisoner tossed the contents of a stein into the face of the agent and then struck his captor a staggering blow on the jaw. The G-Man fell backward and Davis plunged through a glass window, as the sprawled agent fired three times at the fleeing prisoner. A block away, Davis stole a car and raced out of town. Early the next morning, the vehicle was found abandoned near Wheaton, a western suburb of Chicago.

In Washington, D.C., Director Hoover was furious, not only because of Davis's escape, but also due to the two agents' lack of sound judgment and their violation of FBI regulations. Both men were promptly fired.

When Volney Davis had been captured in Kansas City, a slip of paper with a Chicago telephone number on it was found in his possession. Now the number was traced to a brick house in a new real estate development, and for several months, FBI men watched the house.

Then one day, a man answering the description of the fugitive was seen entering the house. An automobile that Davis had stolen was parked outside the place. Word was flashed to the Chicago FBI office, and a squad of agents rushed to the locale.

Melvin Purvis placed his men around the house. In the new housing development, there were no trees or bushes for concealment, so the G-Men had to remain out in the open in broad daylight. One agent remained in a parked car: if Davis managed to elude the others and leap into his car to make a run for it, this agent was to start his engine and ram the fugitive's vehicle.

Tension gripped the waiting lawmen. Mouths were dry, stomachs knotted. Davis, they knew, was desperate and heavily armed. If he came out shooting, the exposed G-Men could be picked off like sitting ducks. The seconds ticked past. It seemed like days or weeks to the agents.

Then a few neighborhood residents walked up and stopped to gawk. If Davis were to peer out a window—a likely possibility—surprise would be lost and a bloody shootout could erupt. Innocent citizens, as well as FBI agents, might be killed.

Purvis, with a sinking heart, flashed his badge at the gapers and, with a frantic motion of his arm, succeeded in getting them to move on. Even then, they walked a short distance before halting briefly to look back over their shoulders.

Finally, Volney Davis emerged from the house, strolled to his car parked along the curb and opened the door. On the seat was a fully loaded .38-caliber pistol.

Before the fugitive could get into the automobile, the G-Men bowled over Davis in a fashion that would have made Notre Dame football coach Knute Rockne proud.

Davis' head was on the seat of the car and his feet were on the curb. He struggled like a wildcat and struck a G-Man's cocked weapon, which discharged with an ear-piercing crack.

Apparently convinced that the men with whom he was grappling intended to kill him, Davis shouted, "I'll give up! I'll give up!"

By now, a flood of neighborhood gawkers descended on the scene and surrounded the automobile. Davis was quickly handcuffed and bundled into an FBI car which rushed him to the Bureau's downtown office in the Bankers Building.

Seated calmly in a chair and questioned by Melvin Purvis and others, Davis seemed to be almost relieved that his days and nights of constant vigilance were over. He was tired of running. Like many desperadoes, Davis had always been gripped by restlessness and could not remain still. He told the G-Men that, on occasion, he had climbed into his automobile in the middle of the night, with no particular destination in mind, and had driven for many hours.

Purvis asked why he had risked his life to flee from the two agents at the hotel in Yorkville. Grinning, Davis shrugged and replied, "Don't you think freedom is worth it?"[4]

Blond, slightly built Volney Davis confessed to playing a role in the Edward Bremer kidnapping and said that his share of the ransom had been $5,000. On June 6, 1935, he pleaded guilty in federal court in St. Paul and was sentenced to life imprisonment in Leavenworth.

With the conviction of Davis, virtually all of the Barker-Karpis gang had been wiped out. Now only slippery Old Creepy Karpis remained at large—and the FBI was hot on his trail.

In mid-1935, famed John D. Rockefeller, the 95-year-old philanthropist billed in the press as the "world's richest man," received letters threatening that he would be kidnapped unless the extortionist received $100,000 in small bills. Instructions were given for leaving the ransom at a designated point in New York City.

Extra bodyguards were hired for the aged Rockefeller and the FBI was called in.

Rockefeller, a native of Richford, New York, and the son of a peddler, amassed a huge fortune in the oil business and gave up active management of his holdings in 1895. Then he began creating foundations that bestowed in excess of $600 million of his wealth.

For two years, G-Men tracked the extortionist, but each lead ran into a blind alley. Then, acting on a tip, Hoover's men swooped down on a rooming house on West 27th Street in New York City, and arrested Giusseppe Queirola, a restaurant employee.

Queirola denied any knowledge of the Rockefeller kidnapping threat, but when G-Men confronted him with the fact that his handwriting matched that in the ransom letters, he confessed to the crime.

Before being sentenced to a long term, he explained to Federal Judge Murray Hulbert the reason for his action: "I wanted to prove my theory that the FBI couldn't find and arrest me."

An agent of the Federal Bureau of Investigation knows that his calling is a highly dangerous one. The potential for sudden violence or an early death is always present, as G-Men have to walk into situations where they are at a distinct disadvantage. While law officers are expected to collar an adversary with the least amount of force necessary, the adversary has the benefit of being able to shoot first—often at point-blank range and before the FBI man can draw his weapon. Despite the handicaps under which he must perform, the G-Man doesn't dwell on his ultimate vulnerability. Rather, he adapts to his situation and continues to carry out his duties—much as an experienced soldier does on the battlefield.

Such was the frame of mind of Agent Nelson B. Klein when he was searching for 49-year-old, gray-haired George W. Barrett, a former Cincinnati streetcar conductor who was wanted for stealing and transporting automobiles to other states. It was early August 1935.

Klein, a 37-year-old native of New Jersey working out of the Cincinnati office, telephoned the chief of police of Hamilton, Ohio, where Barrett had once resided, and advised him that the suspect was wanted by the FBI. From some unknown source, Barrett got word that the G-Men were closing in on him, and he holed up at his brother's farm near College Corner, Indiana, which sits squarely atop the Ohio border, 35 miles southwest of Cincinnati.

On August 16, Agent Klein and Agent Donald McGovern drove to the farm, spotted Barrett near the house, identified themselves, and called on the suspect to surrender. Ignoring the demand, Barrett scampered behind a garage and opened fire. Klein and McGovern blasted away with their revolvers, and bullets hit Barrett in both legs.

When the shooting ceased, McGovern saw that his partner was lying on the ground, bleeding profusely from a bullet wound in the chest. Nelson Klein was rushed to a nearby hospital where he died a few hours later.

In the meantime, Agent McGovern had taken Barrett into custody and he was removed to a hospital in Hamilton. After several weeks of recuperating from his leg wounds, the prisoner was taken by automobile to Indianapolis to stand trial for Agent Klein's murder. During the first week of December 1935, a jury returned a guilty verdict.

On December 14, a scene without precedent in a federal court was enacted as George Barrett was wheeled before the bar of Judge Robert C. Baltzell and sentenced to be hanged. Barrett became the first person to receive the death penalty under a recent federal law that made it a capital offense to kill an FBI agent.

On March 15, 1936, George Barrett was hanged in the yard of the Marion County (Indianapolis) jail—the first official execution in the county in 49 years.

In early 1936, shortly after George Barrett was executed, FBI bloodhounds were hot on the trail of Merle Vandenbush and Harry Brunette, who were wanted for bank robbery and the kidnapping of a New Jersey state trooper. New Jersey officers traced the car used by the two outlaws to New York City, where combined efforts by G-Men and local police eventually discovered that Brunette and his new bride were residing under a phony name in an apartment at 304 West 102nd Street.

An agreement was reached to raid the apartment on a certain day, and J. Edgar Hoover flew in from Washington to lead his men in the assault. A spectacular shootout erupted. Brunette fired a fusillade of bullets from a window, and the G-Men and New York officers sprayed the apartment with a torrent of fire.

For 35 minutes, the melee raged, as other residents in the building cowered under their beds to escape the streams of bullets. Tear-gas canisters were fired into Brunette's apartment, and the old structure caught fire. With sirens blaring, fire engines rushed to the scene, and firefighters found themselves caught in the crossfire, although none of them was hit.

Occupants of the building, frightened thoroughly, rushed outside to escape the blaze. Finally, Harry Brunette, unscathed by the withering burst of bullets, surrendered. His bride was grimacing as the result of a leg wound.

Two months later, Brunette's sidekick, Merle Vandenbush, was apprehended by police in Armonk, New York. On the night of the big shootout on 102nd Street, Vandenbush claimed, he had come to the scene to watch the fireworks and had been so close to J. Edgar Hoover that he could have reached out and touched him. Vandenbush said that after watching the shootout for a while, he strolled away.

Follow That Airplane!

J. Edgar Hoover had a reputation in some circles of being a Simon Legree taskmaster. Some said he was difficult. "That meant he had standards of perfection and expected everybody in the Bureau to live up to them," explained Louis B. Nichols, Hoover's first lobbyist and long-time close associate. "Hoover played no favorites," Nichols said. "The closer you were to him, the more demanding he was."

Hoover had no patience with a person who pulled a blunder, then tried to provide an alibi for it. "But if you made a mistake and when it was called to his attention you said, 'That was a stupid boner,' he'd say, 'It sure was, and don't do it again,' " Nichols added.

Hoover was invariably calm, collected, and courteous when testifying at Congressional hearings, making speeches, receiving visitors to his office, and engaging in public events. Yet, like most top leaders in pressure-cooker endeavors, he swore on occasion. His favorite expression was, "He's a 13-karat son of a bitch." However, no one close to him could recall him using lewd or foul language.

When the situation warranted it, Hoover could build up a full head of steam. One such occasion was a conference of top Bureau leaders in October 1935, when the subject was Old Creepy Karpis, who had eluded Hoover's bloodhounds for more than two years. Banging on the table with his fist and biting off his words, he declared: "I *want* him!"

G-Men had been one step behind the slippery Karpis since he and his sidekick Harry Campbell shot their way out of a police trap at the Danmore Hotel in Atlantic City the previous January. As the fugitive roamed around the nation, he mailed an occasional letter or postcard to Hoover, threatening to kill him.

Hoover shrugged off the taunting messages, which only served as reminders that Old Creepy was still on the loose. He issued a standing order: when agents acquired information on Karpis's whereabouts, Hoover was to be notified immediately so he could take personal charge of the search. Throughout the organization, it was recognized that Karpis was "the boss's man."

Meantime, Karpis hatched a bold scheme that promised to produce riches for him and also give him the chance to thumb his nose at Hoover and his G-Men. Like Jesse James in the Old West, Karpis would rob a train.

Traveling between Cleveland and Toledo, Karpis recruited a gang, which included pal Harry Campbell; aging bank robber Ben Grayson, who had spent half of his long life behind bars and only recently got out of prison once again; Grover "Burrhead" Beady, who had an insatiable craving for liquor, and two small-time hoodlums, Fred Hunter and John Brock.

Karpis targeted Erie train Number 622, which would be hit when it stopped briefly at Garrettsville, Ohio (35 miles southeast of Cleveland) to let off and take on passengers. In the mail car, Karpis had been told by underworld contacts, would be the payrolls of two large corporations, totaling more than $300,000 in cash.

Karpis would add an innovative, twentieth century wrinkle to Jesse James's train robbery technique: instead of on horseback, Creepy would make his getaway in an airplane.

Karpis contacted George Zilter, who was an aviator and worked in a marine garage at Port Clinton, Ohio, and offered him $500 to fly Karpis and two other "businessmen" to Tulsa after the train heist. Zilter was told nothing about the planned robbery, nor did he recognize Karpis as Public Enemy Number 1. Zilter said that he didn't own an airplane, but if he had the $500 in advance, he could get one by making a down payment. In those Great Depression years, airplane dealers would take almost any amount of down payment in order to sell one of their products.

Zilter didn't expect to see again the skinny man with the pallid complexion who insisted on wearing sunglasses while inside. However, three days later, Karpis (who gave a phony name) returned, handed $500 in small bills to Zilter, and departed. The aviator then drove to nearby Toledo, purchased a four-passenger airplane, and flew it to a grassy strip near Port Clinton.

Late in the afternoon of November 7, 1935, Garrettsville station agent W. B. Moses was making preparations for the imminent arrival of Erie train 622 when he heard his office door open. Glancing up, he was gripped by fear. Standing just outside the doorway and aiming a Tommy gun in his direction was a stranger, who snarled, "Get outside or I'll blow your head off!"[1] Moses, despite his terror, slammed the door shut in the bandit's face.

Outside, Old Ben Grayson, wearing a fake mustache and rouged cheeks to disguise himself, and other Karpis gang members were holding at gunpoint a number of citizens who had come to the station to mail letters or to greet arriving passengers.

In the distance the train whistled, then it roared down the tracks and came to a halt alongside the station platform. Three of the bandits swung up into the locomotive and covered the engineer and fireman. Creepy Karpis and Harry Campbell scrambled into the mail car and threatened the workers with Tommy guns, but two clerks and a mail guard leaped out the open door when they saw the gunmen enter.

The head mail clerk remained in the car, surrounded by large piles of mail bags. Not knowing which ones contained the big payrolls, Karpis demanded that the clerk point them out. The clerk remained silent.

"Look," Karpis shouted, "you can play hero if you want. But there's another train coming from the other way and due soon on these (single) tracks. If you don't show me the bags, I'll let the train smash into this one, and there'll be a lot of dead people!"[2]

With a quaking finger, the clerk indicated the payroll sacks, and Karpis and Campbell gathered them and jumped out of the car. Like a well-oiled machine, Karpis and his henchmen loaded nine bulging mail bags into a large Plymouth touring car parked in the station's lot and sped out of Garrettsville over pre-marked roads. At Port Clinton, they dragged the sacks into a rented cottage and eagerly opened them in search of the expected $300,000 in cash.

Creepy and the others cursed loudly: there was only $34,000 in the bags. Rapidly the gang members split the loot and scattered. Karpis, Campbell, and another robber rushed to the seldom-used air strip near Port Clinton, where aviator George Zilter was waiting.

Unaware of the spectacular train robbery, Zilter revved the airplane's engine, steered it along the bumpy runway, and lifted off with Karpis and the other two "businessmen" on board. Winging southward, the plane landed at a small airport outside Hot Springs, Arkansas, where Karpis and Campbell took refuge in a whorehouse located on a hill overlooking the popular resort. Karpis and the madam were old friends.

In Washington, D.C., J. Edgar Hoover got word of the brazen train heist and ordered agents from throughout the Midwest to fly to Garrettsville. There the G-Men interviewed citizens who had been held at gunpoint and had ringside seats for the reenactment of a Jesse James train robbery.

Frightened as the eyewitnesses had been, they provided excellent descriptions of the bandits. Mrs. W. L. Scott, who had come to the station to mail a postcard to her traveling husband, picked out a rouges' gallery mug shot of Alvin Karpis. FBI technicians also lifted Karpis's fingerprints from a windowsill in the mail car.

At Port Clinton, G-Men were told by townspeople of the airplane that had taken off after the robbery. Aircraft flying out of the small town were few and far between. Painstaking investigation by the FBI disclosed that the craft (license number NC12180) had been purchased in Toledo by a George Zilter, and the aviator was traced through the plane's U.S. Department of Commerce listing.

Usually cautious and cunning, Alvin Karpis had pulled a major blunder; he had forgotten that the license numbers of airplanes could not be changed like those of automobiles.

A few days after the Garrettsville affair, J. Edgar Hoover lifted off from an airport outside Washington, D.C., and flew to Tulsa, where he was met by a few of his agents. They whisked him to an isolated house on the outskirts of the city, where two G-Men were with aviator Zilter.

Badly shaken to find himself in the center of a major crime investigation, Zilter told Hoover the story of how he had purchased the airplane. He said that he had flown two of the robbers to Hot Springs, then continued to Tulsa with the third man. FBI men searching for the aircraft had picked up Zilter before he could fly back to Port Clinton.

From photographs, Zilter identified Creepy Karpis as one of the "businessmen" he had dropped off at Hot Springs.

Hoover quickly rushed a few of his agents to Hot Springs, where they posed as hunters and sportsmen. They learned that a tall, thin man and a male companion were living in the bawdy house on the hill.

In the meantime, Karpis apparently had received word from contacts in Hot Springs of the great interest shown in him by the "sportsmen." When his brothel refuge was raided, Public Enemy Number 1 had fled, departing in such haste that he left behind most of his clothing.

Now the FBI intensified its search for Karpis. In Ohio, Arkansas, Oklahoma, Missouri, and Texas, agents swarmed over Karpis's old hideouts. Creepy, the G-Men learned, was holed up in a sharecropper's house owned by the brother of the Hot Springs whorehouse madam, outside Paris, Texas. By the time agents arrived there, the will-o'-the-wisp outlaw had departed.

In New York City, a tip that Karpis planned to attend the heavyweight championship fight between Max Baer and Joe Louis sent FBI men rushing to Madison Square Garden. Karpis, however, was either not present or had slipped away when throngs poured out of the huge building.

Then, on February 26, 1936, G-Men and postal inspectors raided a house in Toledo and collared one of the train robbers, Burrhead Beady, who was trembling with the D.T.'s after losing a bout with John Barleycorn. Beady was taken to Cleveland and charged with robbery of the U.S. mails.

A month later, G-Man Earl Connelly (who had led the Florida operation against Ma and Freddie Barker) and five other agents stepped out of a car on a dark street in Youngstown, Ohio. Four agents took up positions around a house while Connelly and a comrade banged on the front door. No answer. They pounded again. Still no reply. Then, with weapons drawn, Connelly and the other agent used shoulders to crash open the door.

There was a scuffle of feet and Connelly called out: "Okay, Brock, get'em up!"

John Brock, alias Harold Johnson, shrugged. "Well, what in the hell else can I do?" he said. Brock, too, was hauled off to jail in Cleveland and charged in the train holdup.[3]

Meanwhile in the South, David McGee, special agent in charge of the New Orleans FBI office, was advised by a tipster that Creepy Karpis was holed up somewhere in that city. McGee quickly telephoned the news to Hoover in Washington, D.C.

For weeks, Hoover had been hot under the collar as a result of an appearance before a Senate Appropriations Committee chaired by Senator Kenneth D. McKellar of Tennessee. McKellar, who had long been sniping at the FBI boss, seized the occasion to conduct a grilling about Hoover's experience in criminal investigations.

Isn't it true, Director Hoover, that you have never personally apprehended a criminal?'' McKellar queried.

Hoover's face flushed red with anger, but he maintained his composure. McKellar's question was akin to asking General John J. Pershing, commander of the American army in Europe during World War I, if he had ever personally led a bayonet charge against German trenches.

In reply, Hoover made no mention of his rush to Tulsa a month earlier when his agents thought that Karpis was hiding there, nor did he allude to the standing order that he was to be notified of the outlaw's whereabouts so he could personally arrest him. However, he felt that his courage had been publicly challenged and, worse, the senator had implied that Hoover sent G-Men to take chances that he himself would not risk.[4]

Now events moved swiftly. On April 29, Hoover and a few agents made an all-night flight from Washington, D.C. to New Orleans. In Hoover's pocket was one of the letters that Karpis had written him, threatening to kill him on sight. Concerned about a possible leak that might cause Karpis to fly the coop, the New Orleans Police Department was not notified that Hoover was coming to arrest the fugitive.

As Hoover and a group of agents drove from the New Orleans airport toward the Karpis hideout, an apartment a half-mile from the main business district, the Crescent City lay peaceful and quiet except for the heavy bustle of traffic.

> We try to make an arrest at dawn, or some other time when there aren't many people on the street. But we had to do this one at five in the afternoon. Karpis had been holed up in an apartment on Jeff Davis Parkway and it was the rush hour and there were people everywhere.
>
> Karpis and a male companion suddenly walked out of the building and got into a car, I ran up on one side and grabbed him. Another agent went to the other side and grabbed the other fellow.
>
> I said, ''Bring the handcuffs,'' but everybody had forgotten to bring the cuffs. So an agent who had grown up on a cattle ranch said, ''I can tie him up so he can't move.'' And he did, tying his hands behind him with a necktie.
>
> When we got into the car, Karpis called me by name. I asked him how he knew who I was and he said, ''Oh, I saw your picture in the paper in

Miami.'' I'd had my picture taken when I caught a sailfish, the only one I'd ever caught. Karpis said that my luck was better than his, that he'd been trying in catch one for three years.

On the way downtown, the agent driving the car got lost. Karpis spoke up, wanting to know where we were going. I asked him why he cared and he said, ''Well, if it's the post office building, I can tell you how to get there. I was planning to rob it.''

So Karpis directed us. The agent who was driving heard from me later.[5]

Old Creepy was put aboard a chartered airplane and, with Hoover and a few G-Men on board, winged toward St. Paul, where the outlaw would be charged as a participant in the William Hamm, Jr. kidnapping. Perhaps 20 minutes after lifting off from New Orleans, Hoover noticed that Karpis's face was ashen.

''What's the matter, hoodlum?'' Hoover asked. ''Are you sick?''

''Go ahead and get it over with,'' Karpis muttered.

''Get what over with?''

''I know what you're going to do. Your guys are going to pitch me out of the plane and then say it was an accident.''

Hoover scoffed. ''We don't do things that way, hoodlum,'' he replied.

When the airplane stopped at the Kansas City airport to refuel, newspapers were brought on board. One headline blared: ''KARPIS ROBS BANK IN MICHIGAN.'' Old Creepy chuckled. ''Well, this is one time I've got a perfect alibi!'' he exclaimed. Even the customarily reserved Hoover had to laugh over that quip.

During the rough flight to St. Paul, Karpis complained about Hoover always calling him a hoodlum. ''I ain't no hoodlum, Mr. Hoover,'' he declared.

''Well, if you aren't a hoodlum, Karpis, what are you?'' he asked.

''I'm a thief.''[6]

In the meantime, the man who had been captured with Karpis in New Orleans was identified as Fred Hunter, a suspect in the Garrettsville train robbery. He was turned over to postal inspectors for prosecution.

Only later would the FBI learn that it had nearly snared Karpis's long-time pal Harry Campbell, who had been living in the same apartment with Creepy. Campbell had been elsewhere in town when the G-Men grabbed Karpis. Hearing about the fate of his friend, Campbell fled to Toledo and holed up in a four-room apartment over a store.

On May 7, nine days after Karpis's capture, Hoover and several agents took off from the St. Paul airport and landed at an airstrip outside Toledo. The Toledo Police Department was not informed. Armed with Tommy guns, the G-Men drove into the city and surrounded Harry Campbell's apartment.

Hoover and two agents walked to the door of Campbell's unit and crashed it open with their shoulders. Without a shot being fired, Hoover arrested the fugitive. Nearby on a table was a loaded revolver. In Campbell's pocket was $2,132.

Campbell was wanted for the Edward Bremer kidnapping, the murder of Tulsa attorney J. Earl Smith, and the Garrettsville train robbery.[7]

Taken into custody (and later released) was a 15-year-old girl who said she had married the gangster as "Bob Miller" in Bowling Green, Ohio, in May 1935.

Two hours after Campbell was collared, Sam Coker, an Oklahoma badman linked with the Karpis gang, was arrested by a team of FBI agents at his home in the west end of Toledo.

Underworld rumors soon spread that Creepy Karpis, facing execution, sought to save his hide by tipping off FBI interrogators about where Harry Campbell was hiding out.

On May 9, 1936, Karpis was charged with the Bremer and Hamm kidnappings. His bail was fixed at $500,000, the largest amount ever set for any criminal in the United States up to that time. Pleading guilty, the last member of the Barker-Karpis gang had the massive gates of Alcatraz slam shut behind him two months later.[8]

When the FBI closed its books on the Barker-Karpis gang that had terrorized the Midwest for five years, its members were credited with at least ten murders, two kidnappings, countless bank heists, and total loot in excess of $1.5 million.

As though a huge supernatural force had waved a magic wand in the mid-1930s, nearly the entire nation had a new set of heroes—the company of some 410 G-Men who had been slugging it out with America's desperadoes. All over the nation small boys began wearing tin G-Man badges, toting toy G-Man Tommy guns, even wearing G-Man underwear and sleeping in G-Man pajamas.

Hollywood got into the act. In 1935, Warner Brothers came out with a box-office smash entitled *G-Man*, in which a budding young star named James Cagney played the role of a dauntless, intrepid agent tracking down the nation's worst badmen—and getting the girl at the end of the film.

J. Edgar Hoover had become one of America's most admired celebrities. Colleges ranging in size from New York University to Kalamazoo College showered him with honorary degrees. Honors bestowed upon him included the Distinguished Service Medal from the Boys Clubs of America and the Order of the Star of Romania.

Warming to the glare of the spotlight, Hoover took these occasions to lash out at "America's armed forces of crime," which he variously described as ranging in size from 300,000 to three million.

"Don't call or refer to this country's outstanding criminals as public enemies," Hoover told a University of Maryland graduating class in 1936. "I suggest they be called public rats."

Another large group of university students heard him label America's criminals "mad dogs with guns in their hands and murder in their hearts."

Anything Hoover did became news, even when he attended a boxing match or watched a horse race (two of his favorite diversions). On infrequent visits to such plush Manhattan watering holes as Billy Rose's Diamond Horseshoe and Lou Walters's Latin Quarter, the FBI boss became fair game for gossip columnists.

This was the era of Café Society, the Glamour Girl, and the Man About Town in New York City. Although Hoover never had been known to have a date with a woman and drank only an infrequent highball on special occasions, gossip columnists portrayed him as a Broadway Glamour Boy and a swinger.

Speaking requests poured in on him on an average of 100 each month. In the course of a year, time would permit him to accept perhaps a total of 20 invitations. Despite his back-breaking schedule at his office (he considered himself to be on duty around the clock), he insisted on writing his own lengthy speeches, agonizing over each of them.

Although the main thrust of Hoover's speeches was the FBI's attack on "murderers, armed thugs, kidnappers, bank robbers, firebugs and assassins," he also had some choice words for shady politicians.

"The bullets of the underworld are today poisoned by the verdigris of politics," he declared. Broadsides were fired at anyone he felt "sympathized with" or "coddled" criminals and labeled them "sentimental yammerheads."

Speaking to a large group of mothers, he charged that mothers who played bridge instead of minding the kids were contributing to the rise of juvenile delinquency.

Although America's tidal wave of crime had not crested, some liberal members of Congress tried to slash the FBI's meager budget in 1936. At this time, the Bureau's annual budget was one-thirteenth of one percent of the entire cost of federal government.

Tennessee Senator Kenneth McKellar was in the forefront of the forces seeking to slash FBI funds. At a budget hearing, McKellar told Hoover, "It seems to me that your department is just running wild!"

Senator George Norris of Nebraska renewed the charge that Hoover was converting the Bureau into "an American OGPU," the brutal Soviet secret police.

Once again, Hoover declared that "the FBI will always strive to preserve the civil liberties of every American citizen. We could never become an OGPU."

Hoover and the FBI had a warm relationship with a major segment of the media, but he also had a short persona non grata list of correspondents working for what he called the liberal press.

One media critic sneered at the FBI for using ten or 12 agents to seal off avenues of escape when arresting an armed and dangerous criminal. "Hoover, this critic declared, "is using a sledgehammer to knock a fly off a baby's nose." Another columnist even found fault with the fact that Hoover had posed for a photograph with Hollywood child movie star Shirley Temple.

In early 1937, Jack Alexander wrote in *New Yorker* magazine that there was "an undercurrent of feeling" among the denizens of the Washington press corps that Hoover was somehow "undermining the citadel of liberty."

Naming no names, Alexander quoted "the correspondent of a midwestern newspaper" as swearing that FBI agents had been tailing him after word got out that the reporter was collecting material for an unfavorable article on Hoover.

Hoover angrily rejected the charge, explaining that the FBI had far more important things to do than to tail a reporter from one Washington bar to another. The morbid fear of being followed was "a classic instance of pathological behavior," he declared.

Official Washington was thrown into a tizzy when a newspaper dropped a bombshell: wheeler-dealer James A. Farley, President Roosevelt's one-time campaign manager and now his postmaster general, was trying to get Director Hoover sacked. Besides eliminating a personal irritant, the story said, Farley wanted to replace Hoover with a political crony, Val O'Farrell, who operated a private detective agency in New York City.

Hoover reportedly was livid. If Farley, Roosevelt's chief dispenser of patronage, were successful, the FBI would revert to the days of political hacks of the era prior to Hoover cleaning up the organization.

Washington's rumor mill churned night and day. Hoover, it claimed, had struck back by having Jim Farley's office telephone (and those in his Washington and New Jersey homes) tapped in an effort to obtain "derogatory information" on the postmaster's private live.

In 1936 the attacks on Hoover and the FBI reached a pinnacle when the press broke a story that the U.S. Secret Service was quietly investigating the killing of John Dillinger two years earlier. This action was widely interpreted in the media as being an effort by the Secret Service to discredit FBI agents as being trigger-happy amateurs.

Attorney General Cummings leaped to the Bureau chief's defense. "If there is anybody shooting at Hoover, they're shooting at me!" he declared. "Hoover has my entire confidence, and if anybody thinks they are going to get him, they'll have to get me first!"[9]

In the national uproar that erupted, Secretary of the Treasury Henry Morgenthau, under whose jurisdiction the Secret Service functioned, demoted the two officials involved in the "FBI investigation" and wrote an apology to Homer Cummings. His letter said in part: "The irresponsible action taken by these two men is one which I heartily disapprove and will not permit."

As a result of Hoover's ringing salvos on the abuses of the parole system, "sob-sister judges," prisons operated like "country clubs," and "convict-coddling" in general, the National Probation Association tried to gag him. President Roosevelt and Attorney General Cummings were urged to force Hoover to "refrain from issuing statements which are derogatory and destructive to the advancement of probation."

Undaunted, Hoover stressed that he had never denounced the theory or principle of parole or probation, and he wrote to Cummings:

What I have talked about has been the administration of those systems by venal politicians and inefficient and corrupt influences in some of our states, and I have not dozens, but literally hundreds and running into thousands of these cases to prove my point.

I cannot, I believe, be expected to remain silent in the face of this criticism that has been leveled at me.

While being bombarded by some critics, Hoover derived comfort from a framed text kept on top of a radio in his office, which read: "In every field of human endeavor, he that is first must perpetually live in the white light of publicity. . . . When a man's work becomes a standard for the whole world, it also becomes a target for the shafts of an envious few."

Hoover refused to be muzzled. Perhaps his personal sense of security lay in the fact that he remained highly popular with an overwhelming percentage of the American people—and that his staunchest supporter was Franklin D. Roosevelt.

24

"Our Job Is Never Done!"

Early in April 1937, Wimberly W. Baker arrived in Topeka, Kansas, on his first assignment as an agent of the Federal Bureau of Investigation. Four years earlier, the 27-year-old native of Yuma, Arizona, had joined the Bureau as a law clerk, but an urge to meet the challenge of serving in the field caused him to enroll in the special training course for agents.

Baker had been sent to Topeka from his post in the Kansas City office to track down Robert Suhay and Alfred Power, alias Gerald Lewis, both ex-convicts from New York City, who were wanted for the $18,300 robbery of the Northern Westchester Bank of Katonah, New York, a month earlier.

Information had been developed that Suhay and Power had fled to the Midwest and might pick up a package at the general delivery window in the Topeka post office. Baker and two other G-Men staked out the facility for three days. Baker was in the lobby and his comrades were outside, covering the front and back doors.

In midmorning of April 16, Robert Suhay entered the lobby and walked to the general delivery window. The postal clerk flashed Baker a previously designated signal—a tug of the ear lobe—to indicate that his customer was one of the wanted men. Unnoticed by the G-Man, Power entered the lobby just as Baker drew his pistol and stepped forward, ordering Suhay to put up his hands.

Just then Power opened fire and shot the G-man in the back twice. Baker whirled, returned the fire and another slug struck him in the chest. Two more bullets hit him in the legs, and he crumpled to the stone floor, still clutching his now empty weapon.

Meantime, the FBI men posted outside dashed into the lobby and blasted away at Suhay and Power, both of whom shot back. Bullets ricocheted off the floor and walls, causing eerie sounds that echoed throughout the large building.

The lobby was thick with gun-smoke and the pungent odor from the cartridges being fired.

O. D. Harris, a 45-year-old salesman, had been standing at a lobby table addressing an envelope when the violence erupted. Moments later, he was conscious of a stinging pain in his left foot, and looked down to see blood gushing and forming a pool. He ducked under the table beside a thoroughly frightened little woman.

Shooting all the while, Suhay and Power fled through a door to their car parked across the street. The two G-Men followed and emptied their weapons at the fleeing automobile, but the fugitives escaped. Minutes later Wimberly Baker, felled by five bullets, was rushed to a hospital in critical condition.

Several hours after the shootout, Joseph Garver, a farmer, was walking along a road near Sabetha, in northern Kansas near the Nebraska border. Suhay and Power halted their car, threatened Garver with a gun and forced him to take them to his home, which was just over the state line in Nebraska.

While Mrs. Garver stood by in fear, her husband was ordered to telephone Dr. Sam Hibbard, a former mayor of Sabetha, and ask the physician to come to the farmhouse to treat an injured man. When Hibbard arrived, one bank robber brought out his pistol and demanded that Hibbard treat his partner, who had been wounded in the forearm in the Topeka gun battle.

Hibbard pleaded that he did not have the necessary equipment in his medical kit, so the uninjured gunman drove with him to his office to obtain the necessary items, while the wounded man remained to guard the farmer and his wife.

After the doctor was brought back to the farmhouse and had treated the wound, Suhay and Power forced him to drive them several miles north, where they ejected him from his car and continued their flight toward Lincoln, Nebraska.

Late that same afternoon, Sheriff Homer Sylvester and his brother, Deputy Cass Sylvester, were parked along the highway seven miles south of Plattsmouth, Nebraska. They were studying the cars going past after being notified by the FBI office in Omaha to watch for the gunmen in the bloody Topeka episode.

Homer Sylvester had been sheriff for nearly six years, but had never considered himself to have been in peril, except for the time ''a drunk took a pot-shot at me from way off.'' Now, danger loomed. The brothers saw a car bearing the license number furnished by the FBI, and there were two male occupants. The lawmen began tailing the suspects' car.

Aware that they were being followed, the driver of the other car slowed to 35 miles per hour and then to 25 after having been barreling along the highway at speeds in excess of 60 miles per hour. Apparently the occupants hoped they would be regarded as drunken drivers.

''What they wanted was for Cass and me to pull alongside them, then they'd give us the works and speed away,'' Sheriff Sylvester would say.[1]

Refusing to swallow the bait, the lawmen continued to tail the suspects at a safe distance. Driving into Plattsmouth, the driver of the other car suddenly pressed hard on the accelerator and began careening in circles through the town. Near Sixth and Main Streets, the car plunged into a hole and was disabled.

Screeching their vehicle to a halt, Homer and Cass Sylvester, revolvers in hands, leaped out and captured Robert Suhay and Alfred Power.

"We're your guys," Suhay said resignedly.

"You're damned right you are!" the five-foot-four sheriff barked as he snapped on the handcuffs.[2]

Meanwhile, back in Topeka, G-Man Wimberly Baker would never know that his assailants had been captured. Twenty-four hours after being critically wounded, he died.

Suhay and Power were promptly turned over to FBI agents from the Omaha office who whisked the suspects to Kansas City in an overnight, nonstop, high-speed drive. Questioned at the FBI office in the Federal Reserve Bank Building, the two men disclosed that they had stashed part of the New York bank robbery loot in Room 1815 of a Kansas City hotel. Agents hurried there and recovered $6,974, along with five suitcases of clothing and 12 suits, all made of expensive materials.[3]

On June 29—two months and two weeks after Wimberly Baker had been gunned down—Robert Suhay and his partner Power (who now said that his real name was Glen J. Applegate) were put on trial in federal court in Topeka, found guilty by a jury, and sentenced to death. They were executed on October 1, 1937.

Six days after Agent Baker had been slain, Guy Osborne and two other inmates of the county jail in Eufala, Oklahoma, used smuggled hacksaw blades to cut through cell bars and escape. Osborne had been arrested a few days earlier by the local sheriff and charged with stealing a Ford truck at Eufala and transporting it to Fort Smith, Arkansas, a violation of federal law.

FBI investigation disclosed that the 24-year-old Osborne had numerous relatives living in the vicinity of Gallup, New Mexico, and Agent Truett E. Rowe was sent from the El Paso, Texas, office to search for and arrest the Oklahoma fugitive. It appeared to be a matter of tracking down a penny-ante truck thief.

Late on the afternoon of June 1, 1937, Rowe learned that Osborne was hiding at his brother's ranch outside Gallup. So the G-Man and Gallup Chief of Police Kelsey Presley went to the ranch to make the arrest. Guy Osborne meekly surrendered and asked to be permitted to pack some clothes. While Chief Presley stood in the living room to keep an eye on other members of the family, Rowe went into a bedroom with the fugitive.

Moments later, Osborne whipped out a pistol concealed in a dresser drawer, spun and fired point blank at the unsuspecting G-Man, who slumped to the floor with a bullet in his chest. Hearing the shot, Chief Presley pulled out his revolver and, as Osborne bolted out of the bedroom and ran toward the back door, squeezed the trigger. The revolver misfired three times and Osborne plunged into brush and escaped. Presley put the critically wounded Truett Rowe into his squad car and raced for a hospital in Gallup, but the 32-year-old federal agent died en route.

Hoover was in Missouri when word of Rowe's death was flashed to him, and he immediately organized a manhunt by telephone. The search for Osborne centered on the arid Navajo Indian Reservation. Two aircraft with G-Men at the controls were dispatched from El Paso and crisscrossed the desert. Other FBI men and sheriff's deputies, along with Chief Presley and several Gallup policemen, joined in the manhunt.

Osborne was rapidly located hiding in a dilapidated shed and was taken into custody without resistance. On October 5, 1937, he was put on trial in Albuquerque for the murder of Agent Rowe and was sentenced to life imprisonment.

In Washington, D.C., Hoover held no illusions that his personal hazards anywhere near rivaled those of the G-Men in the field. Yet in 1937 he was receiving so many death threats that his staff persuaded him to travel in a bullet-proof Pierce Arrow. James E. Crawford, who had served as Hoover's chauffeur since 1936, recalled that "these threats didn't bother the Boss, but the folks around him (at the Bureau) always got into a dither."

Crawford, who had been one of the first Negroes (he grew angry when called black) in the FBI, said, "They'd always tell him to be careful and they'd go out of their way to make things secure. But the Boss was a fearless man."

Despite the threats to kill him, Hoover would get out of the bullet-proof car most mornings when about six blocks from the Department of Justice Building and walk briskly for the remainder of the way—without a single bodyguard.

Meanwhile in Chicago, 73-year-old Charles S. Ross, who had amassed a fortune in real estate and as a manufacturer of greeting cards, left his home at about 10:00 A.M. on September 25, 1937, after telling his wife May that he was going to his barber and then to the Edgewater Golf Club to play bridge. Ross had retired two years earlier as president of the George S. Carrington Company, with which he had been associated since 1916.

At about 4:30 P.M., Ross left the golf club and drove to the vicinity of the Carrington printing plant, where he met Florence Freihage, who was formerly his personal secretary and now was an officer of the greeting card firm. Since Ross still held a financial interest in the company, he kept in touch with its affairs through the 44-year-old Miss Freihage.

They drove 70 miles to Sycamore, Illinois, where they dined at the Fargo Hotel. Leaving for the drive back to Chicago at about 8:00 P.M., Ross noticed in his rear-view mirror that they were being followed by another automobile. Near the entrance to the Westward Ho golf course on Wolf Road, some 12 miles west of Chicago, the trailing vehicle suddenly whipped around the Ross car and forced it off the road to a halt.

Jumping from the second automobile was 27-year-old John Henry Seadlund, a part-time lumberjack in the Northwest who had recently pulled off three bank robberies in Wisconsin and another in Minnesota. Seadlund thrust the muzzle of a pistol in Ross's face, stole his billfold, and ordered the elderly man to get into the other car.

Seadlund returned to Miss Freihage, who begged him to let Ross go. "He's sick with high blood pressure and has a heart ailment," she said.

"He's rich, ain't he? the gunman asked. "Think he'd be good for a quarter million."

The woman said she didn't think he was.[4]

As soon as Seadlund and his partner James Gray sped off with Charles Ross, Miss Freihage drove to a gasoline station and telephoned police.

With Charles Ross bound and gagged on the rear floorboard and unable to take his prescribed heart medication, the abductors drove through the night to a lonely side road near Emily, Minnesota, 20 miles north of Brainerd. Far back in the woods, they put Ross in a shallow wood dugout, implanted level with the earth. It had been prepared by Seadlund and Gray a few days earlier.

Ross was manacled at hands and ankles and would undergo suffering and privation in the six-foot deep excavation for the next 13 days.

Seven days after Ross had been abducted and no word had been heard from the kidnappers, it was presumed that the victim had been taken across a state line and the FBI entered the case. Inspector Earl Connelly flew from Washington, D.C. to take charge of the investigation.

The first word from the abductors arrived on October 1, when a man who identified himself only as "Bob of New York" informed Mrs. May Ross, through a third person, that the FBI was tapping her telephone line and that "Bob" could not call her.

Six days later, on October 7, a letter, postmarked Savanna, Illinois, arrived at the Ross home. It gave instructions on where and when to deliver a $50,000 ransom in small denominations. After the G-Men had carefully recorded the serial numbers of the bills, the ransom was handed over to the kidnappers on a dark road by a long-time friend of the Ross family.

Days passed, nothing was heard from Charles Ross, and his wife made an emotional appeal through Chicago newspapers and radio stations for the kidnappers to free him. When still no word came two days later, the FBI feared the worst had happened, and began circulating thousands of lists of the serial numbers on the ransom bills throughout the Midwest.

In the meantime, after collecting the $50,000, John Seadlund and James Gray returned to Charles Ross's cold, wet, underground prison. A day later, on October 9, the victim was driven to a lonely woodland spot 12 miles from Spooner, Wisconsin, where an identical dugout had been prepared.

Hardly had the three men reached the new hideout when Seadlund shot and killed his pal Gray and then murdered Charles Ross. After robbing Gray of his clothing, leaving him naked, and taking the $20,000 that was Gray's share of the ransom, Seadlund pushed both dead men into the vault-like burial place, fastened them down with chains, and covered them with brush and debris.

Then Seadlund motored back to Minnesota, and a few miles from the small town of Walker, he cached $30,000 of the ransom money off a lonely road.

Flush with funds, the kidnapper traveled constantly throughout the country, using the alias Peter Anders. FBI agents followed his trail, which was marked by reports of the ransom bills popping up in Omaha, Denver, Chicago, New York City, Philadelphia, Washington, D.C., Miami, and New Orleans.

In the middle of January 1938, the fugitive drove from New Orleans to Los Angeles and registered at a hotel. Aware from previous patterns that Seadlund was fond of horse races, G-Men staked out the Santa Anita racetrack. When Seadlund passed ransom bills through the pari-mutuel windows, FBI agents pounced on and arrested him.[5]

A total of $14,402.28 of the Ross ransom currency was found in Seadlund's pockets and in the glove compartment of his car. He said that a thief had stolen $3,000 from his automobile when it had been parked near the Holland Tunnel in New York City.

On hearing of Seadlund's apprehension, Hoover flew from Washington, D.C. to Los Angeles and interrogated the prisoner all day. The FBI chief had never tolerated third-degree methods and had always believed that psychology played an important role in dealing with criminals.

Near the end of the day, Hoover was near exhaustion, for he had not slept in over 48 hours. "Do you want something to eat?" he asked Seadlund.

"What in the hell do you want to know for?" the prisoner snapped. "You won't get it for me."

Hoover responded: "I said, what do you want to eat?"

Seadlund blinked his eyes, then replied sarcastically, "Steak, potatoes and pie à là mode."

Hoover turned to an agent: "Just double that order."

When Seadlund had consumed his meal, he still denied knowing anything about the kidnapping and disappearance of Charles Ross. Early the next morning, however, he told guards that he wanted to see Hoover.

"Well, you kept your word and got me my steak," the prisoner said evenly. "Now get your steno and I'll tell you what you want to know."[6]

Seadlund not only gave a detailed confession of the Charles Ross kidnapping and murder and that of his crony James Gray, but he also admitted another abduction to which he had not been linked. John and Olive Borcia had been snatched from their Chicago home prior to the Ross affair. Bound and blindfolded, the Borcias had been taken to a hideout near Lake Geneva, Wisconsin, and released two days later when they convinced Seadlund that their relatives had no money for ransom.

Hoover and several of his men flew the swarthy, square-jawed Seadlund to St. Paul. Then, with the prisoner manacled, they drove to Emily, Minnesota, where they dug up the $30,000 that Seadlund had buried months earlier.

The next day, the group motored to Wisconsin, where Seadlund led the FBI men to the locale near Spooner where he had pitched the bodies of Ross and Gray. The country was so heavily covered with snow and brush that it was impossible to drive automobiles into it. Sleighs had to be used on the last leg of the journey.

For two days, Hoover and his agents searched for the bodies of Ross and Gray. Since the temperature had been 78 degrees when the party flew off from Los Angeles and was below zero when the airplane landed in St. Paul, the searchers did not have adequate clothing and suffered from the intense cold and deep snow.

Hoover asked one of his agents to make his way to a nearby town and bring back some warm clothing. A few hours later, the G-Man returned and, with a straight face, handed Hoover some bright red long johns, an impish gag that created great merriment among the search party—Hoover included.

Eventually, the burial vault was located and the bodies of Charles Ross and James Gray were recovered. Seadlund went on trial in Chicago on a kidnapping charge on March 16, 1938. After deliberating for an hour and a half, a jury in the court of Federal Judge John P. Barnes found the defendant guilty and sentenced him to death.

On July 14, John Henry Seadlund was strapped into an electric chair in the Illinois State Penitentiary and a few minutes later, he was dead.

In late April 1938, while the Ross kidnapping probe was in full swing, FBI Agent William R. Ramsey, who had been an intercollegiate boxing champion at the University of Colorado, was hot on the trail of two suspects in the December 1937 robbery of the bank of Lapel, Indiana. During the night, burglars had loosened a grating on a rear window, entered with an acetylene torch, oxygen tank and goggles, and tried to crack the vault. Failing to get the job done, they left their equipment in the bank, stole $5.45 that was lying on a desk, and departed.

It may well have been the smallest loot in bank-robbing history, but the federal crime had been committed and the FBI began an investigation. Information was developed that two Illinois men, Joe Earlywine and John Hulett, may have been the robbers. So Agent Bill Ramsey, 34 years of age, was sent from the Peoria, Illinois, FBI office to Penfield, Illinois, to apprehend the suspects, who were reported to be holed up on a farm owned by Earlywine.

On May 2, 1938, Agent Ramsey and another G-Man, along with Sheriff Harry George of Danville and a few Illinois state policeman, swooped down on the farm. John Hulett was quickly taken into custody, but Earlywine was in the house and refused to respond to shouts to come out with his hands in the air.

Suddenly, Earlywine poked a rifle through an open window and opened fire at Ramsey, who returned the fire. The G-Man was felled by four bullets, but one of his slugs had torn into Earlywine's head, killing him instantly. Ramsey, unconscious and bleeding profusely, was rushed to a hospital and died shortly after arriving.

In Washington, D.C., Hoover was not only saddened by William Ramsey's death, but was furious over the circumstances involved. He claimed that Congress's slashing of the FBI budget from the requested $6.5 million to $6 million the previous year had resulted in the need to furlough agents and was partly responsible for Ramsey's death.

"Two agents were assigned to investigate this gang, suspected of several bank robberies, when ordinarily four men would have been assigned," he told reporters.

Many in Congress agreed with that analysis. Republican Representative Robert Crawford of Michigan promptly took to the floor of the House and offered a bill appropriating $173,000 "to meet the crisis in the Federal Bureau of Investigation." He added: "Our problem is to get FBI agents who had to be furloughed (by the budget slash) back on the job!" Crawford's bill was enacted.[7]

While some members of Congress were hell-bent on hacking away at FBI funds, five-year-old James Bailey Cash was kidnapped from his bed in Princeton, Florida, south of Miami on May 28, 1938. When no word was heard from the abductors in 24 hours, Hoover winged southward to Miami with a contingent of G-Men to take charge of the investigation.

His first act was to request the press not to mention anything about the crime until the ransom had been paid and the child returned. Editors agreed on the condition that reporters be allowed to cover the investigation in order to write future articles. Hoover agreed.

However, 48 hours after Jimmy Cash was spirited away from his home on the edge of the Everglades, the *Miami Herald* broke the agreement with Hoover and plastered the story all over the front page.

Meanwhile, Dade County Sheriff D. C. Coleman picked up Franklin McCall, a local young man who had been "acting mysteriously" and turned him over to Hoover for investigation. Clean-cut and bright, McCall was the son of a highly regarded clergyman in the county.

Like numerous other suspects, McCall was released, then he was arrested once more and this time confessed to the crime. McCall led Hoover, other G-Men, and Sheriff Coleman to a shallow grave where Jimmy Cash's decomposed remains were uncovered. When a platoon of reporters started to tag along, Hoover angrily told them, "If you continue, you'll be arrested for interference with the FBI in the performance of their duties."

The reporters turned back. Hoover feared McCall might be lynched if the news got out, because the Cash boy had been murdered the first night of the kidnapping.

With the arrival of 1939, the FBI was at the height of its popularity. So was Hoover. "Pick a small boy these days and ask him who of all the people in the world he wants to be like," the *New York World-Telegram* said in an editorial, "and ten to one he will reply—J. Edgar Hoover."

After 15 years as to the top G-Man, Hoover, now 44 years of age, continued to awe associates with his enormous energy and drive. He fought crime as thought it were an obsession, and would tackle a dozen fast-breaking cases at once, shooting a barrage of teletype messages to his field offices around the country and barking orders over his battery of telephones. When a big case or two were unfolding, he would often remain at this desk for 72 hours at a stretch—and yet manage to handle much of the Bureau's correspondence and write his own speeches.

Hoover's boss, Attorney General Homer Cummings, warned: "Edgar, you're going to burn yourself out!"

Hoover paid no attention. "Our job is never done!" he responded.

On those rare nights when Hoover was not working late at the office, he would stay at home, reading books of an inspirational theme, such as those by Ralph Waldo Emerson and Edgar Guest. Long ago he had memorized Kipling's *If.* His magazine diet was mainly the *Reader's Digest.* He also had an appetite for law enforcement comic books that portrayed the inevitable triumph of good over evil, such as *Secret Agent X-9* and *Dick Tracy.*

A bachelor, he lived with his elderly mother and a pet dog or two in the same modest frame house on Seward Square where he was born. In her declining years, "Mother" Hoover was an invalid, and he provided her with a nurse until her death in 1938.

A year later, Hoover bought and moved into a seven-room house on 30th Place near Rock Creek Park. The dwelling was far from pretentious by the neighborhood's standards.

On the night of August 24, 1939, Hoover was seated in a parked car amidst the concrete canyons of Manhattan, at the corner of Fifth Avenue and 28th Street. There he was to have secret, prearranged rendezvous with the notorious New York City gangster, Louis "Lepke" Buchalter, who had been vigorously investigated by the FBI for months. Lepke, as he was commonly called, was the Manhattan rackets czar and boss of an organization the press had labeled "Murder, Incorporated."

An ambitious New York district attorney, Thomas E. Dewey, had been trying to nail Buchalter on a murder rap, for running an extortion racket that was hauling in perhaps $100 million per year, and for peddling women on a wholesale scale. In mid-1939, Dewey announced with great fanfare a $25,000 reward for Buchalter's capture.[8]

As the G-Men tightened their net around the crime kingpin, widely known newsman and radio commentator Walter Winchell broadcast an appeal for Buchalter to surrender, promising that his civil rights would be respected by the FBI, which wanted Lepke for the federal crime of drug smuggling.

Fearful that his pals might be tempted by Tom Dewey's $25,000 bounty and turn in to face a murder rap, Buchalter had a go-between launch negotiations with Winchell, resulting in Hoover's lonely vigil on a Manhattan street corner.

That night Winchell picked up Buchalter at Madison Square and drove him to the rendezvous point. There the newsman introduced the two men.

"Mr. Hoover, this is Lepke."

"How do you do," Hoover replied.

Buchalter responded to the sleuth whose men had been on his trail for months: "Glad to meet you."[9]

As promised, the FBI scrupulously respected the racketeer's civil rights. However, a court ordered that Buchalter be handed over to the state of New York, and he was tried for murder, convicted, and executed.

A week after Hoover took the New York rackets czar into custody, haunting events erupted in Europe. On September 1, German dictator Adolf Hitler triggered what would become World War II by sending his military juggernaut, the most powerful that history had known, plunging into Poland.

Ten days later, Hoover rose to speak to a convention of police chiefs in San Francisco. The thunderous applause had barely died down when he dropped a blockbuster. No longer were marauding desperadoes like Pretty Boy Floyd, Baby Face Nelson, John Dillinger, and Old Creepy Karpis the major domestic threat to the nation.

"Now we have a distinct spy menace in this country!" he exclaimed. The audience seemed to be stunned by the alarming disclosure. Spies? What spies?

Few if any of the police chiefs were aware that during the 1930s, while Hoover and his G-Men were tracking down high-powered marauders, Hitler's spymasters had covertly invaded the United States with a formidable army of spies, saboteurs, propagandists, couriers, stringers, go-betweens, and Peeping Toms. It was the most massive espionage penetration of a major power in history.

Incredibly, the United States government never had a single agency designated to thwart insidious forces seeking to subvert the nation. Consequently, Hitler spies roamed America at will and stole nearly all of the nation's defense secrets. Many of the sophisticated technological advances with which Hitler equipped his army, navy, and Luftwaffe had been stolen from the United States.

Finally, Franklin Roosevelt moved to figuratively lock the barn after the horse had been stolen. A few days before Hoover's speech to the police chiefs in San Francisco, the president had called in Hoover and told him that the FBI would now take on the added responsibility of fighting subversion on the home front.

Hoover's shocking warning about widespread Nazi espionage activities in the United States stunned the nation—and Congress. "It is about time we buckle up our belts and start to deal with these things with a firm hand!" Senator Styles Bridges of New Hampshire thundered. "It is time for action. . . . This is no time to twaddle!"

Hoover didn't "twaddle." He plunged into the fight to root out Nazi subversives in the United States with all the vigor he had displayed in the long, bloody, all-out war against the nation's roaming gangs of killers and kidnappers during the nightmare decade of the 1930s.

An alarmed Congress provided funds to beef up the FBI's manpower to deal with the ugly specter of Nazi infiltration of the homefront. By the time the United States was bombed into war at Pearl Harbor on December 7, 1941, there were 2,602 G-Men and the FBI had a total work force of 7,420. Two years later, the number of FBI agents had leaped to 5,072.

Within months after the FBI was designated to combat espionage in the United States until the end of World War II, Hoover and his G-men, with the invaluable support of the entire FBI work force, utterly smashed the Nazi spy apparatus in the United States. In cooperation with the Office of Naval Intelligence and Army Intelligence, the FBI apprehended 92 of Adolf Hitler's spies and saboteurs, who were sent to prison for long terms. Six spies were executed. With G-Men heat searing them, scores of Nazi agents fled the United States and hundreds of others scurried into hiding, unable to function for fear of arrest.

When Hilter's generals surrendered the once powerful German war machine in May 1945, it had been 15 years since Hoover had taken charge of an agency mired in scandal, corruption, confusion, and ineptness. Now, in that relatively short time span, the Federal Bureau of Investigation had become recognized worldwide as the equal of England's Scotland Yard and France's Sûreté, both of which had been in existence for centuries.

While Hoover had established the standards of conduct and investigation and led the pioneering struggle to achieve impartial and effective law enforcement and security for the United States, he always refused to take full credit.

"FBI successes have not come through the efforts of any one person," he declared. "Bureau achievements have resulted from the combined contributions of thousands of dedicated men and women who have served on the team, including many who have given their lives in the line of duty."

Aftermath

In 1965, J. Edgar Hoover reached the mandatory retirement age of 70, but President Lyndon B. Johnson waived the regulation and so did President Richard M. Nixon four years later. Hoover, still energetic, alert, and with his brisk walking style and staccato verbal delivery intact, had frequently given the impression that he hoped to remain on the job as long as he lived.

At 8:30 on the morning of May 2, 1972, James Crawford, Hoover's longtime chauffeur and personal handyman, arrived at his home to plant some roses. A half-hour later, Annie Fields, Hoover's housekeeper, came outside and said that Hoover had not come downstairs at his ritualistic time of 8:00 A.M. sharp.

Sleeping late was unknown to Hoover, so Crawford went upstairs and, as he had feared, found him slumped on the floor beside his bed. Bursting into tears, Annie Fields summoned Hoover's personal physician, who pronounced the 77-year-old lawman dead of a heart attack.

Although J. Edgar Hoover's death in his forty-eighth year at the helm of the FBI was an event that could be expected sooner or later, it hit the Bureau with enormous impact. So ingrained was his mystique that many regarded him subconsciously as being indestructible.

At FBI headquarters, the shocking news was received with an air that some subversive event must have taken place, and a security officer immediately ordered agents to guard all doors leading into the building. None were told what they were guarding against. A few hours later, the agents were withdrawn.

Mrs. Charles S. Robb, daughter of former President Lyndon Johnson, arrived at FBI headquarters at 10:15 A.M. to keep an appointment to interview Hoover. She was working for the *Ladies' Home Journal*. A grim-faced G-Man approached Mrs. Robb and asked, "Can you keep a secret?" She replied that she had kept many while her father was in the White House. Then she was told that Hoover had died during the night.

After FBI offices around the nation and overseas were informed, Attorney General-designate Richard G. Kleindienst gave the news to the media. Virtually every daily newspaper in the United States carried the story on Page 1. So did the press in many foreign countries. Even Tass, the official Soviet news agency, gave the story one sentence.

There was an avalanche of editorials eulogizing Hoover. Said a typical one in the Johnson City, Tennessee *Press-Chronicle*: "J. Edgar Hoover was America's symbol of tough law enforcement. There he stood granite-like through the vicissitudes of a half-century protecting the country against all enemies—be they internal gangsters or external predators."

In the Capitol, members of the Senate and House took to the floor one after the other to sing the praises of Hoover and to mourn his passing. Congress promptly voted its permission for his body to lie in state in the Capitol Rotunda—the first civil servant ever to be accorded that honor. Previously, only 21 persons, eight of whom were presidents or former presidents, received that recognition.

Glowing tributes to the legendary FBI chief poured in. They came from Democrats and Republicans alike, on both sides of the political spectrum.

Senator James O. Eastland: "His courage, integrity and character was a model for all men who dedicate themselves to the protection of the lives and property of their fellow citizens."

Senator Edward H. Kennedy: "The nation has lost a dedicated and loyal public servant."

Speaker of the House Carl Albert: "The Bureau will forever bear the imprint of this dedicated and patriotic man."

Senator Hubert H. Humphrey: "J. Edgar Hoover has been one of the central figures of our time—a man of unquestioned ability, personal integrity and professional competence."

American Bar Association President Leon Jaworski: "I know of no man in modern history who contributed more to law enforcement in our nation than did J. Edgar Hoover."

A few derogatory views were published in the press. Gus Hall, general secretary of the Communist Party USA, branded Hoover "A servant of racism, reaction, and repression" and a "political pervert." Dr. Benjamin Spock, an anti-Vietnam war radical who was the People's Party candidate for president, called his passing "a great relief."

Twenty-four hours after his death, Hoover's flag-draped coffin was placed on the same catafalque that once held the remains of Abraham Lincoln in the Capitol Rotunda. Justices of the Supreme Court, the Cabinet, and members of Congress crushed into the domed chamber to hear Chief Justice Warren E. Burger eulogize him as "this splendid man who dedicated his life to his country in a half-century of unparalleled service."

The body of the man who had served eight presidents and 16 attorneys general was taken the next day from the Capitol to the historic National Presbyterian Church, where he had been a lifelong parishioner, for the final rites. The high and the mighty in Washington were among the 2,000 persons from all walks of life who jammed the modern white stone building. In his eulogy, President Nixon called the day one of sadness but also of pride for ''one of the giants of America.''

At the conclusion of the services, a motorcade of the hearse and ten limousines, carrying only close friends and a few members of Hoover's family, sped across Washington with a motorcycle escort to Congressional Cemetery. There, beside the graves of his parents and a sister who had died in infancy, John Edgar Hoover, a hero to two generations of Americans, was buried—only a few blocks from where he was born.

Like all people, Hoover had his virtues and his faults, his strong characteristics and his weaknesses, his likes and dislikes. Few Americans knew about his lifetime of civic-mindedness. Despite his backbreaking FBI schedule, he served on the boards of his church, his alma mater (George Washington University), and youth groups such as the Boys Club of America and the Explorer Scouts. With his personal funds he began a foundation to support needy families of former G-Men and to contribute to the education of their children.

Another side of Hoover unknown to the public was his compassion for his agents with true hardship cases. As one example among countless others, the Marine son of an FBI agent had been seriously wounded during the Vietnam War. The parents received a telegram that said only that their son had been shot and was not expected to live. The anguished father and mother were unable to get more details. In some manner, Hoover promptly learned of the son's being wounded and telephoned the father. He said he would meet the same day with the Marine Corps commandant and would be back in touch with the agent. Within an hour, Hoover called again, told the agent the nature of his son's wound, said the boy was expected to recover, and reported that arrangements had been made for the parents to speak on the telephone with their son at a naval hospital on Guam.

Most of those who have disagreed with Hoover's tough law enforcement stance, his rooting out of Communist subversives embedded in the U.S. government, his demands that vicious criminals serve their full prison terms, and his strong advocacy of patriotism did not dare to take him on when he was alive and could defend himself. With his death, however, his critics were infused with instant courage, and, along with others who hopped on the anti-Hoover platform, they have spent the intervening 23 years picking him apart vulture-like. Their slick attacks have contained a blend of gossip, rumor, conjecture, lies, and half-truths, backed by facts sifted through their own ideological perspectives.

Although his detractors have had the means to widely disseminate their biased and grotesquely twisted broadsides, the true measure of Hoover rests in how he is regarded by those who have carried out his policies, followed his orders (often in perilous situations), and been subjected to his control and strict discipline. In this respect, the 8,000 members of The Society of Former Special Agents of the FBI today are his staunchest supporters, admirers, and defenders. These men and women view J. Edgar Hoover as one of American history's towering heroes.

Notes

CHAPTER 1

1. *Seattle Post-Intelligencer*, June 5, 1935.
2. Idaho Governor Ross received so much flak after it became known that he had granted a full pardon to William Mahan that he issued a statement that skirted the issue: ''I believe the way to fight crime is to put 100 percent of the criminals in jail. As for (Mahan's) parole, I have nothing to say.''
3. *Washington Herald*, June 17, 1935.
4. Ibid.
5. *Seattle Post-Intelligencer*, June 24, 1935.
6. Ibid.
7. *San Francisco Call-Bulletin*, May 8, 1936.
8. *The New York Times*, May 8, 1936.
9. *Washington Herald*, May 11, 1936.
10. *Seattle Post-Intelligencer*, June 2, 1936.

CHAPTER 2

1. The agency had been known as the Bureau of Investigation prior to 1935, when its title was changed to the Federal Bureau of Investigation (FBI). For purposes of clarity, the organization is identified by the latter name throughout this book.
2. In early 1922, Gaston B. Means had become an embarrassment to even the free-wheeling Daugherty Department of Justice. So the attorney general suspended Means as an agent of the Bureau of Investigation ''until further notice,'' and then the Bureau chief, William J. Burns, put Means on the Bureau's payroll as an informant.
3. Some neutral observers of the Washington scene held that Harry Daugherty was more at fault for what he did not do rather than what he did do.
4. Eleven months after his appointment as attorney general, Harlan Fiske Stone be-

came an associate justice of the U.S. Supreme Court in 1925 and later was chief justice. Stone died in 1946 at the age of 74.

5. *Washington Herald*, February 1, 1934.

6. Don Whitehead, *The FBI Story* (New York: Random House, 1956), p. 79.

7. Martin Durkin served 19 years in the Illinois State Prison. On his release in August 1945, he was taken into custody on another charge and confined in the Leavenworth Federal Penitentiary in Kansas. On expiration of his sentence, Durkin was discharged, in July 1954, at the age of 53.

CHAPTER 3

1. First reports set the amount of valuables taken from the Lincoln National Bank at $40,000. However, the total grew steadily in the days and weeks ahead until the final figure was set at about $3 million.

2. Bank robbers in the 1930s had little trouble disposing of stolen bonds. They would sell them at bargain prices to a financial institution that, to the casual eye, had a reputation for integrity and was engaged in a legitimate business. Numerous shady bankers were involved in these transactions with hot securities.

3. *Nebraska Daily Star*, September 2, 1931.

4. Lie detector findings were not admissible as evidence in trials, as in the case in 1994.

5. *Chicago Tribune*, February 17, 1931.

6. Melvin H. Purvis, *American Agent* (Garden City, N.Y.: Doubleday, Doran, 1936), p. 103.

CHAPTER 4

1. Liberty Bonds were sold during World War I to help finance America's role in the conflict.

2. Ma Barker may have been right in claiming Arthur's innocence in the murder of the Tulsa night watchman. Many years later a thief in California confessed to the killing, and there was evidence that he had been the culprit.

3. Lloyd Barker served his entire sentence. Released in 1947, he got a job as the assistant manager in a snack shop in California. A year later, his wife shot him to death in a domestic dispute.

4. Gangsters often carried Tommy guns in violin cases. The automatic weapons were called "Chicago pianos" by the underworld.

5. Melvin Purvis, *American Agent*, p. 63.

6. *St. Louis Post-Dispatch*, August 16, 1932.

7. In separate trials, three other participants, all Oklahoma prison escapees, were convicted in the Fort Scott bank robbery and were given sentences ranging from 20 to 100 years. They were James Clark, Edward Davis, and Frank Sawyer.

8. FBI Director J. Edgar Hoover said that there was evidence that Freddie Barker and Alvin Karpis had murdered attorney J. Edgar Smith, presumably because he failed to win a not guilty verdict for Harvey Bailey.

9. Ma Barker gave the nickname Dock to her son Arthur, but it became customary for newspapers and detective magazines to spell it Doc.

10. Assistant Director Harold Nathan retired from the FBI in 1945 after 28 years of service.

11. During the national mobilization prior to the United States' entry into World War II, Lieutenant Colonel J. Edgar Hoover of the army reserve and Commander Clyde A. Tolson of the navy reserve (and all Bureau agents and officials holding reserve commissions) were asked by the Secretaries of War and Navy to resign their commissions. This, it was explained, would permit every man to be utilized in a capacity in which he could contribute most to the national defense effort.

12. Clyde Tolson resigned from the FBI two days after J. Edgar Hoover's death in 1972, after serving in the Bureau for 44 years. Hoover, who had never married, left virtually all of his $551,500 estate to Tolson, his friend and close working partner for nearly four decades. Tolson was probably the only FBI person who called Hoover ''Eddie.''

CHAPTER 5

1. Mrs. Anna Lou Boettcher was wealthy in her own right. Her father was H. H. Pigott, managing director of the Helena, Montana, branch of the Federal Agricultural Corporation. Anna Lou Boettcher was chairman of the Women's Organization for Prohibition Reform and was active in the Junior League.

2. Before the passage of the Lindbergh Kidnapping Law in April 1932, Colorado's maximum sentence for abduction was seven years.

3. *Denver Post*, February 22, 1933.

4. Ibid., February 23, 1933.

5. *The New York Times*, March 2, 1933.

6. When told of her husband's suicide, Mrs. Vern Sankey was in jail facing several charges. She screamed hysterically for an hour.

CHAPTER 6

1. A rap-sheet is a law enforcement listing of prisoner's criminal charges and convictions.

2. Authorities never learned how the weapons had been smuggled into the Kansas State Penitentiary.

3. In the wake of the mass escape, Kansas Governor Alfred M. Landon gave six months of ''good time'' to all the inmates who did not take part in the breakout, meaning that this amount of time was deducted from each of their sentences.

4. *Kansas City Times*, June 3, 1933.

5. Quotations are from Warden Kirk Prather's report on his experiences, June 3, 1933.

6. Ibid.

7. When Warden Prather returned to the Kansas penitentiary after his release, he was out of a job. Prather, a Democrat, had been replaced on June 1, 1933 by an appointee of incoming Republican Governor Alfred Landon.

8. In 1936, Governor Landon was the Republican candidate for President of the United States and was soundly trounced by incumbent Franklin D. Roosevelt in the November election.

9. *Daily Oklahoman*, June 2, 1933.

10. Ibid.

11. Twenty-four hours after Wilbur Underhill's capture, three men, believed to be cronies of Underhill, terrorized the town of Vian in the Cookson Hills of northeastern Oklahoma. In an apparent effort to defy the "law," the three men drove wildly through the business district and riddled a hardware store, a restaurant, and the jail with bullets.

12. *Oklahoma City Times*, January 8, 1934.

CHAPTER 7

1. In order to explain her lengthy absence from home while on a crime binge with Clyde Barrow, Bonnie Parker told her deeply religious mother that she had gotten a job in a Houston department store selling cosmetics.

2. The Texas State Prison at Eastham was known to the underworld as "The Burning Hell."

3. Apologists for Clyde Barrow have claimed that the relatively harsh treatment he received at the Eastham prison was the cause of his turning to a life of crime. This neatly skirts the fact that he was in the penitentiary because he was already a convicted criminal.

4. When Clyde and Buck Barrow used barbers for shaves, they took turns. One outlaw remained outside in a car as a lookout while the other was in the barber's chair.

5. At her trial in Texas, Blanche Barrow's defense was that "a wife's role is to be where her husband is." The jury didn't buy her plea, and she received a ten-year sentence.

6. Late in 1933, teenager William Daniel Jones was arrested in Texas and told officers that his time with Clyde and Bonnie had been "18 months of hell."

7. *Minneapolis Tribune*, June 19, 1933.

8. After his acquittal in the Hamm kidnapping, Roger Touhy was arrested again by the FBI and charged with abducting a shady Chicago underworld figure named Jake "The Barber" Factor. Rumors were that Touhy had been framed by the Al Capone gang to get him out of the way in order to move into his lucrative Des Plaines territory. Touhy was found guilty of the Factor abduction (after the first trial ended in a hung jury) and was sentenced to 99 years in prison.

Over the years, Touhy continued to protest his innocence, and in the mid-1950s he won a rehearing of his conviction. After a 36-day hearing, Judge John H. Barnes declared that Jake Factor had never been kidnapped but had disappeared "on his own connivance." In 1959, after 25 years in prison, Touhy was released. Twenty-three days later, "Roger the Terrible" was gunned down on a Chicago street. As he lay dying, Touhy muttered, "I've been expecting it—the bastards never forget!"

9. FBI archives hold 70,910 pages generated during the William Hamm kidnapping investigation.

CHAPTER 8

1. Transcript of trial of Mary McElroy's kidnappers.

2. Henry F. McElroy was not just another city manager. Rather, he was one of Kansas City's most powerful political figures, being a close ally of Tom Pendergast, the Kansas City "boss."

3. On being told of the abductors' praise for his efforts as city manager, Henry McElroy commented drily: "I don't believe a recommendation from kidnappers would do me much good."

4. *Kansas City Star*, May 29, 1933.

5. Although indicted for conspiracy by a Kansas City grand jury, the Johnson and Gilbert couples were later released from charges involving the case.

6. *The New York Times*, July 29, 1933.

7. The brutal kidnappers of the teenaged Herman Miller were arrested, tried, and convicted. "This was a most dastardly crime, and all of you are fortunate you are not charged with murder," Judge Joseph A. Delaney told the kidnappers before sentencing them to terms of 30 years to life.

8. Little Mary Will's nursemaid pleaded guilty to extortion and was sentenced to five years in prison.

CHAPTER 9

1. FBI terminology for a person breaking out of a prison or jail was an "escape," not an "escapee."

2. People from all over the world flocked to Hot Springs to take the mineral-water baths, which some thought could cure or relieve a wide variety of physical ailments and illnesses.

3. Melvin Purvis, special agent in charge of the Chicago FBI office, said, "I doubt manhunters of the future will ever cast their nets for a man as gravely and intelligently dangerous as Vern Miller."

4. According to FBI records, Jelly Nash hadn't bothered to divorce the first Mrs. Nash before he married the second Mrs. Nash.

5. *The Investigator*, January, 1945.

CHAPTER 10

1. The Internal Revenue Service discovered that in one year Thomas Pendergast had made an error in his tax form, neglecting to report $433,500 in income (a sum roughly equivalent to $5,000,000 in 1994). Sentenced as a tax evader in 1939, Boss Tom spend 12 months in prison and his Kansas City organization rapidly fell apart.

2. William "the Killer" Miller pulled off an incredible escape from the Detroit jail in 1929. Charged with the murder of Detective Frank Tradeau, Miller was in a long line of prisoners, all handcuffed together, when he suddenly dashed away with his handcuffs dangling from his wrist. His flight was a success. Authorities would never learn how he had freed himself from the manacles.

3. Underworld rumors were that Pretty Boy Floyd disguised himself as a woman to avoid detection and attended the funeral of his crony George "the Preacher" Birdwell.

4. Months later, the FBI learned of the Vern Miller-Johnny Lazia conference when a gangster named Michael "Jimmy the Needles" La Capra talked after being arrested and faced with several major charges, in order to save his own skin.

5. Johnny Lazia was found murdered in a ditch outside Kansas City a few weeks after his Union Station meeting with Vern Miller. There were 15 bullets in his body.

6. One of the main duties of a special agent in charge of an FBI field office is planning and coordinating raids and other operations.

CHAPTER 11

1. FBI Agent F. Joseph Lackey's serious wounds kept him in a hospital for months and eventually forced his retirement.

2. The FBI archives contain 64 thick volumes on the Kansas City Massacre, from the first teletype on the slaughter to the last piece of mail.

3. J. Edgar Hoover speech manuscript, July 10, 1933.

4. *Kansas City Times*, June 23, 1983.

5. In 1983, retired FBI Agent Hal Bray told a newspaper reporter that he still couldn't determine why he had focused on the two Joplin numbers, an action that played a key role in solving the Kansas City Massacre.

6. When J. Edgar Hoover opened the FBI's own crime laboratory, he received numerous complaints that it would take away business from similar private facilities.

7. When the FBI fingerprint section opened in 1932, local police and sheriffs were often leery about cooperating with the federal agency. But as the months passed their concerns vanished, and within three years more than 5,200 local law enforcement entities were sending fingerprints to Washington.

8. Rose and Beulah Baird had each been grazed by a bullet in the Bowling Green shootout. Later, the two women were released by authorities after spending a short time in jail.

9. *The Investigator*, January 1945.

10. Vi Gibson was taken into custody at her apartment and Bobbie Moore turned herself in to the FBI a few days later. They were indicted for harboring Vern Miller and aiding in his escape. Later, after pleading guilty, both women were sentenced to prison terms of one year. After her release, Vi Gibson was immediately arrested and later plead guilty to a conspiracy charge in connection with the Kansas City Massacre and again went to the penitentiary.

11. The FBI in Chicago picked up underworld rumors that Vern Miller's executioners had located him in Louisville, killed him there after dragging him out of a bathtub full of water, and transported his body in a car for several hundred miles to Michigan.

CHAPTER 12

1. George Kelly's real last name was Barnes.

2. Later, a female friend of Kathryn's told the FBI: "George fell for Kathryn like a ton of bricks."

3. J. Edgar Hoover would write: "Kathryn Thorne Kelly was one of the most coldly deliberate criminals of my experience."

4. While in Leavenworth serving the bootlegging sentence, George Kelly was approached by an inmate who, aware of Kelly's reputation as a fearless desperado, invited him to join in a mass escape that was being planned. "Aw, I'm too old for that," the 35-year-old Kelly replied in declining the invitation.

5. During the robbery of the Wilmer, Texas, bank, a security guard was machine-

gunned. It was never clear which gang member had fired the burst, but Kathryn gave "credit" for the deed to her husband George.

6. One time, during a drunken fling with a fellow bank robber in a Galesburg, Illinois, gambling hall, Eddie Doll became incensed over a slurring remark the other man made toward Doll's girlfriend of the moment. Doll challenged his pal to a duel, presumably with fists. Together with their "seconds," the party drove to a desolate rural area. As soon as Eddie stepped out of the vehicle, his foe drew a pistol and shot him, inflicting a flesh wound. Doll was taken to a shady doctor who patched him up.

CHAPTER 13

1. The FBI was convinced that Kathryn Kelly's powerful 16–cylinder car was one of the two vehicles used in the Urschel kidnapping.

2. Despite intense searches, the FBI never located the typewriter used for the ransom notes. However, investigators believed that either Kathryn Kelly or her mother Ora did the typing.

3. *Kansas City Times*, August 6, 1933.

4. *Daily Oklahoman*, August 8, 1933.

5. Ibid.

6. *The New York Times*, August 9, 1933.

7. *Daily Oklahoman*, August 7, 1933.

8. Files of the Federal Bureau of Investigation contain more than 50,000 pages concerning the Charles Urschel kidnapping.

CHAPTER 14

1. Thomas L. Manion was sentenced to serve two years at Leavenworth and to pay a fine of $10,000. Groover C. Bevill was given a 14-month term in the same institution.

2. J. C. Tichenor and his associate Langford Ramsey stood trial in Jackson, Tennessee, and were found guilty of concealing the Kellys in Memphis. Each was sentenced to two years and six months in prison.

3. When lawman involved in the capture of Machine Gun Kelly told of the gangster's shouting "Don't shoot, G-Men!" it was widely publicized in the media. Although the term *G-Man* had been used much earlier by the underworld to signify any federal investigator or prosecutor, Kelly's plea indelibly attached the monicker G-Man to FBI agents.

4. *Daily Oklahoman*, September 28, 1933.

5. *The New York Times*, October 2, 1933.

6. Armon Shannon apparently received only a probationary sentence because he cooperated with the government in its investigation.

7. In 1954, after George Kelly had been transferred to Leavenworth, he wrote to Charles Urschel, his victim of more than two decades earlier. Kelly had mellowed and lamented in his letter: "These five words seem written in fire on the walls of my cell: Nothing can be worth this. Two weeks later Kelly died of a heart attack.

Kathryn Kelly served four years longer after George's death and was released from the Cincinnati Workhouse in 1958.

8. Clara Feldman, Edward Feldman, and Alvin Scott pleaded guilty to conspiracy

charges and were sentenced to five years in prison. The terms were suspended and each was placed on probation. Lawyer Ben Laska, who defended himself in a stormy trial featuring his own frequent outbursts, was convicted of conspiracy and given a ten-year term.

Edward Barney Berman and Clifford S. Kelley were found guilty of passing ransom money in Minneapolis and each was sentenced to five years in prison.

Cassey Earl Coleman received a one-year-and-a-day term for harboring the Kellys on his Texas ranch, and his associate Will Casey was given a two-year term on the same charge.

9. *Washington Herald*, January 24, 1933.

CHAPTER 15

1. Edgar Singleton gained a degree of fame in later years when he was billed as ''John Dillinger's first partner in crime.'' In 1937, Singleton, in a drunken stupor, fell asleep on a railroad track and was run over by a train.

2. In his late teens, John Dillinger served in the U.S. Navy, and was aboard the USS *Utah* (a battleship), part of the time. He jumped ship, deserted the Navy, and was given a dishonorable discharge.

3. Jay Robert Nash, *Bloodletters and Badmen* (New York: M. Evans, 1973), p. 167.

4. Despite his grievous wounds, 72-year-old Finley C. Carson survived after long hospitalization.

5. Herbert von Valkenburg recovered, but after being injured he could not remember the license number of his own car.

CHAPTER 16

1. John Dillinger had a curious set of principles. Since his girlfriend Billie Frechette was part Menominee and it was a violation of federal law for an Indian to drink booze, he went out of his way to make certain that she did not consume any. In those times, many thought that all Indians invariably got violent when drunk.

2. Law enforcement officials never determined how many robberies, mainly of banks, John Dillinger and his gang should have been ''credited'' for perpetrating, nor could their total haul be figured. Certainly, the loot ran over $1 million. Part of the difficulty in setting total numbers and amounts was that nearly every bank heist pulled in the Midwest for two years was linked to the Dillinger gang, which certainly was responsible for scores of them.

3. *Chicago Tribune*, November 17, 1933.

4. Ibid., December 17, 1933.

CHAPTER 17

1. *Minneapolis Tribune*, February 12, 1934.

2. After Alvin Karpis was captured, he told FBI agents that he had paid Dr. Joseph Moran $350 for the ''face job.'' J. Edgar Hoover would remark: ''It wasn't worth thirty-five cents to him. It changed his jaw a little but we'd recognize him anywhere.''

3. John J. "Boss" McLaughlin was sentenced to a long term and died in prison of a heart attack a few years later. Oliver A. Berg also received a lengthy sentence.

For their part in the William Hamm, Jr. kidnapping, William Weaver, a paroled convict, got life imprisonment; Harry Sawyer, the St. Paul gangland "fixer," received a sentence of life imprisonment; Cassis McDonald, Detroit engineer, who passed some of the ransom money, got 15 years; Harold Alderton and Elmer Farmer, both of Bensenville, Illinois, were sentenced to 20 years; James J. Wilson, a former Northwestern University student, received five years in the reformatory, and Bryon Bolton, who turned state's evidence, got four three-year sentences running concurrently.

4. The Browning automatic rifle (BAR) was a long, cumbersome weapon that many American soldiers and Marines were armed with in World War II and afterward.

5. Melvin Purvis, *American Agent*, p. 112.

6. Arthur "Doc" Barker was sentenced to life imprisonment at Alcatraz and tried to make a break on June 13, 1939, at age 41. He made it over the high walls of "escape-proof" Alcatraz and to the rocky beach of San Francisco Bay far below. He tried to build a raft of sorts by collecting bits of waterlogged wood and tying them together with strips from his shirt.

Barker was spotted from a guard's tower and ordered through a bullhorn to "throw your hands in the air." The convict ignored the command and went back to his frantic work, pushing his makeshift raft a short distance out into the water. Guns from the tower roared and Barker, killed instantly, splashed into the water.

7. "Old Joe" the alligator never enjoyed his sudden celebrity status. By the time the shootout erupted along Lake Weir, Old Joe had died.

8. *Philadelphia Daily News*, January 15, 1985.

9. In January 1985, the Lake Weir Chamber of Commerce sponsored a picnic and reenactment of the shootout to mark the fiftieth anniversary.

10. A short time after her arrest in Atlantic City, Delores Delaney had her baby, who was turned over to the law-abiding parents of Alvin Karpis. Delores was sentenced to a five-year term for harboring a fugitive.

CHAPTER 18

1. *Arizona Star*, January 27, 1934.

2. Ibid.

3. Associated Press, January 27, 1934.

4. *Minneapolis Tribune*, January 28, 1934.

5. Don Sarber succeeded his murdered father Jess as sheriff.

6. Although two eyewitnesses had identified John Dillinger as one of the East Chicago, Indiana, bank robbers, some law enforcement officers later doubted his involvement. Dillinger's girlfriend Billie Frechette, when interviewed in 1968 shortly before her death from cancer, still denied that he had even been in Indiana at the time Officer Patrick O'Malley was shot and killed. As late as 1973, Harry Pierpont's former sweetheart, Mary Kinder, claimed that Dillinger had never left the gang in Florida to pull the East Chicago bank job.

7. Melvin Purvis, *American Agent* (Garden City, N.Y.: Doubleday, Doran, 1936), p. 186.

8. *This Fabulous Century* (New York: Time-Life, 1969), vol. IV, p. 100.

9. *The New York Times*, May 12, 1934.

10. Time/Life Books, *This Fabulous Century*, p. 101.

11. Baby Face Nelson was identified as the man who shot and killed the other driver when an eyewitness jotted down the California license number of Nelson's car.

12. Evelyn ''Billie'' Frechette was taken to St. Paul for trial on a charge of conspiracy to harbor a fugitive (John Dillinger) and was fined $1,000 and sentenced to two years in prison.

CHAPTER 19

1. *Lake Superior Magazine*, May-June 1988.

2. In 1931, Ralph ''Bottles'' Capone was convicted of tax evasion and spent 27 months in prison. In 1945, Bottles purchased the Rex Hotel in Mercer, Wisconsin, for $65,000, according to the FBI. He also owned the Recap Lodge located on Martha Lake near Mercer. For 40 years until his death, Ralph Capone and his wife lived near Mercer.

3. Spider Lake is now called Little Star Lake.

4. *The New York Times*, January 25, 1934.

5. Pat Reilly and his girlfriend Pat Cherington were later captured by the FBI. Reilly was sentenced to two years and Cherington received a two-year term for harboring a fugitive (Reilly).

6. Helen Gillis, Baby Face Nelson's wife, was given a probationary sentence of one year and a day for harboring a fugitive. She promptly rejoined her husband, and they resumed a crime spree.

7. In 1994, Little Bohemia is still being besieged by the curious, armed with John Dillinger and Baby Face Nelson questions. Emil Wanatka Jr., who had been eight years old when caught in the 1934 gun battle, operates a small museum near the main lodge. There, tourists pay $1 to see Dillinger's underwear and a tin of his Ex-Lax pills, among other items the desperado left behind.

8. Frank Hamer retired from the Texas Rangers in 1949. He had always wanted to die when engaged in a shootout with a desperate gang of criminals. Instead, he passed away peacefully, in his bed in Austin, Texas, in 1955 at the age of 71.

9. *Milwaukee Sentinel*, June 1, 1934.

10. *Washington Herald*, May 19, 1934.

11. Hoover's phrasing was recalled later by Samuel Cowley in the *Chicago Tribune*.

12. *Denver Post*, June 9, 1934.

13. Dr. Wilhelm Loeser, who performed the face-lifts on John Dillinger and Homer Van Meter, was sentenced on September 21, 1935, to serve one day on that charge. Then he was returned to federal prison to complete his three-year term on a narcotics charge.

Dr. Harold Cassidy, who assisted Dr. Loeser, was sentenced to serve 11 months on each of three counts, the sentences to run concurrently.

After his arrest, James Probasco, in whose house the Dillinger and Van Meter operations were performed, was taken to the Chicago FBI office on the nineteenth floor of the Bankers Building. Left alone for a few moments, Probasco leaped out the window and plunged to his death.

CHAPTER 20

1. FBI agents Herman Hollis, Charles P. Winstead, and Clarence O. Hurt, all of whom fired at Dillinger, received commendations from J. Edgar Hoover for their courage

and resourcefulness. None of the G-Men involved in the affair at the Biograph would ever disclose which one of them had actually killed John Dillinger.

2. *Chicago Tribune*, July 25, 1934.

3. Ibid., July 29, 1934.

4. *Washington Herald*, July 30, 1934.

5. *The New York Times*, July 5, 1934.

6. Ironically, John Dillinger's final resting place was in an Indianapolis cemetery named Crown Point, which was the name of the Indiana town from which the outlaw had pulled his famous wooden gun escape and first burst into wide ill-fame. All the flowers placed on Dillinger's grave were stolen, presumably as mawkish souvenirs.

7. The John Dillinger Historical Museum was opened in 1977 at Nashville, Indiana, a small town 45 miles south of Indianapolis and near Mooresville, where the outlaw launched his crime career. The museum, a century-old, two-story, red frame house on Nashville's main street, is filled with wax figures depicting scenes of Dillinger's criminal life—and death. Inside, flanked with bouquets, stands a casket holding the wax figure of a man (Dillinger) in a gray suit. A bullet wound is evident under his right eye. Funeral music and the heavy scent of flowers fill the air.

8. FBI archives hold 36,795 pages generated during the hunt for John Dillinger and his gang.

9. Each of the two East Chicago, Indiana, policemen involved in tracking Dillinger to the Biograph received a $2,500 reward from the federal government. FBI regulations prohibit agents from sharing in reward money.

10. A federal judge ruled that even had Samuel Cowley and Melvin Purvis promised that the deportation proceedings against Anna Sage would be dropped, such a promise was not within the jurisdiction of officers outside the Department of Labor. Anna Sage died in 1947 in the little Romanian town of Timisoara.

11. *Minneapolis Tribune*, August 16, 1934.

12. A short time before Homer Van Meter was killed, he visited his brother in Fort Wayne, Indiana, and gave him a new car. Later lawmen confiscated the automobile, but the brother went to court and a judge ordered the vehicle to be returned to him.

13. *Detroit News*, September 25, 1934.

14. *The New York Times*, September 23, 1934.

CHAPTER 21

1. *Youngstown Vindicator*, October 23, 1934.

2. James H. Baum recovered from his gunshot wound and would be a local celebrity of sorts for the remainder of his life.

3. Mrs. Ellen Conkle, Albert Dyke, and a neighboring farmer witnessed the entire episode in which Pretty Boy Floyd was killed.

4. *Chicago Tribune*, October 24, 1934.

5. *Youngstown Vindicator*, October 25, 1934.

6. Press release, American Bankers Association, August 1935.

7. Edward Bentz was sentenced to 20 years in prison for the robbery of the Caledonia Bank.

8. *St. Louis Post-Dispatch*, December 7, 1934.

9. Melvin Purvis, *American Agent*, p. 173.

10. *Washington Herald*, November 29, 1934.

11. Ibid.

12. FBI Agent Herman Hollis was buried in his home town of Des Moines, Iowa. At the funeral mass, the Reverend Francis P. Larkin, rector of St. Ambrose Cathedral, said in closing, "Let us hope that he did not die in vain." A civic funeral was held for FBI Inspector Samuel Cowley in the Assembly Hall in the Latter Day Saints Temple in Salt Lake City, his home town. Hundreds of mourners, including government officials and G-Men, attended the rites in Des Moines and in Salt Lake City.

Mrs. Cowley and Mrs. Hollis (as with the wives of other FBI agents killed in the line of duty) received compensation under a federal law providing a widow 35 percent of his monthly salary and 10 percent for each child. Mrs. Cowley, mother of two young children, received $3,575 annually and Mrs. Hollis got $2,295 per year.

CHAPTER 22

1. *Chicago Tribune*, November 30, 1934.

2. Although John Paul Chase served 20 years for the murder of FBI Inspector Samuel Cowley, he had never been tried on the indictment charging him with Agent Herman Hollis's murder. On October 17, 1955, a district judge in Chicago dismissed the indictment and Chase became eligible for parole. He was released from prison on October 31, 1966, and died seven years later in Palo Alto, California.

3. E. L. Matlock, the owner of the farm on which the airplane landed, and his neighbor William Ford told FBI agents looking into the circumstances of the escape about the shackles being removed from Volney Davis.

4. In July 1935, Melvin Purvis resigned from the FBI "for purely personal reasons." Soon afterward he signed a contract with Post Toasties, a breakfast cereal firm, and organized a Junior G-Man Service, which proved to be highly popular. J. Edgar Hoover reportedly frowned on the project which, he felt, tended to capitalize on the FBI name.

During World War II, Colonel Melvin Purvis was assigned to the U.S. Army War Crimes Office. After the conflict, he practiced law in his home town of Florence, South Carolina. On February 29, 1960, Purvis, who had been in ill health, committed suicide at age 56.

CHAPTER 23

1. *The New York Times*, November 8, 1935.

2. Associated Press, November 7, 1935.

3. *The New York Times*, February 27, 1936.

4. Senator Kenneth McKellar, who had sniped at J. Edgar Hoover for years, eventually became one of his staunchest supporters. At an FBI National Academy graduation attended by Hoover on April 10, 1943, McKellar was introduced but not scheduled to speak. However, he stood up and launched into a ringing tribute: "Let us stand for . . . this great instrument of law and order that has been built up by the grand man who is your director. . . . (Hoover) believes in the Constitution, he believes in the enforcement of law in this country. Let us stand by him!"

Later, J. Edgar Hoover told a friend: "I was so surprised that I looked around to see if Senator McKellar was talking about me!"

5. *Nation's Business*, January 1971.

6. J. Edgar Hoover, *Persons in Hiding* (New York: Random House, 1937), p. 72.

7. Harry Campbell and Fred Hunter were sent to prison for terms in excess of 40 years.

8. Alvin "Old Creepy" Karpis remained at Alcatraz until 1962, when he was transferred to McNeil Island, a federal penitentiary in Washington State, from where he was paroled in 1969. He was deported to Canada and later moved to Spain, where he died from natural causes in the early 1970s.

9. Don Whitehead, *The FBI Story*, p. 111.

CHAPTER 24

1. *Kansas City Star*, April 16, 1937.

2. *The New York Times*, April 18, 1937.

3. At the same time that Robert Suhay and Alfred Power were captured, FBI agents in New York City collared two men who admitted helping to plan the Katohan bank robbery. Some $7,000 in bank loot was recovered from these men, which accounted for virtually all the Katohan money not found in the possession of Suhay and Power.

4. *Chicago Tribune*, September 27, 1937.

5. In gratitude for the arrest of her husband's murderer, Mrs. Charles S. Ross created a fund to go the families of FBI agents killed in the line of duty.

6. *Nation's Business*, January 1971.

7. *Washington Herald*, May 7, 1938.

8. Thomas E. Dewey was the Republican candidate for president of the United States in 1948. Polls favored Dewey to win over incumbent Harry S. Truman, and Dewey initially claimed victory for himself. However, the man from Missouri pulled off an upset and was returned to the White House.

9. *The New York Times*, August 26, 1939.

Index

ALSO BY WILLIAM B. BREUER

American Saga
Bloody Clash at Sadzot
Captain Cool
They Jumped at Midnight
Drop Zone Sicily
Agony at Anzio
Hitler's Fortress Cherbourg
Death of a Nazi Army
Operation Torch
Storming Hitler's Rhine
Retaking the Philippines
Devil Boats
Operation Dragoon
The Secret War with Germany
Hitler's Undercover War
Sea Wolf
Geronimo!
Hoodwinking Hitler
Race to the Moon
The Great Raid on Cabanatuan

About the Author

WILLIAM B. BREUER is a widely acclaimed author with 21 hardcover books published since 1982. Prior to his career as a writer, he operated a St. Louis-based public relations firm, and before that he owned a daily newspaper in Missouri, at one time being the nation's youngest daily publisher. He has written on World War II, the space race, and the FBI. A *New York Times* review described his writing style as "vintage Hemingway." He and his wife Vivien live near Lookout Mountain, Tennessee.